SUPER HOROSCOPE

ARIES

2011

MARCH 21 – APRIL 20

B

BERKLEY BOOKS, NEW YORK

THE BERKLEY PUBLISHING GROUP
Published by the Penguin Group
Penguin Group (USA) Inc.
375 Hudson Street, New York, New York 10014, USA
Penguin Group (Canada), 90 Eglinton Avenue East, Suite 700, Toronto, Ontario M4P 2Y3, Canada
(a division of Pearson Penguin Canada Inc.)
Penguin Books Ltd., 80 Strand, London WC2R 0RL, England
Penguin Group Ireland, 25 St. Stephen's Green, Dublin 2, Ireland (a division of Penguin Books Ltd.)
Penguin Group (Australia), 250 Camberwell Road, Camberwell, Victoria 3124, Australia
(a division of Pearson Australia Group Pty. Ltd.)
Penguin Books India Pvt. Ltd., 11 Community Centre, Panchsheel Park, New Delhi—110 017, India
Penguin Group (NZ), 67 Apollo Drive, Rosedale, North Shore 0632, New Zealand
(a division of Pearson New Zealand Ltd.)
Penguin Books (South Africa) (Pty.) Ltd., 24 Sturdee Avenue, Rosebank, Johannesburg 2196,
South Africa

Penguin Books Ltd., Registered Offices: 80 Strand, London WC2R 0RL, England

The publishers regret that they cannot answer individual letters requesting personal horoscope information.

2011 SUPER HOROSCOPE ARIES

PRINTING HISTORY
Berkley trade paperback edition / July 2010

Berkley trade paperback ISBN: 978-0-425-23285-9

Library of Congress Cataloging-in-Publication Data

ISSN: 1535-8917

PRINTED IN THE UNITED STATES OF AMERICA

10 9 8 7 6 5 4 3 2 1

Contents

THE CUSP-BORN ARIES

Are you *really* an Aries? If your birthday falls during the fourth week of March, at the beginning of Aries, will you still retain the traits of Pisces, the sign of the Zodiac before Aries? And what if you were born late in April—are you more Taurus than Aries? Many people born at the edge, or cusp, of a sign have difficulty determining exactly what sign they are. If you are one of these people, here's how you can figure it out, once and for all.

Consult the cusp table on the facing page, then locate the year of your birth. The table will tell you the precise days on which the Sun entered and left your sign for the year of your birth. In that way you can determine if you are a true Aries—or whether you are a Pisces or Taurus—according to the variations in cusp dates from year to year (see also page 17).

If you were born at the beginning or end of Aries, yours is a lifetime reflecting a process of subtle transformation. Your life on Earth will symbolize a significant change in consciousness, for you are either about to enter a whole new way of living or are leaving one behind.

If your birthday falls at the end of March, you may want to read the horoscope book for Pisces as well as Aries, for Pisces holds the keys to many of your hidden uncertainties, past guilts, weaknesses, sorrows, unspoken wishes, and your cosmic unfoldment.

You are eager to start living, and possess, in a way, the secret of eternal youth. Obstacles enrage you but never beat you, for you usually feel you have sacrificed more than your share. After waiting and suffering long enough, you will assert yourself and your right to make your own decisions.

However, you are often drawn back through Pisces into a sense of responsibility, a duty to others, a selflessness that at times eats away at your confidence and undermines your character. Honor and the vitality of life are your gifts.

If you were born late in April, you may want to read the horoscope book for Taurus as well as Aries. The investment could be revealing and profitable, for Taurus is often your means of putting your talents to practical use and turning your ideas into actual, tangible rewards.

You are headstrong and determined; you have a sense of independence and fight that nothing can destroy. Sometimes you can vacillate and be worried and negative, but you never give up. You have the earthy sense of all your needs to meet responsibilities, do your duties, build, acquire, and collect. You are attracted to all you possess, and the more you possess, the more permanent your life. You are thus less able to simply pick up and go back to zero; what you start you must try to finish.

THE CUSPS OF ARIES

DATES SUN ENTERS ARIES
(LEAVES PISCES)

March 20 every year from 1900 to 2015, except for the following:

March 21

1901	1911	1923	1938	1955
02	13	26	39	59
03	14	27	42	63
05	15	30	43	67
06	18	31	46	71
07	19	34	47	75
09	22	35	51	79
10				

DATES SUN LEAVES ARIES
(ENTERS TAURUS)

April 20 every year from 1900 to 2015, except for the following:

April 19

1948	1972	1988	2000	2012
52	76	89	2001	2013
56	80	92	2004	
60	81	93	2005	
64	84	96	2008	
68	85	97	2009	

THE ASCENDANT: ARIES RISING

Could you be a "double" Aries? That is, could you have Aries as your Rising sign as well as your Sun sign? The tables on pages 8–9 will tell you Aries what your Rising sign happens to be. Just find the hour of your birth, then find the day of your birth, and you will see which sign of the Zodiac is your Ascendant, as the Rising sign is called. The Ascendant is called that because it is the sign rising on the eastern horizon at the time of your birth. For a more detailed discussion of the Rising sign and the twelve houses of the Zodiac, see pages 17–20.

The Ascendant, or Rising sign, is placed on the edge of the 1st house in a horoscope, of which there are twelve houses. The 1st house represents your response to the environment—your unique response. Call it identity, personality, ego, self-image, facade, come-on, body-mind-spirit—whatever term best conveys to you the meaning of the you that acts and reacts in the world. It is a you that is always changing, discovering a new you. Your identity started with birth and early environment, over which you had little conscious control, and continues to experience, to adjust, to express itself. The 1st house also represents how others see you. Has anyone ever guessed your sign to be your Rising sign? People may respond to that personality, that facade, that body type governed by your Rising sign.

Your Ascendant, or Rising sign, modifies your basic Sun sign personality, and it affects the way you act out the daily predictions for your Sun sign. If your Rising sign is indeed Aries, what follows is a description of its effects on your horoscope. If your Rising sign is not Aries, but some other sign of the Zodiac, you may wish to read the horoscope book for that sign as well.

With Aries on the Ascendant, the planet rising in your 1st house is Mars, the ruler of Aries. This is a natural placement for Mars, because the 1st house is the proper home of Aries, the first sign of the Zodiac, and of its ruler Mars. This position gives you undaunted courage and strong recuperative powers. It makes you extraordinarily resistant to stress, strain, and sickness. You are specially lucky in that you probably will live a long life bent on success. The planet Pluto is often regarded as co-ruler of Aries. Pluto rising together with Mars can increase your chances of success. Pluto has a banish-

6

ing effect on enemies and troubles. Just when you feel most hard pressed by personal loss or public enmity, Pluto negates the power of these harmful forces.

Aries Rising people stamp the environment with vitality. You have a great need for instant success, which imparts an urgency to all of your undertakings. You are a picture of boundless energy, unlimited courage, untapped reserves. In love, in work, in study, you want realistic rewards, but you want them right away. As soon as your need is gratified, you may lose interest in a person or project; sometimes you don't stay around to see it through. People may say you lack foresight, but you can honestly answer that you see a brighter horizon elsewhere. Your vision is as bold as your bids for self-actualization.

You are a loner, fiercely guarding your independence. But you are not shy or reticent; rather, you are confident, sometimes boastful. You thrive on challenge; you are reckless of danger; you invite competition and combat. And you frequently gain by these means. You keenly feel oppression; you are more sensitive than others to rank, responsibility, privilege, and the power these confer. If you cannot be at the head of things, you want at least a free hand. But if you are not allowed a free hand, then you don't want to participate. These traits make some of you Aries poor team players, others of you notorious rebels.

Those of you with Aries Rising are blessed with the knack of invention. You know how to start things, to fix things, to make things work. You are quick-witted, a good judge of character and situation; you can size up a scene swiftly and accurately. You are handy and creative. You have a wide repertoire of skills, and you won't get slotted into dead-end routes or stuck in routines. You are always eager to go ahead, to make daring new moves—sometimes overeager, hasty, shortsighted. You scorn defeat, though, so no loss holds you back. Like the Ram, your zodiacal symbol, you butt your way through all the obstacles.

Personal fulfillment is your goal. Because you are so totally absorbed in it, some people find you insensitive. Indeed, your assertive sweep can be a blunt weapon. Your anger, too, can be devastating. Piqued by pride or vanity, it can give rise to passionate revenge, careless actions, disorderly behavior. Combined with righteousness, anger can make you a formidable opponent of antiquated ideas, of a society rigid with formalities. You can reject all that aggressively, fearlessly.

The key words for Aries Rising are impulse and action. Self-fulfillment comes through a balance of these forces in order to meet the challenges of material success and inner growth.

RISING SIGNS FOR ARIES

Hour of Birth*	Date of Birth		
	March 20–25	**March 26–30**	**March 31–April 4**
Midnight	Sagittarius	Sagittarius	Sagittarius
1 AM	Sagittarius Capricorn 3/28	Sagittarius;	Capricorn
2 AM	Capricorn	Capricorn	Capricorn
3 AM	Capricorn	Capricorn; Aquarius 3/27	Aquarius
4 AM	Aquarius	Aquarius	Aquarius; Pisces 4/3
5 AM	Pisces	Pisces	Pisces
6 AM	Pisces; Aries 3/23	Aries	Aries
7 AM	Aries	Aries; Taurus 3/27	Taurus
8 AM	Taurus	Taurus	Taurus; Gemini 4/3
9 AM	Gemini	Gemini	Gemini
10 AM	Gemini	Gemini	Gemini; Cancer 4/2
11 AM	Cancer	Cancer	Cancer
Noon	Cancer	Cancer	Cancer
1 PM	Cancer; Leo 3/23	Leo	Leo
2 PM	Leo	Leo	Leo
3 PM	Leo	Leo	Virgo
4 PM	Virgo	Virgo	Virgo
5 PM	Virgo	Virgo	Virgo
6 PM	Virgo; Libra 3/24	Libra	Libra
7 PM	Libra	Libra	Libra
8 PM	Libra	Libra	Scorpio
9 PM	Scorpio	Scorpio	Scorpio
10 PM	Scorpio	Scorpio	Scorpio
11 PM	Scorpio; Sagittarius 3/22	Sagittarius	Sagittarius

Hour of Birth*	Date of Birth		
	April 5–9	April 10–14	April 15–20
Midnight	Sagittarius	Sagittarius Capricorn 4/12	Capricorn
1 AM	Capricorn	Capricorn	Capricorn
2 AM	Capricorn	Capricorn; Aquarius 4/11	Aquarius
3 AM	Aquarius	Aquarius	Aquarius; Pisces 4/18
4 AM	Pisces	Pisces	Pisces
5 AM	Pisces; Aries 4/7	Aries	Aries
6 AM	Aries	Aries; Taurus 4/11	Taurus
7 AM	Taurus	Taurus	Taurus; Gemini 4/18
8 AM	Gemini	Gemini	Gemini
9 AM	Gemini	Gemini	Gemini; Cancer 4/17
10 AM	Cancer	Cancer	Cancer
11 AM	Cancer	Cancer	Cancer
Noon	Cancer; Leo 4/8	Leo	Leo
1 PM	Leo	Leo	Leo
2 PM	Leo	Leo	Virgo
3 PM	Virgo	Virgo	Virgo
4 PM	Virgo	Virgo	Virgo
5 PM	Virgo;	Libra	Libra
6 PM	Libra Libra 4/7	Libra	Libra
7 PM	Libra	Libra; Scorpio 4/14	Scorpio
8 PM	Scorpio	Scorpio	Scorpio
9 PM	Scorpio	Scorpio	Scorpio
10 PM	Scorpio; Sagittarius 4/1	Sagittarius	Sagittarius
11 PM	Sagittarius	Sagittarius	Sagittarius

*Hour of birth given here is for Standard Time in any time zone. If your hour of birth was recorded in Daylight Saving Time, subtract one hour from it and consult that hour in the table above. For example, if you were born at 6 AM D.S.T., see 5 AM above.

THE PLACE OF ASTROLOGY IN TODAY'S WORLD

Does astrology have a place in the fast-moving, ultra-scientific world we live in today? Can it be justified in a sophisticated society whose outriders are already preparing to step off the moon into the deep space of the planets themselves? Or is it just a hangover of ancient superstition, a psychological dummy for neurotics and dreamers of every historical age?

These are the kind of questions that any inquiring person can be expected to ask when they approach a subject like astrology which goes beyond, but never excludes, the materialistic side of life.

The simple, single answer is that astrology works. It works for many millions of people in the western world alone. In the United States there are 10 million followers and in Europe, an estimated 25 million. America has more than 4000 practicing astrologers, Europe nearly three times as many. Even down-under Australia has its hundreds of thousands of adherents. In the eastern countries, astrology has enormous followings, again, because it has been proved to work. In India, for example, brides and grooms for centuries have been chosen on the basis of their astrological compatibility.

Astrology today is more vital than ever before, more practicable because all over the world the media devotes much space and time to it, more valid because science itself is confirming the precepts of astrological knowledge with every new exciting step. The ordinary person who daily applies astrology intelligently does not have to wonder whether it is true nor believe in it blindly. He can see it working for himself. And, if he can use it—and this book is designed to help the reader to do just that—he can make living a far richer experience, and become a more developed personality and a better person.

Astrology and Relationships

Astrology is the science of relationships. It is not just a study of planetary influences on man and his environment. It is the study of man himself.

We are at the center of our personal universe, of all our relationships. And our happiness or sadness depends on how we act, how we relate to the people and things that surround us. The emotions that we generate have a distinct effect—for better or worse—on the world around us. Our friends and our enemies will confirm this. Just look in the mirror the next time you are angry. In other words, each of us is a kind of sun or planet or star radiating our feelings on the environment around us. Our influence on our personal universe, whether loving, helpful, or destructive, varies with our changing moods, expressed through our individual character.

Our personal "radiations" are potent in the way they affect our moods and our ability to control them. But we usually are able to throw off our emotion in some sort of action—we have a good cry, walk it off, or tell someone our troubles—before it can build up too far and make us physically ill. Astrology helps us to understand the universal forces working on us, and through this understanding, we can become more properly adjusted to our surroundings so that we find ourselves coping where others may flounder.

The Challenge of Love

The challenge of love lies in recognizing the difference between infatuation, emotion, sex, and, sometimes, the intentional deceit of the other person. Mankind, with its record of broken marriages, despair, and disillusionment, is obviously not very good at making these distinctions.

Can astrology help?

Yes. In the same way that advance knowledge can usually help in any human situation. And there is probably no situation as human, as poignant, as pathetic and universal, as the failure of man's love.

Love, of course, is not just between man and woman. It involves love of children, parents, home, and friends. But the big problems usually involve the choice of partner.

Astrology has established degrees of compatibility that exist between people born under the various signs of the Zodiac. Because people are individuals, there are numerous variations and modifications. So the astrologer, when approached on mate and marriage matters, makes allowances for them. But the fact remains that some groups of people are suited for each other and some are not, and astrology has expressed this in terms of characteristics we all can study and use as a personal guide.

No matter how much enjoyment and pleasure we find in the different aspects of each other's character, if it is not an overall compatibility, the chances of our finding fulfillment or enduring happiness in each other are pretty hopeless. And astrology can help us to find someone compatible.

Astrology and Science

Closely related to our emotions is the "other side" of our personal universe, our physical welfare. Our body, of course, is largely influenced by things around us over which we have very little control. The phone rings, we hear it. The train runs late. We snag our stocking or cut our face shaving. Our body is under a constant bombardment of events that influence our daily lives to varying degrees.

The question that arises from all this is, what makes each of us act so that we have to involve other people and keep the ball of activity and evolution rolling? This is the question that both science and astrology are involved with. The scientists have attacked it from different angles: anthropology, the study of human evolution as body, mind and response to environment; anatomy, the study of bodily structure; psychology, the science of the human mind; and so on. These studies have produced very impressive classifications and valuable information, but because the approach to the problem is fragmented, so is the result. They remain "branches" of science. Science generally studies effects. It keeps turning up wonderful answers but no lasting solutions. Astrology, on the other hand, approaches the question from the broader viewpoint. Astrology began its inquiry with the totality of human experience and saw it as an effect. It then looked to find the cause, or at least the prime movers, and during thousands of years of observation of man and his *universal* environment came up with the extraordinary principle of planetary influence—or astrology, which, from the Greek, means the science of the stars.

Modern science, as we shall see, has confirmed much of astrology's foundations—most of it unintentionally, some of it reluctantly, but still, indisputably.

It is not difficult to imagine that there must be a connection between outer space and Earth. Even today, scientists are not too sure how our Earth was created, but it is generally agreed that it is only a tiny part of the universe. And as a part of the universe, people on Earth see and feel the influence of heavenly bodies in almost every aspect of our existence. There is no doubt that the Sun has the greatest influence on life on this planet. Without it there would be no life, for without it there would be no warmth, no division into day and night, no cycles of time or season at all. This is clear and easy to see. The influence of the Moon, on the other hand, is more subtle, though no less definite.

There are many ways in which the influence of the Moon manifests itself here on Earth, both on human and animal life. It is a well-known fact, for instance, that the large movements of water on our planet—that is the ebb and flow of the tides—are caused by the

Moon's gravitational pull. Since this is so, it follows that these water movements do not occur only in the oceans, but that all bodies of water are affected, even down to the tiniest puddle.

The human body, too, which consists of about 70 percent water, falls within the scope of this lunar influence. For example the menstrual cycle of most women corresponds to the 28-day lunar month; the period of pregnancy in humans is 273 days, or equal to nine lunar months. Similarly, many illnesses reach a crisis at the change of the Moon, and statistics in many countries have shown that the crime rate is highest at the time of the Full Moon. Even human sexual desire has been associated with the phases of the Moon. But it is in the movement of the tides that we get the clearest demonstration of planetary influence, which leads to the irresistible correspondence between the so-called metaphysical and the physical.

Tide tables are prepared years in advance by calculating the future positions of the Moon. Science has known for a long time that the Moon is the main cause of tidal action. But only in the last few years has it begun to realize the possible extent of this influence on mankind. To begin with, the ocean tides do not rise and fall as we might imagine from our personal observations of them. The Moon as it orbits around Earth sets up a circular wave of attraction which pulls the oceans of the world after it, broadly in an east to west direction. This influence is like a phantom wave crest, a loop of power stretching from pole to pole which passes over and around the Earth like an invisible shadow. It travels with equal effect across the land masses and, as scientists were recently amazed to observe, caused oysters placed in the dark in the middle of the United States where there is no sea to open their shells to receive the nonexistent tide. If the land-locked oysters react to this invisible signal, what effect does it have on us who not so long ago in evolutionary time came out of the sea and still have its salt in our blood and sweat?

Less well known is the fact that the Moon is also the primary force behind the circulation of blood in human beings and animals, and the movement of sap in trees and plants. Agriculturists have established that the Moon has a distinct influence on crops, which explains why for centuries people have planted according to Moon cycles. The habits of many animals, too, are directed by the movement of the Moon. Migratory birds, for instance, depart only at or near the time of the Full Moon. And certain sea creatures, eels in particular, move only in accordance with certain phases of the Moon.

Know Thyself—Why?

In today's fast-changing world, everyone still longs to know what the future holds. It is the one thing that everyone has in common: rich and poor, famous and infamous, all are deeply concerned about tomorrow.

But the key to the future, as every historian knows, lies in the past. This is as true of individual people as it is of nations. You cannot understand your future without first understanding your past, which is simply another way of saying that you must first of all know yourself.

The motto "know thyself" seems obvious enough nowadays, but it was originally put forward as the foundation of wisdom by the ancient Greek philosophers. It was then adopted by the "mystery religions" of the ancient Middle East, Greece, Rome, and is still used in all genuine schools of mind training or mystical discipline, both in those of the East, based on yoga, and those of the West. So it is universally accepted now, and has been through the ages.

But how do you go about discovering what sort of person you are? The first step is usually classification into some sort of system of types. Astrology did this long before the birth of Christ. Psychology has also done it. So has modern medicine, in its way.

One system classifies people according to the source of the impulses they respond to most readily: the muscles, leading to direct bodily action; the digestive organs, resulting in emotion; or the brain and nerves, giving rise to thinking. Another such system says that character is determined by the endocrine glands, and gives us such labels as "pituitary," "thyroid," and "hyperthyroid" types. These different systems are neither contradictory nor mutually exclusive. In fact, they are very often different ways of saying the same thing.

Very popular, useful classifications were devised by Carl Jung, the eminent disciple of Freud. Jung observed among the different faculties of the mind, four which have a predominant influence on character. These four faculties exist in all of us without exception, but not in perfect balance. So when we say, for instance, that someone is a "thinking type," it means that in any situation he or she tries to be rational. Emotion, which may be the opposite of thinking, will be his or her weakest function. This thinking type can be sensible and reasonable, or calculating and unsympathetic. The emotional type, on the other hand, can often be recognized by exaggerated language—everything is either marvelous or terrible—and in extreme cases they even invent dramas and quarrels out of nothing just to make life more interesting.

The other two faculties are intuition and physical sensation. The sensation type does not only care for food and drink, nice clothes and furniture; he or she is also interested in all forms of physical experience. Many scientists are sensation types as are athletes and nature-lovers. Like sensation, intuition is a form of perception and we all possess it. But it works through that part of the mind which is not under conscious control—consequently it sees meanings and connections which are not obvious to thought or emotion. Inventors and original thinkers are always intuitive, but so, too, are superstitious people who see meanings where none exist.

Thus, sensation tells us what is going on in the world, feeling (that is, emotion) tells us how important it is to ourselves, thinking enables us to interpret it and work out what we should do about it, and intuition tells us what it means to ourselves and others. All four faculties are essential, and all are present in every one of us. But some people are guided chiefly by one, others by another. In addition, Jung also observed a division of the human personality into the extrovert and the introvert, which cuts across these four types.

A disadvantage of all these systems of classification is that one cannot tell very easily where to place oneself. Some people are reluctant to admit that they act to please their emotions. So they deceive themselves for years by trying to belong to whichever type they think is the "best." Of course, there is no best; each has its faults and each has its good points.

The advantage of the signs of the Zodiac is that they simplify classification. Not only that, but your date of birth is personal—it is unarguably yours. What better way to know yourself than by going back as far as possible to the very moment of your birth? And this is precisely what your horoscope is all about, as we shall see in the next section.

WHAT IS A HOROSCOPE?

If you had been able to take a picture of the skies at the moment of your birth, that photograph would be your horoscope. Lacking such a snapshot, it is still possible to recreate the picture—and this is at the basis of the astrologer's art. In other words, your horoscope is a representation of the skies with the planets in the exact positions they occupied at the time you were born.

The year of birth tells an astrologer the positions of the distant, slow-moving planets Jupiter, Saturn, Uranus, Neptune, and Pluto. The month of birth indicates the Sun sign, or birth sign as it is commonly called, as well as indicating the positions of the rapidly moving planets Venus, Mercury, and Mars. The day and time of birth will locate the position of our Moon. And the moment—the exact hour and minute—of birth determines the houses through what is called the Ascendant, or Rising sign.

With this information the astrologer consults various tables to calculate the specific positions of the Sun, Moon, and other planets relative to your birthplace at the moment you were born. Then he or she locates them by means of the Zodiac.

The Zodiac

The Zodiac is a band of stars (constellations) in the skies, centered on the Sun's apparent path around the Earth, and is divided into twelve equal segments, or signs. What we are actually dividing up is the Earth's path around the Sun. But from our point of view here on Earth, it seems as if the Sun is making a great circle around our planet in the sky, so we say it is the Sun's apparent path. This twelvefold division, the Zodiac, is a reference system for the astrologer. At any given moment the planets—and in astrology both the Sun and Moon are considered to be planets—can all be located at a specific point along this path.

Now where in all this are you, the subject of the horoscope? Your character is largely determined by the sign the Sun is in. So that is where the astrologer looks first in your horoscope, at your Sun sign.

The Sun Sign and the Cusp

There are twelve signs in the Zodiac, and the Sun spends approximately one month in each sign. But because of the motion of the Earth around the Sun—the Sun's apparent motion—the dates when the Sun enters and leaves each sign may change from year to year. Some people born near the cusp, or edge, of a sign have difficulty determining which is their Sun sign. But in this book a Table of Cusps is provided for the years 1900 to 2015 (page 5) so you can find out what your true Sun sign is.

Here are the twelve signs of the Zodiac, their ancient zodiacal symbol, and the dates when the Sun enters and leaves each sign for the year 2011. Remember, these dates may change from year to year.

ARIES	Ram	March 20–April 20
TAURUS	Bull	April 20–May 21
GEMINI	Twins	May 21–June 21
CANCER	Crab	June 21–July 22
LEO	Lion	July 23–August 23
VIRGO	Virgin	August 23–September 23
LIBRA	Scales	September 23–October 23
SCORPIO	Scorpion	October 23–November 22
SAGITTARIUS	Archer	November 22–December 22
CAPRICORN	Sea Goat	December 22–January 20
AQUARIUS	Water Bearer	January 20–February 18
PISCES	Fish	February 18–March 20

It is possible to draw significant conclusions and make meaningful predictions based simply on the Sun sign of a person. There are many people who have been amazed at the accuracy of the description of their own character based only on the Sun sign. But an astrologer needs more information than just your Sun sign to interpret the photograph that is your horoscope.

The Rising Sign and the Zodiacal Houses

An astrologer needs the exact time and place of your birth in order to construct and interpret your horoscope. The illustration on the next page shows the flat chart, or natural wheel, an astrologer uses. Note the inner circle of the wheel labeled 1 through 12. These 12 divisions are known as the houses of the Zodiac.

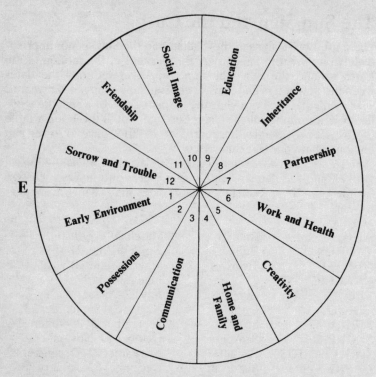

The 1st house always starts from the position marked E, which corresponds to the eastern horizon. The rest of the houses 2 through 12 follow around in a "counterclockwise" direction. The point where each house starts is known as a cusp, or edge.

The cusp, or edge, of the 1st house (point E) is where an astrologer would place your Rising sign, the Ascendant. And, as already noted, the exact time of your birth determines your Rising sign. Let's see how this works.

As the Earth rotates on its axis once every 24 hours, each one of the twelve signs of the Zodiac appears to be "rising" on the horizon, with a new one appearing about every 2 hours. Actually it is the turning of the Earth that exposes each sign to view, but in our astrological work we are discussing apparent motion. This Rising sign marks the Ascendant, and it colors the whole orientation of a horoscope. It indicates the sign governing the 1st house of the chart, and will thus determine which signs will govern all the other houses.

To visualize this idea, imagine two color wheels with twelve divisions superimposed upon each other. For just as the Zodiac is divided into twelve constellations that we identify as the signs, another twelvefold division is used to denote the houses. Now imagine one wheel (the signs) moving slowly while the other wheel (the houses) remains still. This analogy may help you see how the signs keep shifting the "color" of the houses as the Rising sign continues to change every two hours. To simplify things, a Table of Rising Signs has been provided (pages 8–9) for your specific Sun sign.

Once your Rising sign has been placed on the cusp of the 1st house, the signs that govern the rest of the 11 houses can be placed on the chart. In any individual's horoscope the signs do not necessarily correspond with the houses. For example, it could be that a sign covers part of two adjacent houses. It is the interpretation of such variations in an individual's horoscope that marks the professional astrologer.

But to gain a workable understanding of astrology, it is not necessary to go into great detail. In fact, we just need a description of the houses and their meanings, as is shown in the illustration above and in the table below.

THE 12 HOUSES OF THE ZODIAC

1st	Individuality, body appearance, general outlook on life	Personality house
2nd	Finance, possessions, ethical principles, gain or loss	Money house
3rd	Relatives, communication, short journeys, writing, education	Relatives house
4th	Family and home, parental ties, land and property, security	Home house
5th	Pleasure, children, creativity, entertainment, risk	Pleasure house
6th	Health, harvest, hygiene, work and service, employees	Health house
7th	Marriage and divorce, the law, partnerships and alliances	Marriage house
8th	Inheritance, secret deals, sex, death, regeneration	Inheritance house
9th	Travel, sports, study, philosophy, religion	Travel house
10th	Career, social standing, success and honor	Business house
11th	Friendship, social life, hopes and wishes	Friends house
12th	Troubles, illness, secret enemies, hidden agendas	Trouble house

The Planets in the Houses

An astrologer, knowing the exact time and place of your birth, will use tables of planetary motion in order to locate the planets in your horoscope chart. He or she will determine which planet or planets are in which sign and in which house. It is not uncommon, in an individual's horoscope, for there to be two or more planets in the same sign and in the same house.

The characteristics of the planets modify the influence of the Sun according to their natures and strengths.

Sun: Source of life. Basic temperament according to the Sun sign. The conscious will. Human potential.

Moon: Emotions. Moods. Customs. Habits. Changeable. Adaptive. Nurturing.

Mercury: Communication. Intellect. Reasoning power. Curiosity. Short travels.

Venus: Love. Delight. Charm. Harmony. Balance. Art. Beautiful possessions.

Mars: Energy. Initiative. War. Anger. Adventure. Courage. Daring. Impulse.

Jupiter: Luck. Optimism. Generous. Expansive. Opportunities. Protection.

Saturn: Pessimism. Privation. Obstacles. Delay. Hard work. Research. Lasting rewards after long struggle.

Uranus: Fashion. Electricity. Revolution. Independence. Freedom. Sudden changes. Modern science.

Neptune: Sensationalism. Theater. Dreams. Inspiration. Illusion. Deception.

Pluto: Creation and destruction. Total transformation. Lust for power. Strong obsessions.

Superimpose the characteristics of the planets on the functions of the house in which they appear. Express the result through the character of the Sun sign, and you will get the basic idea.

Of course, many other considerations have been taken into account in producing the carefully worked out predictions in this book: the aspects of the planets to each other; their strength according to position and sign; whether they are in a house of exaltation or decline; whether they are natural enemies or not; whether a planet occupies its own sign; the position of a planet in relation to its own house or sign; whether the sign is male or female; whether the sign is a fire, earth, water, or air sign. These are only a few of the colors on the astrologer's pallet which he or she must mix with the inspiration of the artist and the accuracy of the mathematician.

How To Use These Predictions

A person reading the predictions in this book should understand that they are produced from the daily position of the planets for a group of people and are not, of course, individually specialized. To get the full benefit of them our readers should relate the predictions to their own character and circumstances, coordinate them, and draw their own conclusions from them.

If you are a serious observer of your own life, you should find a definite pattern emerging that will be a helpful and reliable guide.

The point is that we always retain our free will. The stars indicate certain directional tendencies but we are not compelled to follow. We can do or not do, and wisdom must make the choice.

We all have our good and bad days. Sometimes they extend into cycles of weeks. It is therefore advisable to study daily predictions in a span ranging from the day before to several days ahead.

Daily predictions should be taken very generally. The word "difficult" does not necessarily indicate a whole day of obstruction or inconvenience. It is a warning to you to be cautious. Your caution will often see you around the difficulty before you are involved. This is the correct use of astrology.

In another section (pages 78–84), detailed information is given about the influence of the Moon as it passes through each of the twelve signs of the Zodiac. There are instructions on how to use the Moon Tables (pages 85–92), which provide Moon Sign Dates throughout the year as well as the Moon's role in health and daily affairs. This information should be used in conjunction with the daily forecasts to give a fuller picture of the astrological trends.

HISTORY OF ASTROLOGY

The origins of astrology have been lost far back in history, but we do know that reference is made to it as far back as the first written records of the human race. It is not hard to see why. Even in primitive times, people must have looked for an explanation for the various happenings in their lives. They must have wanted to know why people were different from one another. And in their search they turned to the regular movements of the Sun, Moon, and stars to see if they could provide an answer.

It is interesting to note that as soon as man learned to use his tools in any type of design, or his mind in any kind of calculation, he turned his attention to the heavens. Ancient cave dwellings reveal dim crescents and circles representative of the Sun and Moon, rulers of day and night. Mesopotamia and the civilization of Chaldea, in itself the foundation of those of Babylonia and Assyria, show a complete picture of astronomical observation and well-developed astrological interpretation.

Humanity has a natural instinct for order. The study of anthropology reveals that primitive people—even as far back as prehistoric times—were striving to achieve a certain order in their lives. They tried to organize the apparent chaos of the universe. They had the desire to attach meaning to things. This demand for order has persisted throughout the history of man. So that observing the regularity of the heavenly bodies made it logical that primitive peoples should turn heavenward in their search for an understanding of the world in which they found themselves so random and alone.

And they did find a significance in the movements of the stars. Shepherds tending their flocks, for instance, observed that when the cluster of stars now known as the constellation Aries was in sight, it was the time of fertility and they associated it with the Ram. And they noticed that the growth of plants and plant life corresponded with different phases of the Moon, so that certain times were favorable for the planting of crops, and other times were not. In this way, there grew up a tradition of seasons and causes connected with the passage of the Sun through the twelve signs of the Zodiac.

Astrology was valued so highly that the king was kept informed of the daily and monthly changes in the heavenly bodies, and the results of astrological studies regarding events of the future. Head astrologers were clearly men of great rank and position, and the office was said to be a hereditary one.

Omens were taken, not only from eclipses and conjunctions of the Moon or Sun with one of the planets, but also from storms and earthquakes. In the eastern civilizations, particularly, the reverence inspired by astrology appears to have remained unbroken since the very earliest days. In ancient China, astrology, astronomy, and religion went hand in hand. The astrologer, who was also an astronomer, was part of the official government service and had his own corner in the Imperial Palace. The duties of the Imperial astrologer, whose office was one of the most important in the land, were clearly defined, as this extract from early records shows:

> This exalted gentleman must concern himself with the stars in the heavens, keeping a record of the changes and movements of the Planets, the Sun and the Moon, in order to examine the movements of the terrestrial world with the object of prognosticating good and bad fortune. He divides the territories of the nine regions of the empire in accordance with their dependence on particular celestial bodies. All the fiefs and principalities are connected with the stars and from this their prosperity or misfortune should be ascertained. He makes prognostications according to the twelve years of the Jupiter cycle of good and evil of the terrestrial world. From the colors of the five kinds of clouds, he determines the coming of floods or droughts, abundance or famine. From the twelve winds, he draws conclusions about the state of harmony of heaven and earth, and takes note of good and bad signs that result from their accord or disaccord. In general, he concerns himself with five kinds of phenomena so as to warn the Emperor to come to the aid of the government and to allow for variations in the ceremonies according to their circumstances.

The Chinese were also keen observers of the fixed stars, giving them such unusual names as Ghost Vehicle, Sun of Imperial Concubine, Imperial Prince, Pivot of Heaven, Twinkling Brilliance, Weaving Girl. But, great astrologers though they may have been, the Chinese lacked one aspect of mathematics that the Greeks applied to astrology—deductive geometry. Deductive geometry was the basis of much classical astrology in and after the time of the Greeks, and this explains the different methods of prognostication used in the East and West.

Down through the ages the astrologer's art has depended, not so much on the uncovering of new facts, though this is important, as on the interpretation of the facts already known. This is the essence of the astrologer's skill.

But why should the signs of the Zodiac have any effect at all on the formation of human character? It is easy to see why people thought they did, and even now we constantly use astrological expressions in our everyday speech. The thoughts of "lucky star," "ill-fated," "star-crossed," "mooning around," are interwoven into the very structure of our language.

Wherever the concept of the Zodiac is understood and used, it could well appear to have an influence on the human character. Does this mean, then, that the human race, in whose civilization the idea of the twelve signs of the Zodiac has long been embedded, is divided into only twelve types? Can we honestly believe that it is really as simple as that? If so, there must be pretty wide ranges of variation within each type. And if, to explain the variation, we call in heredity and environment, experiences in early childhood, the thyroid and other glands, and also the four functions of the mind together with extroversion and introversion, then one begins to wonder if the original classification was worth making at all. No sensible person believes that his favorite system explains everything. But even so, he will not find the system much use at all if it does not even save him the trouble of bothering with the others.

In the same way, if we were to put every person under only one sign of the Zodiac, the system becomes too rigid and unlike life. Besides, it was never intended to be used like that. It may be convenient to have only twelve types, but we know that in practice there is every possible gradation between aggressiveness and timidity, or between conscientiousness and laziness. How, then, do we account for this?

A person born under any given Sun sign can be mainly influenced by one or two of the other signs that appear in their individual horoscope. For instance, famous persons born under the sign of Gemini include Henry VIII, whom nothing and no one could have induced to abdicate, and Edward VIII, who did just that. Obviously, then, the sign Gemini does not fully explain the complete character of either of them.

Again, under the opposite sign, Sagittarius, were both Stalin, who was totally consumed with the notion of power, and Charles V, who freely gave up an empire because he preferred to go into a monastery. And we find under Scorpio many uncompromising characters such as Luther, de Gaulle, Indira Gandhi, and Montgomery, but also Petain, a successful commander whose name later became synonymous with collaboration.

A single sign is therefore obviously inadequate to explain the differences between people; it can only explain resemblances, such as the combativeness of the Scorpio group, or the far-reaching devotion of Charles V and Stalin to their respective ideals—the Christian heaven and the Communist utopia.

But very few people have only one sign in their horoscope chart. In addition to the month of birth, the day and, even more, the hour to the nearest minute if possible, ought to be considered. Without this, it is impossible to have an actual horoscope, for the word horoscope literally means "a consideration of the hour."

The month of birth tells you only which sign of the Zodiac was occupied by the Sun. The day and hour tell you what sign was occupied by the Moon. And the minute tells you which sign was rising on the eastern horizon. This is called the Ascendant, and, as some astrologers believe, it is supposed to be the most important thing in the whole horoscope.

The Sun is said to signify one's heart, that is to say, one's deepest desires and inmost nature. This is quite different from the Moon, which signifies one's superficial way of behaving. When the ancient Romans referred to the Emperor Augustus as a Capricorn, they meant that he had the Moon in Capricorn. Or, to take another example, a modern astrologer would call Disraeli a Scorpion because he had Scorpio Rising, but most people would call him Sagittarius because he had the Sun there. The Romans would have called him Leo because his Moon was in Leo.

So if one does not seem to fit one's birth month, it is always worthwhile reading the other signs, for one may have been born at a time when any of them were rising or occupied by the Moon. It also seems to be the case that the influence of the Sun develops as life goes on, so that the month of birth is easier to guess in people over the age of forty. The young are supposed to be influenced mainly by their Ascendant, the Rising sign, which characterizes the body and physical personality as a whole.

It is nonsense to assume that all people born at a certain time will exhibit the same characteristics, or that they will even behave in the same manner. It is quite obvious that, from the very moment of its birth, a child is subject to the effects of its environment, and that this in turn will influence its character and heritage to a decisive extent. Also to be taken into account are education and economic conditions, which play a very important part in the formation of one's character as well.

People have, in general, certain character traits and qualities which, according to their environment, develop in either a positive or a negative manner. Therefore, selfishness (inherent selfishness, that is) might emerge as unselfishness; kindness and consideration as cruelty and lack of consideration toward others. In the same way, a naturally constructive person may, through frustration, become destructive, and so 'on. The latent characteristics with which people are born can, therefore, through environment and good or bad training, become something that would appear to be its opposite, and so give the lie to the astrologer's description of their character. But this is not the case. The true character is still there, but it is buried deep beneath these external superficialities.

Careful study of the character traits of various signs of the Zodiac are of immeasurable help, and can render beneficial service to the intelligent person. Undoubtedly, the reader will already have discovered that, while he is able to get on very well with some people, he just "cannot stand" others. The causes sometimes seem inexplicable. At times there is intense dislike, at other times immediate sympathy. And there is, too, the phenomenon of love at first sight, which is also apparently inexplicable. People appear to be either sympathetic or unsympathetic toward each other for no apparent reason.

Now if we look at this in the light of the Zodiac, we find that people born under different signs are either compatible or incompatible with each other. In other words, there are good and bad interrelating factors among the various signs. This does not, of course, mean that humanity can be divided into groups of hostile camps. It would be quite wrong to be hostile or indifferent toward people who happen to be born under an incompatible sign. There is no reason why everybody should not, or cannot, learn to control and adjust their feelings and actions, especially after they are aware of the positive qualities of other people by studying their character analyses, among other things.

Every person born under a certain sign has both positive and negative qualities, which are developed more or less according to our free will. Nobody is entirely good or entirely bad, and it is up to each of us to learn to control ourselves on the one hand and at the same time to endeavor to learn about ourselves and others.

It cannot be emphasized often enough that it is free will that determines whether we will make really good use of our talents and abilities. Using our free will, we can either overcome our failings or allow them to rule us. Our free will enables us to exert sufficient willpower to control our failings so that they do not harm ourselves or others.

Astrology can reveal our inclinations and tendencies. Astrology can tell us about ourselves so that we are able to use our free will to overcome our shortcomings. In this way astrology helps us do our best to become needed and valuable members of society as well as helpmates to our family and our friends. Astrology also can save us a great deal of unhappiness and remorse.

Yet it may seem absurd that an ancient philosophy could be a prop to modern men and women. But below the materialistic surface of modern life, there are hidden streams of feeling and thought. Symbology is reappearing as a study worthy of the scholar; the psychosomatic factor in illness has passed from the writings of the crank to those of the specialist; spiritual healing in all its forms is no longer a pious hope but an accepted phenomenon. And it is into this context that we consider astrology, in the sense that it is an analysis of human types.

Astrology and medicine had a long journey together, and only parted company a couple of centuries ago. There still remain in medical language such astrological terms as "saturnine," "choleric," and "mercurial," used in the diagnosis of physical tendencies. The herbalist, for long the handyman of the medical profession, has been dominated by astrology since the days of the Greeks. Certain herbs traditionally respond to certain planetary influences, and diseases must therefore be treated to ensure harmony between the medicine and the disease.

But the stars are expected to foretell and not only to diagnose.

Astrological forecasting has been remarkably accurate, but often it is wide of the mark. The brave person who cares to predict world events takes dangerous chances. Individual forecasting is less clear cut; it can be a help or a disillusionment. Then we come to the nagging question: if it is possible to foreknow, is it right to foretell? This is a point of ethics on which it is hard to pronounce judgment. The doctor faces the same dilemma if he finds that symptoms of a mortal disease are present in his patient and that he can only prognosticate a steady decline. How much to tell an individual in a crisis is a problem that has perplexed many distinguished scholars. Honest and conscientious astrologers in this modern world, where so many people are seeking guidance, face the same problem.

Five hundred years ago it was customary to call in a learned man who was an astrologer who was probably also a doctor and a philosopher. By his knowledge of astrology, his study of planetary influences, he felt himself qualified to guide those in distress. The world has moved forward at a fantastic rate since then, and yet people are still uncertain of themselves. At first sight it seems fantastic in the light of modern thinking that they turn to the most ancient of all studies, and get someone to calculate a horoscope for them. But is it really so fantastic if you take a second look? For astrology is concerned with tomorrow, with survival. And in a world such as ours, tomorrow and survival are the keywords for the twenty-first century.

SPECIAL OVERVIEW 2011–2020

The second decade of the twenty-first century opens on major planetary shifts that set the stage for challenge, opportunity, and change. The personal planets—notably Jupiter and Saturn—and the generational planets—Uranus, Neptune, and Pluto—have all moved forward into new signs of the zodiac. These fresh planetary influences act to shape unfolding events and illuminate pathways to the future.

Jupiter, the big planet that attracts luck, spends about one year in each zodiacal sign. It takes approximately twelve years for Jupiter to travel through all twelve signs of the zodiac in order to complete a cycle. In 2011 a new Jupiter cycle is initiated with Jupiter transiting Aries, the first sign of the zodiac. As each year progresses over the course of the decade, Jupiter moves forward into the next sign, following the natural progression of the zodiac. Jupiter visits Taurus in 2012, Gemini in 2013, Cancer in 2014, Leo in 2015, Virgo in 2016, Libra in 2017, Scorpio in 2018, Sagittarius in 2019, Capricorn in 2020. Then in late December 2020 Jupiter enters Aquarius just two weeks before the decade closes. Jupiter's vibrations are helpful and fruitful, a source of good luck and a protection against bad luck. Opportunity swells under Jupiter's powerful rays. Learning takes leaps of faith.

Saturn, the beautiful planet of reason and responsibility, spends about two and a half years in each zodiacal sign. A complete Saturn cycle through all twelve signs of the zodiac takes about twenty-nine to thirty years. Saturn is known as the lawgiver: setting boundaries and codes of conduct, urging self-discipline and structure within a creative framework. The rule of law, the role of government, the responsibility of the individual are all sourced from Saturn. Saturn gives as it takes. Once a lesson is learned, Saturn's reward is just and full.

Saturn transits Libra throughout 2011 until early autumn of 2012. Here Saturn seeks to harmonize, to balance, to bring order out of chaos. Saturn in Libra ennobles the artist, the judge, the high-minded, the honest. Saturn next visits Scorpio from autumn 2012 until late December 2014. With Saturn in Scorpio, tactic and strategy combine to get workable solutions and desired results. Saturn's problem-solving tools here can harness dynamic energy for the common good. Saturn in Sagittarius, an idealistic and humanistic transit that stretches from December 2014 into the last day of autumn 2017, promotes activism over mere dogma and debate. Saturn in Sagittarius can be a driving force for good. Saturn tours Capricorn, the sign that Saturn rules, from the first day of winter 2017 into early spring 2020. Saturn in Capricorn is a consolidating transit, bringing things forth and into fruition. Here a plan can be made right, made whole, then launched for success. Saturn starts to visit Aquarius, a sign that Saturn corules and a very good sign for Saturn to visit, in the very last year of the decade. Saturn in Aquarius fosters team spirit, the unity of effort amid diversity. The transit of Saturn in Aquarius until early 2023 represents a period of enlightened activism and unprecedented growth.

Uranus, Neptune, and Pluto spend more than several years in each sign. They produce the differences in attitude, belief, behavior, and taste that distinguish one generation from another—and so are called the generational planets.

Uranus, planet of innovation and surprise, is known as the awakener. Uranus spends seven to eight years in each sign. Uranus started a new cycle when it entered Aries, the first sign of the zodiac, in May 2010. Uranus tours Aries until May 2018. Uranus in Aries accents originality, freedom, independence, unpredictability. There can be a start-stop quality to undertakings given this transit. Despite contradiction and confrontation, significant invention and productivity mark this transit. Uranus next visits Taurus through the end of the decade into 2026. Strategic thinking and timely action characterize the transit of Uranus in Taurus. Here intuition is backed up by common sense, leading to fresh discoveries upon which new industries can be built.

Neptune spends about fourteen years in each sign. Neptune, the visionary planet, enters Pisces, the sign Neptune rules and the final sign of the zodiac, in early April 2011. Neptune journeys through Pisces until 2026 to complete the Neptune cycle of visiting all twelve zodiacal signs. Neptune's tour of Pisces ushers in a long period of great potentiality: universal understanding, universal good, universal love, universal generosity, universal forgiveness—the universal spirit affects all. Neptune in Pisces can oversee the fruition of such noble aims as human rights for all and liberation from all forms of tyranny. Neptune in Pisces is a pervasive influence that changes concepts, consciences, attitudes, actions. The impact of Neptune in Pisces is to illuminate and to inspire.

Pluto, dwarf planet of beginnings and endings, entered the earthy sign of Capricorn in 2008 and journeys there for sixteen years into late 2024. Pluto in Capricorn over the course of this extensive visit has the capacity to change the landscape as well as the humanscape. The transforming energy of Pluto combines with the persevering power of Capricorn to give depth and character to potential change. Pluto in Capricorn brings focus and cohesion to disparate, diverse creativities. As new forms arise and take root, Pluto in Capricorn organizes the rebuilding process. Freedom versus limitation, freedom versus authority is in the framework during this transit. Reasonableness struggles with recklessness to solve divisive issues. Pluto in Capricorn teaches important lessons about adversity, and the lessons will be learned.

THE SIGNS OF THE ZODIAC

Dominant Characteristics

Aries: March 21–April 20

The Positive Side of Aries

The Aries has many positive points to his character. People born under this first sign of the Zodiac are often quite strong and enthusiastic. On the whole, they are forward-looking people who are not easily discouraged by temporary setbacks. They know what they want out of life and they go out after it. Their personalities are strong. Others are usually quite impressed by the Ram's way of doing things. Quite often they are sources of inspiration for others traveling the same route. Aries men and women have a special zest for life that can be contagious; for others, they are a fine example of how life should be lived.

The Aries person usually has a quick and active mind. He is imaginative and inventive. He enjoys keeping busy and active. He generally gets along well with all kinds of people. He is interested in mankind, as a whole. He likes to be challenged. Some would say he thrives on opposition, for it is when he is set against that he often does his best. Getting over or around obstacles is a challenge he generally enjoys. All in all, Aries is quite positive and young-thinking. He likes to keep abreast of new things that are happening in the world. Aries are often fond of speed. They like things to be done quickly, and this sometimes aggravates their slower colleagues and associates.

The Aries man or woman always seems to remain young. Their whole approach to life is youthful and optimistic. They never say die, no matter what the odds. They may have an occasional setback, but it is not long before they are back on their feet again.

The Negative Side of Aries

Everybody has his less positive qualities—and Aries is no exception. Sometimes the Aries man or woman is not very tactful in communicating with others; in his hurry to get things done he is apt to be a little callous or inconsiderate. Sensitive people are likely to find him somewhat sharp-tongued in some situations. Often in his eagerness to get the show on the road, he misses the mark altogether and cannot achieve his aims.

At times Aries can be too impulsive. He can occasionally be stubborn and refuse to listen to reason. If things do not move quickly enough to suit the Aries man or woman, he or she is apt to become rather nervous or irritable. The uncultivated Aries is not unfamiliar with moments of doubt and fear. He is capable of being destructive if he does not get his way. He can overcome some of his emotional problems by steadily trying to express himself as he really is, but this requires effort.

Taurus: April 21–May 20

The Positive Side of Taurus

The Taurus person is known for his ability to concentrate and for his tenacity. These are perhaps his strongest qualities. The Taurus man or woman generally has very little trouble in getting along with others; it's his nature to be helpful toward people in need. He can always be depended on by his friends, especially those in trouble.

Taurus generally achieves what he wants through his ability to persevere. He never leaves anything unfinished but works on something until it has been completed. People can usually take him at his word; he is honest and forthright in most of his dealings. The Taurus person has a good chance to make a success of his life because of his many positive qualities. The Taurus who aims high seldom falls short of his mark. He learns well by experience. He is thorough and does not believe in shortcuts of any kind. The Bull's thoroughness pays off in the end, for through his deliberateness he learns how to rely on himself and what he has learned. The Taurus person tries to get along with others, as a rule. He is not overly critical and likes people to be themselves. He is a tolerant person and enjoys peace and harmony—especially in his home life.

Taurus is usually cautious in all that he does. He is not a person who believes in taking unnecessary risks. Before adopting any one line of action, he will weigh all of the pros and cons. The Taurus person is steadfast. Once his mind is made up it seldom changes. The person born under this sign usually is a good family person—reliable and loving.

The Negative Side of Taurus

Sometimes the Taurus man or woman is a bit too stubborn. He won't listen to other points of view if his mind is set on something. To others, this can be quite annoying. Taurus also does not like to be told what to do. He becomes rather angry if others think him not too bright. He does not like to be told he is wrong, even when he is. He dislikes being contradicted.

Some people who are born under this sign are very suspicious of others—even of those persons close to them. They find it difficult to trust people fully. They are often afraid of being deceived or taken advantage of. The Bull often finds it difficult to forget or forgive. His love of material things sometimes makes him rather avaricious and petty.

Gemini: May 21–June 20
The Positive Side of Gemini

The person born under this sign of the Heavenly Twins is usually quite bright and quick-witted. Some of them are capable of doing many different things. The Gemini person very often has many different interests. He keeps an open mind and is always anxious to learn new things.

Gemini is often an analytical person. He is a person who enjoys making use of his intellect. He is governed more by his mind than by his emotions. He is a person who is not confined to one view; he can often understand both sides to a problem or question. He knows how to reason, how to make rapid decisions if need be.

He is an adaptable person and can make himself at home almost anywhere. There are all kinds of situations he can adapt to. He is a person who seldom doubts himself; he is sure of his talents and his ability to think and reason. Gemini is generally most satisfied when

he is in a situation where he can make use of his intellect. Never short of imagination, he often has strong talents for invention. He is rather a modern person when it comes to life; Gemini almost always moves along with the times—perhaps that is why he remains so youthful throughout most of his life.

Literature and art appeal to the person born under this sign. Creativity in almost any form will interest and intrigue the Gemini man or woman.

The Gemini is often quite charming. A good talker, he often is the center of attraction at any gathering. People find it easy to like a person born under this sign because he can appear easygoing and usually has a good sense of humor.

The Negative Side of Gemini

Sometimes the Gemini person tries to do too many things at one time—and as a result, winds up finishing nothing. Some Twins are easily distracted and find it rather difficult to concentrate on one thing for too long a time. Sometimes they give in to trifling fancies and find it rather boring to become too serious about any one thing. Some of them are never dependable, no matter what they promise.

Although the Gemini man or woman often appears to be well-versed on many subjects, this is sometimes just a veneer. His knowledge may be only superficial, but because he speaks so well he gives people the impression of erudition. Some Geminis are sharp-tongued and inconsiderate; they think only of themselves and their own pleasure.

Cancer: June 21–July 20

The Positive Side of Cancer

The Moon Child's most positive point is his understanding nature. On the whole, he is a loving and sympathetic person. He would never go out of his way to hurt anyone. The Cancer man or woman is often very kind and tender; they give what they can to others. They hate to see others suffering and will do what they can to help someone in less fortunate circumstances than themselves. They are often very concerned about the world. Their interest in people generally goes beyond that of just their own families and close friends; they have a deep sense of community and respect humanitarian values. The Moon Child means what he says, as a rule; he is honest about his feelings.

The Cancer man or woman is a person who knows the art of patience. When something seems difficult, he is willing to wait until the situation becomes manageable again. He is a person who knows how to bide his time. Cancer knows how to concentrate on one thing at a time. When he has made his mind up he generally sticks with what he does, seeing it through to the end.

Cancer is a person who loves his home. He enjoys being surrounded by familiar things and the people he loves. Of all the signs, Cancer is the most maternal. Even the men born under this sign often have a motherly or protective quality about them. They like to take care of people in their family—to see that they are well loved and well provided for. They are usually loyal and faithful. Family ties mean a lot to the Cancer man or woman. Parents and in-laws are respected and loved. Young Cancer responds very well to adults who show faith in him. The Moon Child has a strong sense of tradition. He is very sensitive to the moods of others.

The Negative Side of Cancer

Sometimes Cancer finds it rather hard to face life. It becomes too much for him. He can be a little timid and retiring, when things don't go too well. When unfortunate things happen, he is apt to just shrug and say, "Whatever will be will be." He can be fatalistic to a fault. The uncultivated Cancer is a bit lazy. He doesn't have very much ambition. Anything that seems a bit difficult he'll gladly leave to others. He may be lacking in initiative. Too sensitive, when he feels he's been injured, he'll crawl back into his shell and nurse his imaginary wounds. The immature Moon Child often is given to crying when the smallest thing goes wrong.

Some Cancers find it difficult to enjoy themselves in environments outside their homes. They make heavy demands on others, and need to be constantly reassured that they are loved. Lacking such reassurance, they may resort to sulking in silence.

Leo: July 21–August 21

The Positive Side of Leo

Often Leos make good leaders. They seem to be good organizers and administrators. Usually they are quite popular with others. Whatever group it is that they belong to, the Leo man or woman is almost sure to be or become the leader. Loyalty, one of the Lion's noblest traits, enables him or her to maintain this leadership position.

Leo is generous most of the time. It is his best characteristic. He or she likes to give gifts and presents. In making others happy, the Leo person becomes happy himself. He likes to splurge when spending money on others. In some instances it may seem that the Lion's generosity knows no boundaries. A hospitable person, the Leo man or woman is very fond of welcoming people to his house and entertaining them. He is never short of company.

Leo has plenty of energy and drive. He enjoys working toward some specific goal. When he applies himself correctly, he gets what he wants most often. The Leo person is almost never unsure of himself. He has plenty of confidence and aplomb. He is a person who is direct in almost everything he does. He has a quick mind and can make a decision in a very short time.

He usually sets a good example for others because of his ambitious manner and positive ways. He knows how to stick to something once he's started. Although Leo may be good at making a joke, he is not superficial or glib. He is a loving person, kind and thoughtful.

There is generally nothing small or petty about the Leo man or woman. He does what he can for those who are deserving. He is a person others can rely upon at all times. He means what he says. An honest person, generally speaking, he is a friend who is valued and sought out.

The Negative Side of Leo

Leo, however, does have his faults. At times, he can be just a bit too arrogant. He thinks that no one deserves a leadership position except him. Only he is capable of doing things well. His opinion of himself is often much too high. Because of his conceit, he is sometimes rather unpopular with a good many people. Some Leos are too materialistic; they can only think in terms of money and profit.

Some Leos enjoy lording it over others—at home or at their place of business. What is more, they feel they have the right to. Egocentric to an impossible degree, this sort of Leo cares little about how others think or feel. He can be rude and cutting.

Virgo: August 22–September 22

The Positive Side of Virgo

The person born under the sign of Virgo is generally a busy person. He knows how to arrange and organize things. He is a good planner. Above all, he is practical and is not afraid of hard work.

Often called the sign of the Harvester, Virgo knows how to attain what he desires. He sticks with something until it is finished. He never shirks his duties, and can always be depended upon. The Virgo person can be thoroughly trusted at all times.

The man or woman born under this sign tries to do everything to perfection. He doesn't believe in doing anything halfway. He always aims for the top. He is the sort of a person who is always learning and constantly striving to better himself—not because he wants more money or glory, but because it gives him a feeling of accomplishment.

The Virgo man or woman is a very observant person. He is sensitive to how others feel, and can see things below the surface of a situation. He usually puts this talent to constructive use.

It is not difficult for the Virgo to be open and earnest. He believes in putting his cards on the table. He is never secretive or underhanded. He's as good as his word. The Virgo person is generally plainspoken and down to earth. He has no trouble in expressing himself.

The Virgo person likes to keep up to date on new developments in his particular field. Well-informed, generally, he sometimes has a keen interest in the arts or literature. What he knows, he knows well. His ability to use his critical faculties is well-developed and sometimes startles others because of its accuracy.

Virgos adhere to a moderate way of life; they avoid excesses. Virgo is a responsible person and enjoys being of service.

The Negative Side of Virgo

Sometimes a Virgo person is too critical. He thinks that only he can do something the way it should be done. Whatever anyone else does is inferior. He can be rather annoying in the way he quibbles over insignificant details. In telling others how things should be done, he can be rather tactless and mean.

Some Virgos seem rather emotionless and cool. They feel emotional involvement is beneath them. They are sometimes too tidy, too neat. With money they can be rather miserly. Some Virgos try to force their opinions and ideas on others.

Libra: September 23–October 22

The Positive Side of Libra

Libras love harmony. It is one of their most outstanding character traits. They are interested in achieving balance; they admire beauty and grace in things as well as in people. Generally speaking, they are kind and considerate people. Libras are usually very sympathetic. They go out of their way not to hurt another person's feelings. They are outgoing and do what they can to help those in need.

People born under the sign of Libra almost always make good friends. They are loyal and amiable. They enjoy the company of others. Many of them are rather moderate in their views; they believe in keeping an open mind, however, and weighing both sides of an issue fairly before making a decision.

Alert and intelligent, Libra, often known as the Lawgiver, is always fair-minded and tries to put himself in the position of the other person. They are against injustice; quite often they take up for the underdog. In most of their social dealings, they try to be tactful and kind. They dislike discord and bickering, and most Libras strive for peace and harmony in all their relationships.

The Libra man or woman has a keen sense of beauty. They appreciate handsome furnishings and clothes. Many of them are artistically inclined. Their taste is usually impeccable. They know how to use color. Their homes are almost always attractively arranged and inviting. They enjoy entertaining people and see to it that their guests always feel at home and welcome.

Libra gets along with almost everyone. He is well-liked and socially much in demand.

The Negative Side of Libra

Some people born under this sign tend to be rather insincere. So eager are they to achieve harmony in all relationships that they will even go so far as to lie. Many of them are escapists. They find facing the truth an ordeal and prefer living in a world of make-believe.

In a serious argument, some Libras give in rather easily even when they know they are right. Arguing, even about something they believe in, is too unsettling for some of them.

Libras sometimes care too much for material things. They enjoy possessions and luxuries. Some are vain and tend to be jealous.

Scorpio: October 23–November 22

The Positive Side of Scorpio

The Scorpio man or woman generally knows what he or she wants out of life. He is a determined person. He sees something through to the end. Scorpio is quite sincere, and seldom says anything he doesn't mean. When he sets a goal for himself he tries to go about achieving it in a very direct way.

The Scorpion is brave and courageous. They are not afraid of hard work. Obstacles do not frighten them. They forge ahead until they achieve what they set out for. The Scorpio man or woman has a strong will.

Although Scorpio may seem rather fixed and determined, inside he is often quite tender and loving. He can care very much for others. He believes in sincerity in all relationships. His feelings about someone tend to last; they are profound and not superficial.

The Scorpio person is someone who adheres to his principles no matter what happens. He will not be deterred from a path he believes to be right.

Because of his many positive strengths, the Scorpion can often achieve happiness for himself and for those that he loves.

He is a constructive person by nature. He often has a deep understanding of people and of life, in general. He is perceptive and unafraid. Obstacles often seem to spur him on. He is a positive person who enjoys winning. He has many strengths and resources; challenge of any sort often brings out the best in him.

The Negative Side of Scorpio

The Scorpio person is sometimes hypersensitive. Often he imagines injury when there is none. He feels that others do not bother to recognize him for his true worth. Sometimes he is given to excessive boasting in order to compensate for what he feels is neglect.

Scorpio can be proud, arrogant, and competitive. They can be sly when they put their minds to it and they enjoy outwitting persons or institutions noted for their cleverness.

Their tactics for getting what they want are sometimes devious and ruthless. They don't care too much about what others may think. If they feel others have done them an injustice, they will do their best to seek revenge. The Scorpion often has a sudden, violent temper; and this person's interest in sex is sometimes quite unbalanced or excessive.

Sagittarius: November 23–December 20

The Positive Side of Sagittarius

People born under this sign are honest and forthright. Their approach to life is earnest and open. Sagittarius is often quite adult in his way of seeing things. They are broad-minded and tolerant people. When dealing with others the person born under the sign of the Archer is almost always open and forthright. He doesn't believe in deceit or pretension. His standards are high. People who associate with Sagittarius generally admire and respect his tolerant viewpoint.

The Archer trusts others easily and expects them to trust him. He is never suspicious or envious and almost always thinks well of others. People always enjoy his company because he is so friendly and easygoing. The Sagittarius man or woman is often good-humored. He can always be depended upon by his friends, family, and co-workers.

The person born under this sign of the Zodiac likes a good joke every now and then. Sagittarius is eager for fun and laughs, which makes him very popular with others.

A lively person, he enjoys sports and outdoor life. The Archer is fond of animals. Intelligent and interesting, he can begin an ani-

mated conversation with ease. He likes exchanging ideas and discussing various views.

He is not selfish or proud. If someone proposes an idea or plan that is better than his, he will immediately adopt it. Imaginative yet practical, he knows how to put ideas into practice.

The Archer enjoys sport and games, and it doesn't matter if he wins or loses. He is a forgiving person, and never sulks over something that has not worked out in his favor.

He is seldom critical, and is almost always generous.

The Negative Side of Sagittarius

Some Sagittarius are restless. They take foolish risks and seldom learn from the mistakes they make. They don't have heads for money and are often mismanaging their finances. Some of them devote much of their time to gambling.

Some are too outspoken and tactless, always putting their feet in their mouths. They hurt others carelessly by being honest at the wrong time. Sometimes they make promises which they don't keep. They don't stick close enough to their plans and go from one failure to another. They are undisciplined and waste a lot of energy.

Capricorn: December 21–January 19

The Positive Side of Capricorn

The person born under the sign of Capricorn, known variously as the Mountain Goat or Sea Goat, is usually very stable and patient. He sticks to whatever tasks he has and sees them through. He can always be relied upon and he is not averse to work.

An honest person, Capricorn is generally serious about whatever he does. He does not take his duties lightly. He is a practical person and believes in keeping his feet on the ground.

Quite often the person born under this sign is ambitious and knows how to get what he wants out of life. The Goat forges ahead and never gives up his goal. When he is determined about something, he almost always wins. He is a good worker—a hard worker. Although things may not come easy to him, he will not complain, but continue working until his chores are finished.

He is usually good at business matters and knows the value of money. He is not a spendthrift and knows how to put something away for a rainy day; he dislikes waste and unnecessary loss.

Capricorn knows how to make use of his self-control. He can apply himself to almost anything once he puts his mind to it. His ability to concentrate sometimes astounds others. He is diligent and does well when involved in detail work.

The Capricorn man or woman is charitable, generally speaking, and will do what is possible to help others less fortunate. As a friend, he is loyal and trustworthy. He never shirks his duties or responsibilities. He is self-reliant and never expects too much of the other fellow. He does what he can on his own. If someone does him a good turn, then he will do his best to return the favor.

The Negative Side of Capricorn

Like everyone, Capricorn, too, has faults. At times, the Goat can be overcritical of others. He expects others to live up to his own high standards. He thinks highly of himself and tends to look down on others.

His interest in material things may be exaggerated. The Capricorn man or woman thinks too much about getting on in the world and having something to show for it. He may even be a little greedy.

He sometimes thinks he knows what's best for everyone. He is too bossy. He is always trying to organize and correct others. He may be a little narrow in his thinking.

Aquarius: January 20–February 18

The Positive Side of Aquarius

The Aquarius man or woman is usually very honest and forthright. These are his two greatest qualities. His standards for himself are generally very high. He can always be relied upon by others. His word is his bond.

Aquarius is perhaps the most tolerant of all the Zodiac personalities. He respects other people's beliefs and feels that everyone is entitled to his own approach to life.

He would never do anything to injure another's feelings. He is never unkind or cruel. Always considerate of others, the Water

Bearer is always willing to help a person in need. He feels a very strong tie between himself and all the other members of mankind.

The person born under this sign, called the Water Bearer, is almost always an individualist. He does not believe in teaming up with the masses, but prefers going his own way. His ideas about life and mankind are often quite advanced. There is a saying to the effect that the average Aquarius is fifty years ahead of his time.

Aquarius is community-minded. The problems of the world concern him greatly. He is interested in helping others no matter what part of the globe they live in. He is truly a humanitarian sort. He likes to be of service to others.

Giving, considerate, and without prejudice, Aquarius have no trouble getting along with others.

The Negative Side of Aquarius

Aquarius may be too much of a dreamer. He makes plans but seldom carries them out. He is rather unrealistic. His imagination has a tendency to run away with him. Because many of his plans are impractical, he is always in some sort of a dither.

Others may not approve of him at all times because of his unconventional behavior. He may be a bit eccentric. Sometimes he is so busy with his own thoughts that he loses touch with the realities of existence.

Some Aquarius feel they are more clever and intelligent than others. They seldom admit to their own faults, even when they are quite apparent. Some become rather fanatic in their views. Their criticism of others is sometimes destructive and negative.

Pisces: February 19–March 20

The Positive Side of Pisces

Known as the sign of the Fishes, Pisces has a sympathetic nature. Kindly, he is often dedicated in the way he goes about helping others. The sick and the troubled often turn to him for advice and assistance. Possessing keen intuition, Pisces can easily understand people's deepest problems.

He is very broad-minded and does not criticize others for their faults. He knows how to accept people for what they are. On the whole, he is a trustworthy and earnest person. He is loyal to his friends and will do what he can to help them in time of need. Generous and good-natured, he is a lover of peace; he is often willing to help others solve their differences. People who have taken a wrong turn in life often interest him and he will do what he can to persuade them to rehabilitate themselves.

He has a strong intuitive sense and most of the time he knows how to make it work for him. Pisces is unusually perceptive and often knows what is bothering someone before that person, himself, is aware of it. The Pisces man or woman is an idealistic person, basically, and is interested in making the world a better place in which to live. Pisces believes that everyone should help each other. He is willing to do more than his share in order to achieve cooperation with others.

The person born under this sign often is talented in music or art. He is a receptive person; he is able to take the ups and downs of life with philosophic calm.

The Negative Side of Pisces

Some Pisces are often depressed; their outlook on life is rather glum. They may feel that they have been given a bad deal in life and that others are always taking unfair advantage of them. Pisces sometimes feel that the world is a cold and cruel place. The Fishes can be easily discouraged. The Pisces man or woman may even withdraw from the harshness of reality into a secret shell of his own where he dreams and idles away a good deal of his time.

Pisces can be lazy. He lets things happen without giving the least bit of resistance. He drifts along, whether on the high road or on the low. He can be lacking in willpower.

Some Pisces people seek escape through drugs or alcohol. When temptation comes along they find it hard to resist. In matters of sex, they can be rather permissive.

Sun Sign Personalities

ARIES: Hans Christian Andersen, Pearl Bailey, Marlon Brando, Wernher Von Braun, Charlie Chaplin, Joan Crawford, Da Vinci, Bette Davis, Doris Day, W.C. Fields, Alec Guinness, Adolf Hitler, William Holden, Thomas Jefferson, Nikita Khrushchev, Elton John, Arturo Toscanini, J.P. Morgan, Paul Robeson, Gloria Steinem, Sarah Vaughn, Vincent van Gogh, Tennessee Williams

TAURUS: Fred Astaire, Charlotte Brontë, Carol Burnett, Irving Berlin, Bing Crosby, Salvador Dali, Tchaikovsky, Queen Elizabeth II, Duke Ellington, Ella Fitzgerald, Henry Fonda, Sigmund Freud, Orson Welles, Joe Louis, Lenin, Karl Marx, Golda Meir, Eva Peron, Bertrand Russell, Shakespeare, Kate Smith, Benjamin Spock, Barbra Streisand, Shirley Temple, Harry Truman

GEMINI: Ruth Benedict, Josephine Baker, Rachel Carson, Carlos Chavez, Walt Whitman, Bob Dylan, Ralph Waldo Emerson, Judy Garland, Paul Gauguin, Allen Ginsberg, Benny Goodman, Bob Hope, Burl Ives, John F. Kennedy, Peggy Lee, Marilyn Monroe, Joe Namath, Cole Porter, Laurence Olivier, Harriet Beecher Stowe, Queen Victoria, John Wayne, Frank Lloyd Wright

CANCER: "Dear Abby," Lizzie Borden, David Brinkley, Yul Brynner, Pearl Buck, Marc Chagall, Princess Diana, Babe Didrikson, Mary Baker Eddy, Henry VIII, John Glenn, Ernest Hemingway, Lena Horne, Oscar Hammerstein, Helen Keller, Ann Landers, George Orwell, Nancy Reagan, Rembrandt, Richard Rodgers, Ginger Rogers, Rubens, Jean-Paul Sartre, O.J. Simpson

LEO: Neil Armstrong, James Baldwin, Lucille Ball, Emily Brontë, Wilt Chamberlain, Julia Child, William J. Clinton, Cecil B. De Mille, Ogden Nash, Amelia Earhart, Edna Ferber, Arthur Goldberg, Alfred Hitchcock, Mick Jagger, George Meany, Annie Oakley, George Bernard Shaw, Napoleon, Jacqueline Onassis, Henry Ford, Francis Scott Key, Andy Warhol, Mae West, Orville Wright

VIRGO: Ingrid Bergman, Warren Burger, Maurice Chevalier, Agatha Christie, Sean Connery, Lafayette, Peter Falk, Greta Garbo, Althea Gibson, Arthur Godfrey, Goethe, Buddy Hackett, Michael Jackson, Lyndon Johnson, D.H. Lawrence, Sophia Loren, Grandma Moses, Arnold Palmer, Queen Elizabeth I, Walter Reuther, Peter Sellers, Lily Tomlin, George Wallace

LIBRA: Brigitte Bardot, Art Buchwald, Truman Capote, Dwight D. Eisenhower, William Faulkner, F. Scott Fitzgerald, Gandhi, George Gershwin, Micky Mantle, Helen Hayes, Vladimir Horowitz, Doris Lessing, Martina Navratalova, Eugene O'Neill, Luciano Pavarotti, Emily Post, Eleanor Roosevelt, Bruce Springsteen, Margaret Thatcher, Gore Vidal, Barbara Walters, Oscar Wilde

SCORPIO: Vivien Leigh, Richard Burton, Art Carney, Johnny Carson, Billy Graham, Grace Kelly, Walter Cronkite, Marie Curie, Charles de Gaulle, Linda Evans, Indira Gandhi, Theodore Roosevelt, Rock Hudson, Katherine Hepburn, Robert F. Kennedy, Billie Jean King, Martin Luther, Georgia O'Keeffe, Pablo Picasso, Jonas Salk, Alan Shepard, Robert Louis Stevenson

SAGITTARIUS: Jane Austen, Louisa May Alcott, Woody Allen, Beethoven, Willy Brandt, Mary Martin, William F. Buckley, Maria Callas, Winston Churchill, Noel Coward, Emily Dickinson, Walt Disney, Benjamin Disraeli, James Doolittle, Kirk Douglas, Chet Huntley, Jane Fonda, Chris Evert Lloyd, Margaret Mead, Charles Schulz, John Milton, Frank Sinatra, Steven Spielberg

CAPRICORN: Muhammad Ali, Isaac Asimov, Pablo Casals, Dizzy Dean, Marlene Dietrich, James Farmer, Ava Gardner, Barry Goldwater, Cary Grant, J. Edgar Hoover, Howard Hughes, Joan of Arc, Gypsy Rose Lee, Martin Luther King, Jr., Rudyard Kipling, Mao Tse-tung, Richard Nixon, Gamal Nasser, Louis Pasteur, Albert Schweitzer, Stalin, Benjamin Franklin, Elvis Presley

AQUARIUS: Marian Anderson, Susan B. Anthony, Jack Benny, John Barrymore, Mikhail Baryshnikov, Charles Darwin, Charles Dickens, Thomas Edison, Clark Gable, Jascha Heifetz, Abraham Lincoln, Yehudi Menuhin, Mozart, Jack Nicklaus, Ronald Reagan, Jackie Robinson, Norman Rockwell, Franklin D. Roosevelt, Gertrude Stein, Charles Lindbergh, Margaret Truman

PISCES: Edward Albee, Harry Belafonte, Alexander Graham Bell, Chopin, Adelle Davis, Albert Einstein, Golda Meir, Jackie Gleason, Winslow Homer, Edward M. Kennedy, Victor Hugo, Mike Mansfield, Michelangelo, Edna St. Vincent Millay, Liza Minelli, John Steinbeck, Linus Pauling, Ravel, Renoir, Diana Ross, William Shirer, Elizabeth Taylor, George Washington

The Signs and Their Key Words

		POSITIVE	NEGATIVE
ARIES	self	courage, initiative, pioneer instinct	brash rudeness, selfish impetuosity
TAURUS	money	endurance, loyalty, wealth	obstinacy, gluttony
GEMINI	mind	versatility	capriciousness, unreliability
CANCER	family	sympathy, homing instinct	clannishness, childishness
LEO	children	love, authority, integrity	egotism, force
VIRGO	work	purity, industry, analysis	faultfinding, cynicism
LIBRA	marriage	harmony, justice	vacillation, superficiality
SCORPIO	sex	survival, regeneration	vengeance, discord
SAGITTARIUS	travel	optimism, higher learning	lawlessness
CAPRICORN	career	depth	narrowness, gloom
AQUARIUS	friends	human fellowship, genius	perverse unpredictability
PISCES	confine-ment	spiritual love, universality	diffusion, escapism

The Elements and Qualities of The Signs

Every sign has both an *element* and a *quality* associated with it. The element indicates the basic makeup of the sign, and the quality describes the kind of activity associated with each.

Element	Sign	Quality	Sign
FIRE...........	ARIES LEO SAGITTARIUS	CARDINAL......	ARIES LIBRA CANCER CAPRICORN
EARTH	TAURUS VIRGO CAPRICORN	FIXED	TAURUS LEO SCORPIO AQUARIUS
AIR..............	GEMINI LIBRA AQUARIUS		
WATER	CANCER SCORPIO PISCES	MUTABLE	GEMINI VIRGO SAGITTARIUS PISCES

Signs can be grouped together according to their element and quality. Signs of the same element share many basic traits in common. They tend to form stable configurations and ultimately harmonious relationships. Signs of the same quality are often less harmonious, but they share many dynamic potentials for growth as well as profound fulfillment.

Further discussion of each of these sign groupings is provided on the following pages.

The Fire Signs

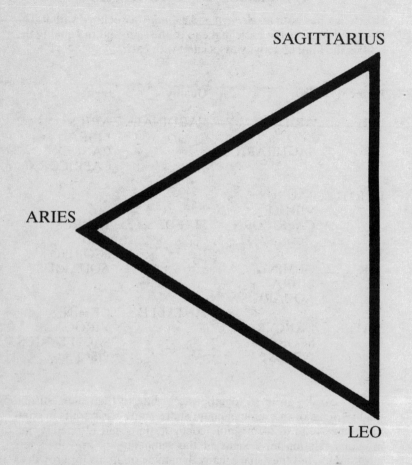

This is the fire group. On the whole these are emotional, volatile types, quick to anger, quick to forgive. They are adventurous, powerful people and act as a source of inspiration for everyone. They spark into action with immediate exuberant impulses. They are intelligent, self-involved, creative, and idealistic. They all share a certain vibrancy and glow that outwardly reflects an inner flame and passion for living.

The Earth Signs

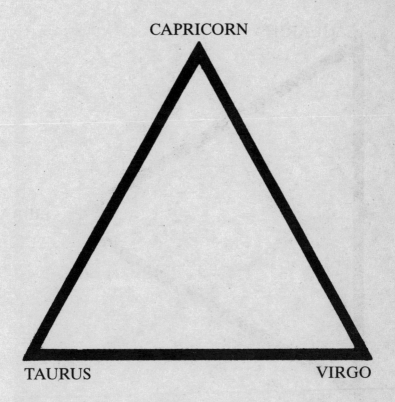

CAPRICORN

TAURUS

VIRGO

This is the earth group. They are in constant touch with the material world and tend to be conservative. Although they are all capable of spartan self-discipline, they are earthy, sensual people who are stimulated by the tangible, elegant, and luxurious. The thread of their lives is always practical, but they do fantasize and are often attracted to dark, mysterious, emotional people. They are like great cliffs overhanging the sea, forever married to the ocean but always resisting erosion from the dark, emotional forces that thunder at their feet.

The Air Signs

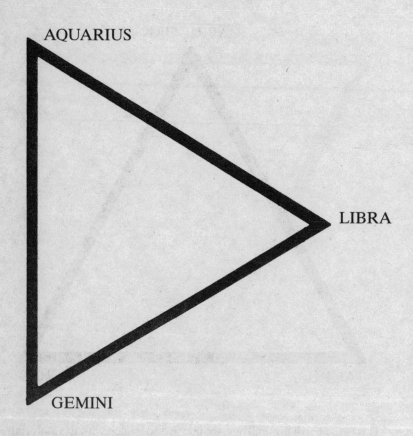

This is the air group. They are light, mental creatures desirous of contact, communication, and relationship. They are involved with people and the forming of ties on many levels. Original thinkers, they are the bearers of human news. Their language is their sense of word, color, style, and beauty. They provide an atmosphere suitable and pleasant for living. They add change and versatility to the scene, and it is through them that we can explore new territory of human intelligence and experience.

The Water Signs

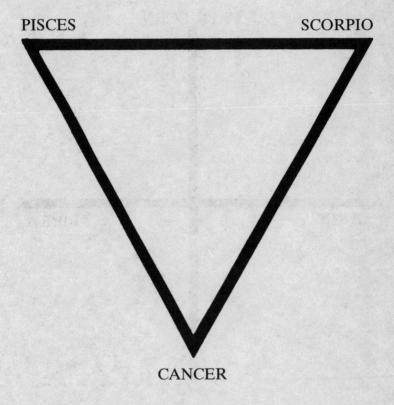

PISCES

SCORPIO

CANCER

This is the water group. Through the water people, we are all joined together on emotional, nonverbal levels. They are silent, mysterious types whose magic hypnotizes even the most determined realist. They have uncanny perceptions about people and are as rich as the oceans when it comes to feeling, emotion, or imagination. They are sensitive, mystical creatures with memories that go back beyond time. Through water, life is sustained. These people have the potential for the depths of darkness or the heights of mysticism and art.

The Cardinal Signs

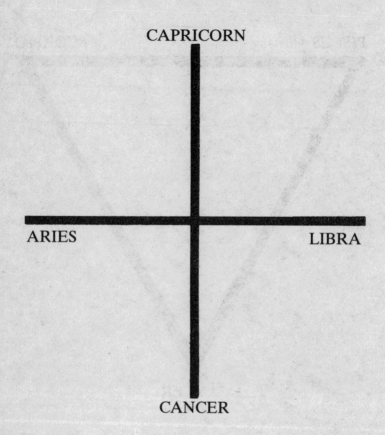

Put together, this is a clear-cut picture of dynamism, activity, tremendous stress, and remarkable achievement. These people know the meaning of great change since their lives are often characterized by significant crises and major successes. This combination is like a simultaneous storm of summer, fall, winter, and spring. The danger is chaotic diffusion of energy; the potential is irrepressible growth and victory.

The Fixed Signs

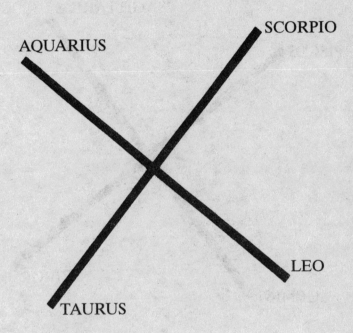

Fixed signs are always establishing themselves in a given place or area of experience. Like explorers who arrive and plant a flag, these people claim a position from which they do not enjoy being deposed. They are staunch, stalwart, upright, trusty, honorable people, although their obstinacy is well-known. Their contribution is fixity, and they are the angels who support our visible world.

The Mutable Signs

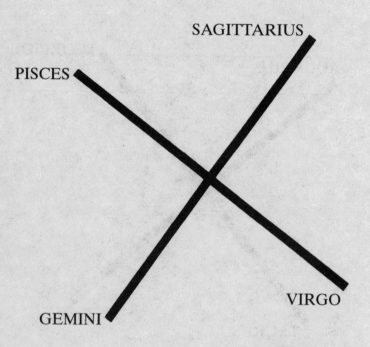

Mutable people are versatile, sensitive, intelligent, ner vous, and deeply curious about life. They are the translators of all energy. They often carry out or complete tasks initiated by others. Combinations of these signs have highly developed minds; they are imaginative and jumpy and think and talk a lot. At worst their lives are a Tower of Babel. At best they are adaptable and ready creatures who can assimilate one kind of experience and enjoy it while anticipating coming changes.

THE PLANETS
OF THE SOLAR SYSTEM

This section describes the planets of the solar system. In astrology, both the Sun and the Moon are considered to be planets. Because of the Moon's influence in our day-to-day lives, the Moon is described in a separate section following this one.

The Planets and the Signs
They Rule

The signs of the Zodiac are linked to the planets in the following way. Each sign is governed or ruled by one or more planets. No matter where the planets are located in the sky at any given moment, they still rule their respective signs, and when they travel through the signs they rule, they have special dignity and their effects are stronger.

Following is a list of the planets and the signs they rule. After looking at the list, read the definitions of the planets and see if you can determine how the planet ruling *your* Sun sign has affected your life.

SIGNS	RULING PLANETS
Aries	Mars, Pluto
Taurus	Venus
Gemini	Mercury
Cancer	Moon
Leo	Sun
Virgo	Mercury
Libra	Venus
Scorpio	Mars, Pluto
Sagittarius	Jupiter
Capricorn	Saturn
Aquarius	Saturn, Uranus
Pisces	Jupiter, Neptune

Characteristics of the Planets

The following pages give the meaning and characteristics of the planets of the solar system. They all travel around the Sun at different speeds and different distances. Taken with the Sun, they all distribute individual intelligence and ability throughout the entire chart.

The planets modify the influence of the Sun in a chart according to their own particular natures, strengths, and positions. Their positions must be calculated for each year and day, and their function and expression in a horoscope will change as they move from one area of the Zodiac to another.

We start with a description of the sun.

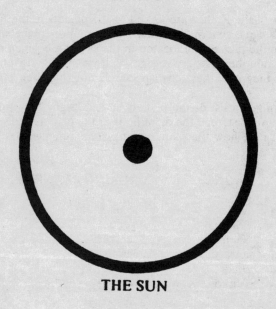

THE SUN

SUN

This is the center of existence. Around this flaming sphere all the planets revolve in endless orbits. Our star is constantly sending out its beams of light and energy without which no life on Earth would be possible. In astrology it symbolizes everything we are trying to become, the center around which all of our activity in life will always revolve. It is the symbol of our basic nature and describes the natural and constant thread that runs through everything that we do from birth to death on this planet.

To early astrologers, the Sun seemed to be another planet because it crossed the heavens every day, just like the rest of the bodies in the sky.

It is the only star near enough to be seen well—it is, in fact, a dwarf star. Approximately 860,000 miles in diameter, it is about ten times as wide as the giant planet Jupiter. The next nearest star is nearly 300,000 times as far away, and if the Sun were located as far away as most of the bright stars, it would be too faint to be seen without a telescope.

Everything in the horoscope ultimately revolves around this singular body. Although other forces may be prominent in the charts of some individuals, still the Sun is the total nucleus of being and symbolizes the complete potential of every human being alive. It is vitality and the life force. Your whole essence comes from the position of the Sun.

You are always trying to express the Sun according to its position by house and sign. Possibility for all development is found in the Sun, and it marks the fundamental character of your personal radiations all around you.

It is the symbol of strength, vigor, wisdom, dignity, ardor, and generosity, and the ability for a person to function as a mature individual. It is also a creative force in society. It is consciousness of the gift of life.

The underdeveloped solar nature is arrogant, pushy, undependable, and proud, and is constantly using force.

MERCURY

Mercury is the planet closest to the Sun. It races around our star, gathering information and translating it to the rest of the system. Mercury represents your capacity to understand the desires of your own will and to translate those desires into action.

In other words it is the planet of mind and the power of communication. Through Mercury we develop an ability to think, write, speak, and observe—to become aware of the world around us. It colors our attitudes and vision of the world, as well as our capacity to communicate our inner responses to the outside world. Some people who have serious disabilities in their power of verbal communication have often wrongly been described as people lacking intelligence.

Although this planet (and its position in the horoscope) indicates your power to communicate your thoughts and perceptions to the world, intelligence is something deeper. Intelligence is distributed throughout all the planets. It is the relationship of the planets to each other that truly describes what we call intelligence. Mercury rules speaking, language, mathematics, draft and design, students, messengers, young people, offices, teachers, and any pursuits where the mind of man has wings.

VENUS

Venus is beauty. It symbolizes the harmony and radiance of a rare and elusive quality: beauty itself. It is refinement and delicacy, softness and charm. In astrology it indicates grace, balance, and the aesthetic sense. Where Venus is we see beauty, a gentle drawing in of energy and the need for satisfaction and completion. It is a special touch that finishes off rough edges. It is sensitivity, and affection, and it is always the place for that other elusive phenomenon: love. Venus describes our sense of what is beautiful and loving. Poorly developed, it is vulgar, tasteless, and self-indulgent. But its ideal is the flame of spiritual love—Aphrodite, goddess of love, and the sweetness and power of personal beauty.

MARS

Mars is raw, crude energy. The planet next to Earth but outward from the Sun is a fiery red sphere that charges through the horoscope with force and fury. It represents the way you reach out for new adventure and new experience. It is energy and drive, initiative, courage, and daring. It is the power to start something and see it through. It can be thoughtless, cruel and wild, angry and hostile, causing cuts, burns, scalds, and wounds. It can stab its way through a chart, or it can be the symbol of healthy spirited adventure, well-channeled constructive power to begin and keep up the drive. If you have trouble starting things, if you lack the get-up-and-go to start the ball rolling, if you lack aggressiveness and self-confidence, chances are there's another planet influencing your Mars. Mars rules soldiers, butchers, surgeons, salesmen—any field that requires daring, bold skill, operational technique, or self-promotion.

JUPITER

This is the largest planet of the solar system. Scientists have recently learned that Jupiter reflects more light than it receives from the Sun. In a sense it is like a star itself. In astrology it rules good luck and good cheer, health, wealth, optimism, happiness, success, and joy. It is the symbol of opportunity and always opens the way for new possibilities in your life. It rules exuberance, enthusiasm, wisdom, knowledge, generosity, and all forms of expansion in general. It rules actors, statesmen, clerics, professional people, religion, publishing, and the distribution of many people over large areas.

Sometimes Jupiter makes you think you deserve everything, and you become sloppy, wasteful, careless and rude, prodigal and lawless, in the illusion that nothing can ever go wrong. Then there is the danger of overconfidence, exaggeration, undependability, and overindulgence.

Jupiter is the minimization of limitation and the emphasis on spirituality and potential. It is the thirst for knowledge and higher learning.

SATURN

Saturn circles our system in dark splendor with its mysterious rings, forcing us to be awakened to what ever we have neglected in the past. It will present real puzzles and problems to be solved, causing delays, obstacles, and hindrances. By doing so, Saturn stirs our own sensitivity to those areas where we are laziest.

Here we must patiently develop *method*, and only through pains-taking effort can our ends be achieved. It brings order to a horoscope and imposes reason just where we are feeling least reasonable. By creating limitations and boundary, Saturn shows the consequences of being human and demands that we accept the changing cycles inevitable in human life. Saturn rules time, old age, and sobriety. It can bring depression, gloom, jealousy, and greed, or serious ac cep tance of responsibilities out of which success will develop. With Saturn there is nothing to do but face facts. It rules laborers, stones, granite, rocks, and crystals of all kinds.

THE OUTER PLANETS:
URANUS, NEPTUNE, PLUTO

Uranus, Neptune, Pluto are the outer planets. They liberate human beings from cultural conditioning, and in that sense are the lawbreakers. In early times it was thought that Saturn was the last planet of the system—the outer limit beyond which we could never go. The discovery of the next three planets ushered in new phases of human history, revolution, and technology.

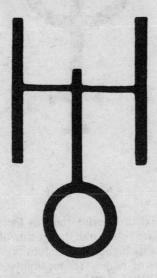

URANUS

Uranus rules unexpected change, upheaval, revolution. It is the symbol of total independence and asserts the freedom of an individual from all restriction and restraint. It is a breakthrough planet and indicates talent, originality, and genius in a horoscope. It usually causes last-minute reversals and changes of plan, unwanted separations, accidents, catastrophes, and eccentric behavior. It can add irrational rebelliousness and perverse bohemianism to a personality or a streak of unaffected brilliance in science and art. It rules technology, aviation, and all forms of electrical and electronic advancement. It governs great leaps forward and topsy-turvy situations, and *always* turns things around at the last minute. Its effects are difficult to predict, since it rules sudden last-minute decisions and events that come like lightning out of the blue.

NEPTUNE

Neptune dissolves existing reality the way the sea erodes the cliffs beside it. Its effects are subtle like the ringing of a buoy's bell in the fog. It suggests a reality higher than definition can usually describe. It awakens a sense of higher responsibility often causing guilt, worry, anxieties, or delusions. Neptune is associated with all forms of escape and can make things seem a certain way so convincingly that you are absolutely sure of something that eventually turns out to be quite different.

It is the planet of illusion and therefore governs the invisible realms that lie beyond our ordinary minds, beyond our simple factual ability to prove what is "real." Treachery, deceit, disillusionment, and disappointment are linked to Neptune. It describes a vague reality that promises eternity and the divine, yet in a manner so complex that we cannot really fathom it at all. At its worst Neptune is a cheap intoxicant; at its best it is the poetry, music, and inspiration of the higher planes of spiritual love. It has dominion over movies, photographs, and much of the arts.

PLUTO

Pluto lies at the outpost of our system and therefore rules finality in a horoscope—the final closing of chapters in your life, the passing of major milestones and points of development from which there is no return. It is a final wipeout, a closeout, an evacuation. It is a distant, subtle but powerful catalyst in all transformations that occur. It creates, destroys, then re creates. Sometimes Pluto starts its influence with a minor event or insignificant incident that might even go unnoticed. Slowly but surely, little by little, everything changes, until at last there has been a total transformation in the area of your life where Pluto has been operating. It rules mass thinking and the trends that society first rejects, then adopts, and finally outgrows.

Pluto rules the dead and the underworld—all the powerful forces of creation and destruction that go on all the time beneath, around, and above us. It can bring a lust for power with strong obsessions.

It is the planet that rules the metamorphosis of the caterpillar into a butterfly, for it symbolizes the capacity to change totally and forever a person's lifestyle, way of thought, and behavior.

THE MOON IN EACH SIGN

The Moon is the nearest planet to the Earth. It exerts more observable influence on us from day to day than any other planet. The effect is very personal, very intimate, and if we are not aware of how it works it can make us quite unstable in our ideas. And the annoying thing is that at these times we often see our own instability but can do nothing about it. A knowledge of what can be expected may help considerably. We can then be prepared to stand strong against the Moon's negative influences and use its positive ones to help us to get ahead. Who has not heard of going with the tide?

The Moon reflects, has no light of its own. It reflects the Sun—the life giver—in the form of vital movement. The Moon controls the tides, the blood rhythm, the movement of sap in trees and plants. Its nature is inconstancy and change so it signifies our moods, our superficial behavior—walking, talking, and especially thinking. Being a true reflector of other forces, the Moon is cold, watery like the surface of a still lake, brilliant and scintillating at times, but easily ruffled and disturbed by the winds of change.

The Moon takes about 27⅓ days to make a complete transit of the Zodiac. It spends just over 2¼ days in each sign. During that time it reflects the qualities, energies, and characteristics of the sign and, to a degree, the planet which rules the sign. When the Moon in its transit occupies a sign incompatible with our own birth sign, we can expect to feel a vague uneasiness, perhaps a touch of irritableness. We should not be discouraged nor let the feeling get us down, or, worse still, allow ourselves to take the discomfort out on others. Try to remember that the Moon has to change signs within 55 hours and, provided you are not physically ill, your mood will probably change with it. It is amazing how frequently depression lifts with the shift in the Moon's position. And, of course, when the Moon is transiting a sign compatible or sympathetic to yours, you will probably feel some sort of stimulation or just be plain happy to be alive.

In the horoscope, the Moon is such a powerful indicator that competent astrologers often use the sign it occupied at birth as the birth sign of the person. This is done particularly when the Sun is on the cusp, or edge, of two signs. Most experienced astrologers, however, coordinate both Sun and Moon signs by reading and confirming from one to the other and secure a far more accurate and personalized analysis.

For these reasons, the Moon tables which follow this section (see pages 86–92) are of great importance to the individual. They show the days and the exact times the Moon will enter each sign of the Zodiac for the year. Remember, you have to adjust the indicated times to local time. The corrections, already calculated for most of the main cities, are at the beginning of the tables. What follows now is a guide to the influences that will be reflected to the Earth by the Moon while it transits each of the twelve signs. The influence is at its peak about 26 hours after the Moon enters a sign. As you read the daily forecast, check the Moon sign for any given day and glance back at this guide.

MOON IN ARIES
This is a time for action, for reaching out beyond the usual self-imposed limitations and faint-hearted cautions. If you have plans in your head or on your desk, put them into practice. New ventures, applications, new jobs, new starts of any kind—all have a good chance of success. This is the period when original and dynamic impulses are being reflected onto Earth. Such energies are extremely vital and favor the pursuit of pleasure and adventure in practically every form. Sick people should feel an improvement. Those who are well will probably find themselves exuding confidence and optimism. People fond of physical exercise should find their bodies growing with tone and well-being. Boldness, strength, determination should characterize most of your activities with a readiness to face up to old challenges. Yesterday's problems may seem petty and exaggerated—so deal with them. Strike out alone. Self-reliance will attract others to you. This is a good time for making friends. Business and marriage partners are more likely to be impressed with the man and woman of action. Opposition will be overcome or thrown aside with much less effort than usual. CAUTION: Be dominant but not domineering.

MOON IN TAURUS
The spontaneous, action-packed person of yesterday gives way to the cautious, diligent, hardworking "thinker." In this period ideas will probably be concentrated on ways of improving finances. A great deal of time may be spent figuring out and going over

schemes and plans. It is the right time to be careful with detail. People will find themselves working longer than usual at their desks. Or devoting more time to serious thought about the future. A strong desire to put order into business and financial arrangements may cause extra work. Loved ones may complain of being neglected and may fail to appreciate that your efforts are for their ultimate benefit. Your desire for system may extend to criticism of arrangements in the home and lead to minor upsets. Health may be affected through overwork. Try to secure a reasonable amount of rest and relaxation, although the tendency will be to "keep going" despite good advice. Work done conscientiously in this period should result in a solid contribution to your future security. CAUTION: Try not to be as serious with people as the work you are engaged in.

MOON IN GEMINI

The humdrum of routine and too much work should suddenly end. You are likely to find yourself in an expansive, quicksilver world of change and self-expression. Urges to write, to paint, to experience the freedom of some sort of artistic outpouring, may be very strong. Take full advantage of them. You may find yourself finishing something you began and put aside long ago. Or embarking on something new which could easily be prompted by a chance meeting, a new acquaintance, or even an advertisement. There may be a yearning for a change of scenery, the feeling to visit another country (not too far away), or at least to get away for a few days. This may result in short, quick journeys. Or, if you are planning a single visit, there may be some unexpected changes or detours on the way. Familiar activities will seem to give little satisfaction unless they contain a fresh element of excitement or expectation. The inclination will be toward untried pursuits, particularly those that allow you to express your inner nature. The accent is on new faces, new places. CAUTION: Do not be too quick to commit yourself emotionally.

MOON IN CANCER

Feelings of uncertainty and vague insecurity are likely to cause problems while the Moon is in Cancer. Thoughts may turn frequently to the warmth of the home and the comfort of loved ones. Nostalgic impulses could cause you to bring out old photographs and letters and reflect on the days when your life seemed to be much more rewarding and less demanding. The love and understanding of parents and family may be important, and, if it is not forthcoming, you may have to fight against bouts of self-pity. The cordiality of friends and the thought of good times with them that are sure to be repeated will help to restore you to a happier frame of mind. The desire to be alone may follow minor setbacks or rebuffs at this time, but solitude is unlikely to help. Better to get on the telephone or visit someone. This period often causes peculiar dreams and upsurges of imaginative thinking which can be helpful to authors of occult and mystical works. Preoccupation with the personal world of simple human needs can overshadow any material strivings. CAUTION: Do not spend too much time thinking—seek the company of loved ones or close friends.

MOON IN LEO
New horizons of exciting and rather extravagant activity open up. This is the time for exhilarating entertainment, glamorous and lavish parties, and expensive shopping sprees. Any merrymaking that relies upon your generosity as a host has every chance of being a spectacular success. You should find yourself right in the center of the fun, either as the life of the party or simply as a person whom happy people like to be with. Romance thrives in this heady atmosphere and friendships are likely to explode unexpectedly into serious attachments. Children and younger people should be attracted to you and you may find yourself organizing a picnic or a visit to a fun-fair, the movies, or the beach. The sunny company and vitality of youthful companions should help you to find some unsuspected energy. In career, you could find an opening for promotion or advancement. This should be the time to make a direct approach. The period favors those engaged in original research. CAUTION: Bask in popularity, not in flattery.

MOON IN VIRGO
Off comes the party cap and out steps the busy, practical worker. He wants to get his personal affairs straight, to rearrange them, if necessary, for more efficiency, so he will have more time for more work. He clears up his correspondence, pays outstanding bills, makes numerous phone calls. He is likely to make inquiries, or sign up for some new insurance and put money into gilt-edged investment. Thoughts probably revolve around the need for future security—to tie up loose ends and clear the decks. There may be a tendency to be "finicky," to interfere in the routine of others, particularly friends and family members. The motive may be a genuine desire to help with suggestions for updating or streamlining their affairs, but these will probably not be welcomed. Sympathy may be felt for less fortunate sections of the community and a flurry of some sort of voluntary service is likely. This may be accompanied by strong feelings of responsibility on several fronts and health may suffer from extra efforts made. CAUTION: Everyone may not want your help or advice.

MOON IN LIBRA

These are days of harmony and agreement and you should find yourself at peace with most others. Relationships tend to be smooth and sweet-flowing. Friends may become closer and bonds deepen in mutual understanding. Hopes will be shared. Progress by cooperation could be the secret of success in every sphere. In business, established partnerships may flourish and new ones get off to a good start. Acquaintances could discover similar interests that lead to congenial discussions and rewarding exchanges of some sort. Love, as a unifying force, reaches its optimum. Marriage partners should find accord. Those who wed at this time face the prospect of a happy union. Cooperation and tolerance are felt to be stronger than dissension and impatience. The argumentative are not quite so loud in their bellowings, nor as inflexible in their attitudes. In the home, there should be a greater recognition of the other point of view and a readiness to put the wishes of the group before selfish insistence. This is a favorable time to join an art group. CAUTION: Do not be too independent—let others help you if they want to.

MOON IN SCORPIO

Driving impulses to make money and to economize are likely to cause upsets all around. No area of expenditure is likely to be spared the ax, including the household budget. This is a time when the desire to cut down on extravagance can become near fanatical. Care must be exercised to try to keep the aim in reasonable perspective. Others may not feel the same urgent need to save and may retaliate. There is a danger that possessions of sentimental value will be sold to realize cash for investment. Buying and selling of stock for quick profit is also likely. The attention turns to organizing, reorganizing, tidying up at home and at work. Neglected jobs could suddenly be done with great bursts of energy. The desire for solitude may intervene. Self-searching thoughts could disturb. The sense of invisible and mysterious energies in play could cause some excitability. The reassurance of loves ones may help. CAUTION: Be kind to the people you love.

MOON IN SAGITTARIUS

These are days when you are likely to be stirred and elevated by discussions and reflections of a religious and philosophical nature. Ideas of faraway places may cause unusual response and excitement. A decision may be made to visit someone overseas, perhaps a person whose influence was important to your earlier character development. There could be a strong resolution to get away from present intellectual patterns, to learn new subjects, and to meet more interesting people. The superficial may be rejected in all its forms. An impatience with old ideas and unimaginative contacts could lead to a change of companions and interests. There may be an upsurge of religious feeling and metaphysical inquiry. Even a new insight into the significance of astrology and other occult studies is likely under the curious stimulus of the Moon in Sagittarius. Physically, you may express this need for fundamental change by spending more time outdoors: sports, gardening, long walks appeal. CAUTION: Try to channel any restlessness into worthwhile study.

MOON IN CAPRICORN
Life in these hours may seem to pivot around the importance of gaining prestige and honor in the career, as well as maintaining a spotless reputation. Ambitious urges may be excessive and could be accompanied by quite acquisitive drives for money. Effort should be directed along strictly ethical lines where there is no possibility of reproach or scandal. All endeavors are likely to be characterized by great earnestness, and an air of authority and purpose which should impress those who are looking for leadership or reliability. The desire to conform to accepted standards may extend to sharp criticism of family members. Frivolity and unconventional actions are unlikely to amuse while the Moon is in Capricorn. Moderation and seriousness are the orders of the day. Achievement and recognition in this period could come through community work or organizing for the benefit of some amateur group. CAUTION: Dignity and esteem are not always self-awarded.

MOON IN AQUARIUS
Moon in Aquarius is in the second last sign of the Zodiac where ideas can become disturbingly fine and subtle. The result is often a mental "no-man's land" where imagination cannot be trusted with the same certitude as other times. The dangers for the individual are the extremes of optimism and pessimism. Unless the imagination is held in check, situations are likely to be misread, and rosy conclusions drawn where they do not exist. Consequences for the unwary can be costly in career and business. Best to think twice and not speak or act until you think again. Pessimism can be a cruel self-inflicted penalty for delusion at this time. Between the two extremes are strange areas of self-deception which, for example, can make the selfish person think he is actually being generous. Eerie dreams which resemble the reality and even seem to continue into the waking state are also possible. CAUTION: Look for the fact and not just for the image in your mind.

MOON IN PISCES

Everything seems to come to the surface now. Memory may be crystal clear, throwing up long-forgotten information which could be valuable in the career or business. Flashes of clairvoyance and intuition are possible along with sudden realizations of one's own nature, which may be used for self-improvement. A talent, never before suspected, may be discovered. Qualities not evident before in friends and marriage partners are likely to be noticed. As this is a period in which the truth seems to emerge, the discovery of false characteristics is likely to lead to disenchantment or a shift in attachments. However, when qualities are accepted, it should lead to happiness and deeper feeling. Surprise solutions could bob up for old problems. There may be a public announcement of the solving of a crime or mystery. People with secrets may find someone has "guessed" correctly. The secrets of the soul or the inner self also tend to reveal themselves. Religious and philosophical groups may make some interesting discoveries. CAUTION: Not a time for activities that depend on secrecy.

NOTE: When you read your daily forecasts, use the Moon Sign Dates that are provided in the following section of Moon Tables. Then you may want to glance back here for the Moon's influence in a given sign.

MOON TABLES

CORRECTION FOR NEW YORK TIME, FIVE HOURS
WEST OF GREENWICH

Atlanta, Boston, Detroit, Miami, Washington, Montreal,
   Ottawa, Quebec, Bogota,Havana, Lima, Santiago...... Same time
Chicago, New Orleans, Houston, Winnipeg, Churchill,
   Mexico City .... Deduct 1 hour
Albuquerque, Denver, Phoenix, El Paso, Edmonton,
   Helena.. Deduct 2 hours
Los Angeles, San Francisco, Reno, Portland,
   Seattle, Vancouver .... Deduct 3 hours
Honolulu, Anchorage, Fairbanks, Kodiak .... Deduct 5 hours
Nome, Samoa, Tonga, Midway .... Deduct 6 hours
Halifax, Bermuda, San Juan, Caracas, La Paz,
   Barbados.. Add 1 hour
St. John's, Brasilia, Rio de Janeiro, Sao Paulo,
   Buenos Aires, Montevideo .... Add 2 hours
Azores, Cape Verde Islands... Add 3 hours
Canary Islands, Madeira, Reykjavik............................. Add 4 hours
London, Paris, Amsterdam, Madrid, Lisbon,
   Gibraltar, Belfast, Raba .... Add 5 hours
Frankfurt, Rome, Oslo, Stockholm, Prague,
   Belgrade... Add 6 hours
Bucharest, Beirut, Tel Aviv, Athens, Istanbul, Cairo,
   Alexandria, Cape Town, Johannesburg..................... Add 7 hours
Moscow, Leningrad, Baghdad, Dhahran,
   Addis Ababa, Nairobi, Teheran, Zanzibar .... Add 8 hours
Bombay, Calcutta, Sri Lanka.................................... Add 10½
Hong Kong, Shanghai, Manila, Peking, Perth............. Add 13 hours
Tokyo, Okinawa, Darwin, Pusan .... Add 14 hours
Sydney, Melbourne, Port Moresby, Guam .... Add 15 hours
Auckland, Wellington, Suva, Wake .... Add 17 hours

2011 MOON SIGN DATES— NEW YORK TIME

JANUARY		FEBRUARY		MARCH	
Day Moon Enters		**Day Moon Enters**		**Day Moon Enters**	
1. Sagitt.		1. Aquar.	6:22 pm	1. Aquar.	12:15 am
2. Sagitt.		2. Aquar.		2. Aquar.	
3. Capric.	2:40 am	3. Aquar.		3. Pisces	11:48 am
4. Capric.		4. Pisces	6:25 am	4. Pisces	
5. Aquar.	11:09 am	5. Pisces		5. Pisces	
6. Aquar.		6. Aries	5:47 pm	6. Aries	12:15 am
7. Pisces	9:58 pm	7. Aries		7. Aries	
8. Pisces		8. Aries		8. Taurus	12:53 pm
9. Pisces		9. Taurus	6:24 am	9. Taurus	
10. Aries	10:25 am	10. Taurus		10. Taurus	
11. Aries		11. Gemini	5:22 pm	11. Gemini	12:32 am
12. Taurus	10:38 pm	12. Gemini		12. Gemini	
13. Taurus		13. Gemini		13. Cancer	9:31 am
14. Taurus		14. Cancer	12:50 am	14. Cancer	
15. Gemini	8:24 am	15. Cancer		15. Leo	2:34 pm
16. Gemini		16. Leo	4:15 am	16. Leo	
17. Cancer	2:30 pm	17. Leo		17. Virgo	3:54 pm
18. Cancer		18. Virgo	4:40 am	18. Virgo	
19. Leo	5:17 pm	19. Virgo		19. Libra	3:04 pm
20. Leo		20. Libra	4:02 am	20. Libra	
21. Virgo	6:11 pm	21. Libra		21. Scorp.	2:18 pm
22. Virgo		22. Scorp.	4:30 am	22. Scorp.	
23. Libra	7:00 pm	23. Scorp.		23. Sagitt.	3:48 pm
24. Libra		24. Sagitt.	7:47 am	24. Sagitt.	
25. Scorp.	9:17 pm	25. Sagitt.		25. Capric.	8:58 pm
26. Scorp.		26. Capric.	2:33 pm	26. Capric.	
27. Scorp.		27. Capric.		27. Capric.	
28. Sagitt.	1:56 am	28. Capric.		28. Aquar.	6:01 am
29. Sagitt.				29. Aquar.	
30. Capric.	9:05 am			30. Pisces	5:39 pm
31. Capric.				31. Pisces	

Daylight saving time to be considered where applicable.

2011 MOON SIGN DATES—
NEW YORK TIME

APRIL Day Moon Enters		MAY Day Moon Enters		JUNE Day Moon Enters	
1. Pisces		1. Aries		1. Gemini	
2. Aries	6:17 pm	2. Taurus	12:59 am	2. Gemini	
3. Aries		3. Taurus		3. Cancer	3:37 am
4. Taurus	6:47 pm	4. Gemini	12:10 pm	4. Cancer	
5. Taurus		5. Gemini		5. Leo	10:04 am
6. Taurus		6. Cancer	9:33 pm	6. Leo	
7. Gemini	6:23 am	7. Cancer		7. Virgo	2:34 pm
8. Gemini		8. Cancer		8. Virgo	
9. Cancer	4:03 pm	9. Leo	4:36 am	9. Libra	5:32 pm
10. Cancer		10. Leo		10. Libra	
11. Leo	10:38 pm	11. Virgo	9:00 am	11. Scorp.	7:34 pm
12. Leo		12. Virgo		12. Scorp.	
13. Leo		13. Libra	10:58 am	13. Sagitt.	9:39 pm
14. Virgo	1:41 am	14. Libra		14. Sagitt.	
15. Virgo		15. Scorp.	11:33 am	15. Sagitt.	
16. Libra	2:00 am	16. Scorp.		16. Capric.	1:00 am
17. Libra		17. Sagitt.	12:24 pm	17. Capric.	
18. Scorp.	1:20 am	18. Sagitt.		18. Aquar.	5:48 am
19. Scorp.		19. Capric.	3:17 pm	19. Aquar.	
20. Sagitt.	1:51 am	20. Capric.		20. Pisces	3:46 pm
21. Sagitt.		21. Aquar.	9:33 pm	21. Pisces	
22. Capric.	5:25 am	22. Aquar.		22. Pisces	
23. Capric.		23. Aquar.		23. Aries	3:25 am
24. Aquar.	1:00 pm	24. Pisces	7:25 am	24. Aries	
25. Aquar.		25. Pisces		25. Taurus	3:54 pm
26. Pisces	11:59 pm	26. Aries	7:37 pm	26. Taurus	
27. Pisces		27. Aries		27. Taurus	
28. Pisces		28. Aries		28. Gemini	2:57 am
29. Aries	12:34 pm	29. Taurus	8:03 am	29. Gemini	
30. Aries		30. Taurus		30. Cancer	11:14 am
		31. Gemini	6:57 pm		

Daylight saving time to be considered where applicable.

2011 MOON SIGN DATES—
NEW YORK TIME

JULY		AUGUST		SEPTEMBER	
Day Moon Enters		**Day Moon Enters**		**Day Moon Enters**	
1. Cancer		1. Virgo	3:43 am	1. Scorp.	1:49 pm
2. Leo	4:44 pm	2. Virgo		2. Scorp.	
3. Leo		3. Libra	5:05 am	3. Sagitt.	4:05 am
4. Virgo	8:16 pm	4. Libra		4. Sagitt.	
5. Virgo		5. Scorp.	6:58 am	5. Capric.	9:05 pm
6. Libra	10:55 pm	6. Scorp.		6. Capric.	
7. Libra		7. Sagitt.	10:22 am	7. Capric.	
8. Libra		8. Sagitt.		8. Aquar.	4:43 am
9. Scorp.	1:32 am	9. Capric.	3:39 pm	9. Aquar.	
10. Scorp.		10. Capric.		10. Pisces	2:28 pm
11. Sagitt.	4:48 am	11. Aquar.	10:49 pm	11. Pisces	
12. Sagitt.		12. Aquar.		12. Pisces	
13. Capric.	9:14 am	13. Aquar.		13. Aries	1:50 am
14. Capric.		14. Pisces	7:55 am	14. Aries	
15. Aquar.	3:31 pm	15. Pisces		15. Taurus	2:26 pm
16. Aquar.		16. Aries	7:03 pm	16. Taurus	
17. Aquar.		17. Aries		17. Taurus	
18. Pisces	12:14 am	18. Aries		18. Gemini	3:07 am
19. Pisces		19. Taurus	7:37 am	19. Gemini	
20. Aries	11:26 am	20. Taurus		20. Cancer	1:55 pm
21. Aries		21. Gemini	7:54 am	21. Cancer	
22. Taurus	11:59 pm	22. Gemini		22. Leo	8:56 pm
23. Taurus		23. Gemini		23. Leo	
24. Taurus		24. Cancer	5:32 am	24. Virgo	11:50 pm
25. Gemini	11:35 am	25. Cancer		25. Virgo	
26. Gemini		26. Leo	11:10 am	26. Libra	11:52 pm
27. Cancer	8:13 pm	27. Leo		27. Libra	
28. Cancer		28. Virgo	1:14 pm	28. Scorp.	11:06 pm
29. Cancer		29. Virgo		29. Scorp.	
30. Leo	1:17 am	30. Libra	1:26 pm	30. Sagitt.	11:42 pm
31. Leo		31. Libra			

Daylight saving time to be considered where applicable.

2011 MOON SIGN DATES—
NEW YORK TIME

OCTOBER Day Moon Enters		NOVEMBER Day Moon Enters		DECEMBER Day Moon Enters	
1. Sagitt.		1. Aquar.	5:09 pm	1. Pisces	9:46 pm
2. Sagitt.		2. Aquar.		2. Pisces	
3. Capric.	3:17 am	3. Aquar.		3. Aries	8:52 pm
4. Capric.		4. Pisces	2:19 am	4. Aries	
5. Aquar.	10:19 am	5. Pisces		5. Aries	
6. Aquar.		6. Aries	2:03 pm	6. Taurus	9:36 am
7. Pisces	8:14 pm	7. Aries		7. Taurus	
8. Pisces		8. Aries		8. Gemini	9:53 pm
9. Pisces		9. Taurus	2:46 am	9. Gemini	
10. Aries	7:58 am	10. Taurus		10. Gemini	
11. Aries		11. Gemini	3:11 pm	11. Cancer	8:27 am
12. Taurus	8:36 pm	12. Gemini		12. Cancer	
13. Taurus		13. Gemini		13. Leo	4:49 pm
14. Taurus		14. Cancer	2:20 am	14. Leo	
15. Gemini	9:16 am	15. Cancer		15. Virgo	11:00 pm
16. Gemini		16. Leo	11:18 am	16. Virgo	
17. Cancer	8:39 pm	17. Leo		17. Virgo	
18. Cancer		18. Virgo	5:20 pm	18. Libra	3:07 am
19. Cancer		19. Virgo		19. Libra	
20. Leo	5:07 am	20. Libra	8:17 pm	20. Scorp.	5:34 am
21. Leo		21. Libra		21. Scorp.	
22. Virgo	9:42 am	22. Scorp.	8:59 pm	22. Sagitt.	7:04 am
23. Virgo		23. Scorp.		23. Sagitt.	
24. Libra	10:50 am	24. Sagitt.	8:58 pm	24. Capric.	8:58 am
25. Libra		25. Sagitt.		25. Capric.	
26. Scorp.	10:09 am	26. Capric.	10:06 pm	26. Aquar.	12:15 pm
27. Scorp.		27. Capric.		27. Aquar.	
28. Sagitt.	9:46 am	28. Capric.		28. Pisces	6:46 pm
29. Sagitt.		29. Aquar.	2:03 am	29. Pisces	
30. Capric.	11:40 am	30. Aquar.		30. Pisces	
31. Capric.				31. Aries	4:49 am

Daylight saving time to be considered where applicable.

2011 PHASES OF THE MOON—
NEW YORK TIME

New Moon	First Quarter	Full Moon	Last Quarter
Jan. 4	Jan. 12	Jan. 19	Jan. 26
Feb. 2	Feb. 11	Feb. 18	Feb. 24
March 4	March 12	March 19	March 26
April 3	April 11	April 17	April 24
May 3	May 10	May 17	May 24
June 1	June 8	June 15	June 23
July 1	July 8	July 15	July 23
July 30	August 6	August 13	August 21
August 28	Sept. 4	Sept. 12	Sept. 20
Sept. 27	Oct. 3	Oct. 11	Oct. 19
Oct. 26	Nov. 2	Nov. 10	Nov. 18
Nov. 25	Dec. 2	Dec. 10	Dec. 17
Dec. 24	Jan. 1 ('12)	Jan. 9 ('12)	Jan. 16 ('12)

Each phase of the Moon lasts approximately seven to eight days, during which the Moon's shape gradually changes as it comes out of one phase and goes into the next.

There will be a solar eclipse during the New Moon phase on January 4, on June 1, on July 1, and on November 25.

There will be a lunar eclipse during the Full Moon phase on June 15 and on December 10.

2011 FISHING GUIDE

	Good	Best
January	3-4-6-9-14-20-28-31	2-8-18-27
February	2-10-14-19-24-28	5-15-23
March	5-7-12-14-20-25-27	4-13-22-31
April	1-6-10-11-13-21-25-27	2-10-19-28
May	3-5-11-12-18-21-26	8-16-25
June	1-18-12-17-20-22	4-12-21
July	6-11-21-22-26-28-31	1-2-10-19-29
August	2-5-10-18-26-28-30	6-15-25
September	1-6-9-17-23-24-25	2-11-21-29
October	6-16-20-22-24-28	8-18-27
November	5-10-15-19-25	4-14-23
December	3-8-13-17-20-22-23-35	2-12-21-29

2011 PLANTING GUIDE

	Aboveground Crops	Root Crops
January	1-4-8-9-10-18-19	24-25-26-31
February	5-6-15-16	1-21-22-28
March	5-6-14-15-18	1-20-21-27-28-29
April	10-11-12-15-16	18-22-23-24
May	8-9-12-13-16-17	20-21-30-31
June	4-5-8-9-12-13-14	17-18-19-27-38
July	18-19-20-29-30	14-15-23-24-25
August	15-16-25-26-29	20-21
September	12-22-23-26-27	17-18-27-28
October	19-20-23-24	13-14-15-25
November	15-16-19-20-23	10-11-21-22-23
December	12-13-17-18-21-22	19-20

	Pruning	Weeds and Pests
January	11-12	20-21
February	13-14	17-18
March	13-16-17	29-30
April	13-14	25-26-27
May	10-11	24
June	15-16	29-30
July	12-13	13-14-15
August	8-9-10	12-13
September	4-5	9-10
October	11-12	6-7
November	8-9	2-3-4
December	4-5-6	1-10-11

MOON'S INFLUENCE OVER PLANTS

Centuries ago it was established that seeds planted when the Moon is in signs and phases called Fruitful will produce more growth than seeds planted when the Moon is in a Barren sign.

Fruitful Signs: Taurus, Cancer, Libra, Scorpio, Capricorn, Pisces
Barren Signs: Aries, Gemini, Leo, Virgo, Sagittarius, Aquarius
Dry Signs: Aries, Gemini, Sagittarius, Aquarius

Activity	Moon In
Mow lawn, trim plants	**Fruitful sign:** 1st & 2nd quarter
Plant flowers	**Fruitful sign:** 2nd quarter; best in Cancer and Libra
Prune	**Fruitful sign:** 3rd & 4th quarter
Destroy pests; spray	**Barren sign:** 4th quarter
Harvest potatoes, root crops	**Dry sign:** 3rd & 4th quarter; Taurus, Leo, and Aquarius

MOON'S INFLUENCE OVER YOUR HEALTH

ARIES   Head, brain, face, upper jaw
TAURUS   Throat, neck, lower jaw
GEMINI   Hands, arms, lungs, shoulders, ner vous system
CANCER   Esophagus, stomach, breasts, womb, liver
LEO   Heart, spine
VIRGO   Intestines, liver
LIBRA   Kidneys, lower back
SCORPIO   Sex and eliminative organs
SAGITTARIUS   Hips, thighs, liver
CAPRICORN   Skin, bones, teeth, knees
AQUARIUS   Circulatory system, lower legs
PISCES   Feet, tone of being

Try to avoid work being done on that part of the body when the Moon is in the sign governing that part.

MOON'S INFLUENCE OVER DAILY AFFAIRS

The Moon makes a complete transit of the Zodiac every 27 days 7 hours and 43 minutes. In making this transit the Moon forms different aspects with the planets and consequently has favorable or unfavorable bearings on affairs and events for persons according to the sign of the Zodiac under which they were born.

When the Moon is in conjunction with the Sun it is called a New Moon; when the Moon and Sun are in opposition it is called a Full Moon. From New Moon to Full Moon, first and second quarter—which takes about two weeks—the Moon is increasing or waxing. From Full Moon to New Moon, third and fourth quarter, the Moon is decreasing or waning.

Activity	Moon In
Business: buying and selling new, requiring public support	Sagittarius, Aries, Gemini, Virgo 1st and 2nd quarter
meant to be kept quiet	3rd and 4th quarter
Investigation	3rd and 4th quarter
Signing documents	1st & 2nd quarter, Cancer, Scorpio, Pisces
Advertising	2nd quarter, Sagittarius
Journeys and trips	1st & 2nd quarter, Gemini, Virgo
Renting offices, etc.	Taurus, Leo, Scorpio, Aquarius
Painting of house/apartment	3rd & 4th quarter, Taurus, Scorpio, Aquarius
Decorating	Gemini, Libra, Aquarius
Buying clothes and accessories	Taurus, Virgo
Beauty salon or barber shop visit	1st & 2nd quarter, Taurus, Leo, Libra, Scorpio, Aquarius
Weddings	1st & 2nd quarter

Aries

ARIES

Character Analysis

People born under the astrological sign of Aries are often strong-willed and energetic. Aries are seldom afraid of taking a risk, provided that it is well-calculated. They are people who dare; they are sometimes impulsive but almost never irrational. The Aries man or woman likes to keep busy. They are not a people who like to while away the time in an aimless fashion. Aries are known for their drive and their boldness. They generally know how to make proper use of their energies; they are positive and productive people who seldom doubt themselves. They know what they want out of life and they go after it. They generally have a pioneering sort of spirit and are always anxious to begin something new. They know how to make use of opportunity when it appears. Many Aries have no trouble in achieving success.

The strong and positive sort of Aries knows how to channel his energies properly so that he will get the most out of what life has to offer. He is a sensible, practical person, who does not only think about himself but does what he can to help those in less fortunate positions than himself. If a plan goes awry, he does not hesitate to see what he can do to fix it. Aries is usually quick to initiate a change if it seems necessary to do so. He is an activist, generally, and does not believe in sitting around waiting for good things to tumble into his lap. If good fortune does not appear, the positive Aries will go out and look for it; his search does not end until he has it. Obstacles do not frighten the Aries man or woman. In fact, contrary situations or people seem to spur him on. Aries often thrives on adversity. He knows how to turn a disadvantage to an advantage in short order. Not easily discouraged, he will forge ahead on a plan or idea until it is exactly the way he wants it. The Aries knows how to shift for himself. He won't wait for others to lend a helping hand, but starts himself, without assistance. Some find the Aries person a little too ruthless in his manner for getting what he wants. Patience is a virtue some Aries lack; they are people who are usually interested in fast results. They want to see the fruits of their investments as quickly as possible.

The average Aries is a person who has many ideas; he is never at a loss for a new approach to an old or familiar situation. He is ever adaptable and knows how to make a profit out of a loss. In emergency situations, Aries is always quick to act. When an accident occurs, he often knows the proper remedy. Decision making does not frighten the strong Aries man or woman. They have the ability to think clearly and to direct their interests and energies toward their ultimate goal. Aries people are easily attracted to anything that is new and interesting. They have naturally inquiring minds.

Although Aries are often alert and quick to act, they are sometimes easily distracted by side issues. Almost everything interests them and this can have its disadvantages, especially when a one-track mind is needed in order to solve a problem. Aries can sometimes make a mess of things in their eagerness to get things done as soon as possible.

The weak or poorly directed Aries sometimes has a problem trying to put all of his eggs in one basket. He is easily distracted and often argumentative. He sometimes finds it difficult to see the forest for the trees. In trying to get many things accomplished at one time, he achieves nothing. In spite of his shortcomings, he is apt to be quite caught up with what he fancies to be his virtues. He will underestimate the intelligence and abilities of others, especially if they seem to threaten his position in one way or another. The confused Aries is always ready for a quarrel. He will often refuse to see the other person's point of view and dismiss their opinions as so much nonsense. The Aries man or woman who does not know how to concentrate his or her energies effectively easily jumps from one mistake to another, leaving things in an incomplete and jumbled state. The weak Aries will seldom admit his faults, although he will eagerly point out those of others or what he imagines to be those of others.

The misdirected Aries more often than not misses his mark. He is too anxious to succeed. He wants success fast and is in too much of a hurry to prepare himself adequately. The weak Aries man or woman can be as stubborn as a mule. When intent on some illusory goal they will seldom take the time to listen to others. Not afraid of taking a risk, the ill-prepared Aries often finds himself leaping from one unsuccessful plan to the other. His optimism often makes a fool of him. He is the type of person who leaps before looking. Although he is easy to anger, his temper quickly cools off. When hurt, he can rant and rave for an hour but once he has defended himself, he will drop the matter altogether and move on to something else. Aries seldom carries a grudge. In love, too, the Aries man or woman who has not learned how to curb impulsiveness, often finds himself or herself in a pot of hot water. Love at first sight is not uncommon to this sort of Aries person; he is romantic for as long as the impulse carries him. He is not averse to fly-by-night romances, and is likely to throw caution to the winds when in love.

Because the Aries person has an enterprising nature, he never finds it difficult to keep busy. He is an extremely independent person—sometimes to a fault. Others sometimes find him rather haughty and arrogant. This weak sort of Aries finds it difficult to be objective in anything. He resents criticism even when it is due, yet he will not find it difficult to criticize others. He is the kind of person who takes any dare as an opportunity to prove his worth. Others are often annoyed by the manner in which he presses an issue. He is capable of becoming quite aggressive when the situation calls for tact and understanding. If the weak Aries made an attempt to see or understand both sides of one story, he could improve his own insight into problems. He should do what he can to develop a balanced sense of judgment. It is important for this sort of Aries person to prepare himself adequately before taking on a new project. He should avoid overdoing as that only ends in total exhaustion and very little actual progress is made.

Health

People born under the sign of Aries are generally quite healthy. Their physical condition tends to be good. Still, it is necessary that they take steps not to abuse their health by overdoing. Aries is sometimes accident-prone because he is careless in his actions, particularly when intent on achieving a particular goal. The head and the face are areas of the body that are often injured. It is important that Aries learn to relax. The Aries man or woman usually does fairly well in sports. Their bodies are generally well-developed and lithe. The Aries constitution is almost always good. He is capable of great physical strength for short periods of time. This, of course, has its disadvantages as well as advantages. Aries can achieve more if he learns how to apply his spurts of strength correctly. Sports where staying power is important are not likely to be ones in which he can excel.

The sign of Aries governs the head; nerves, head, and stomach are apt to be the weak points under this sign. Headaches and fevers are not uncommon complaints.

As was mentioned before, it is essential that men and women born under this first sign of the Zodiac learn how to relax. It is often the case that they wear out easily because they are impulsive and headstrong; they do not know how to channel their energies in a consistent manner. This can sometimes lead to a breakdown.

Self-control must also be learned. Sometimes fiery Aries is too free in expressing himself—this can lead to emotional bankruptcy. He is a person who is quick to anger; he worries. Controlling negative emotions is vitally important as bad moods can often affect his health.

Proper rest is vital. Adequate sleep helps an exhausted Aries to regain his strength. A sensible, well-balanced diet is also important. Overeating or immoderate drinking habits can, to some extent, incorrectly influence the general disposition of the Aries man or woman. Aries does not like to be ill. Sickness makes him restless and impatient. He does not like to spend too much time recuperating from an illness. Because of his drive and enthusiasm, Aries often recovers more quickly than others. An illness may strike him hard, but he is soon on his feet again.

Aries generally lead long and active lives; to some, they never seem to grow old. The Aries who learns how to conserve his energies as well as to correctly channel them can add years to his life span. Good health habits should be continually observed.

Occupation

The Aries is an active, industrious person. He should find a career in which he can best put his talents to use. Although an Aries is apt to have many interests, he should try to find out which interest is the most suited to his actual means and abilities. He is a person who is sincerely interested in getting on in the world and making a success of himself.

The sign of Aries governs the head and the intellect. The person born during the period March 21 to April 20 is usually quite ambitious and enterprising. He is not a person who can sit still when there is something to do. Some Aries have an artistic bent and do well in creative work. Others have some trouble in making up their minds about what kind of work they should do because they are interested in so many things and can handle them all reasonably well. Generally speaking, whatever profession Aries chooses to enter, he makes a good job of it.

The Aries man or woman is never lacking in personality and charm. They are dynamic and creative. Often they do well in work that requires them to come in direct contact with the public. Quite often they are clever conversationalists. They know how to deal with people—how to amuse them, how to convince them. Others often turn to Aries for advice or counsel when in difficulty. The Aries person can usually handle a position that requires authoritative behavior without any problem at all. They make good leaders and advisers. Aries are inventive and forward-looking. They have plenty of energy and drive; many have a talent for successfully realizing their plans and dreams.

Aries is a person of action. Quite often he does well in the military or in organized sports. Some Aries make excellent doctors and nurses. Other do remarkably well as artists and designers. They are a resourceful people—men and women who often know what they want to achieve in life.

The person born under the sign of Aries is more often than not an individualist. He prefers giving orders to taking them. He is not a "group" sort of person. He enjoys working by himself more than working in a team. A modern person, he usually sees to it that he keeps abreast of the new developments in his field.

One fault often found in the underdeveloped Aries is that he will undertake a project with much enthusiasm, then as his interest flags he will readily give it up for something new. In such cases, he will often pass the unfinished chore or project on to someone else. Some Aries make a habit of starting things, then turning them over to others. The sort of Aries who falls into this habit often does it unknowingly. New plans and ideas attract people of this sign quickly. They are always off for new fields to conquer. The strong Aries, however, seldom has difficulties of this sort; he knows how to stick with one job until it is done. He will do his utmost to direct his efforts and energies toward one goal. This sort of Ram makes a success of his life without much effort.

The Aries man or woman is seldom a person who is only interested in work and material gain. He or she knows how to go about having a good time. Some are quite happy when they are able to combine business with pleasure. Aries usually are not hard materialists, but they know well what money can do. They busy themselves earning money, but they sometimes spend it as soon as it comes into their pockets. The Aries man or woman is generally honest when it comes to money matters. If he or she directs him or herself to one goal, there is a good chance that it will be attained without too much effort. Aries has a driving and courageous personality. In work, this often stands him in good stead.

People born under the sign of Aries generally like to be surrounded by fashionable furnishings and the like. Luxury makes them feel comfortable and successful and often has an important influence in making them positive and enterprising. Shabby or old surroundings are apt to depress the Aries person. He is modern and forward-looking; he must live in an environment that is suited to his general disposition.

Some Aries tend to be rather careless with their money. Saving is something of a problem for them. They would rather spend what they earn instead of putting something aside for a rainy day. They know how to live for the moment. The weak Aries often invests unwisely or mismanages his joint finances without regard for his partner or mate. The wise Aries avoids impulsive spending and thinks of the future. He sees to it that he learns how to budget his expenses in an effective manner.

Home and Family

The Aries man or woman is a home-loving person by nature. Home means a lot to the Ram. Here he can relax at the end of a hard day and enjoy the comfort of his surroundings. Aries women are generally excellent homemakers. They have a way with furnishings and color arrangement. They know how to make a home radiate harmony and comfort. Invariably, they have good taste. They can beautify a room or a home without much difficulty. The Aries home usually gives one the feeling of freedom and roominess. A guest is not apt to feel himself confined or uncomfortable.

The Aries enjoys entertaining his friends and family. Nothing pleases him more than people dropping in. He knows how to make the best of a social situation even if it occurs on the spur of the moment. They know how to please visitors and enjoy company. Friends generally respect them and their homes.

In family matters, the Aries man or woman is very emotional—in the good sense of the word. Affection and love between members of his or her immediate family are essential for getting along. The Aries is keenly interested in keeping his home peaceful and harmonious. If possible, the Aries husband or wife tries to exert a strong influence in household matters. The Aries feels that his guidance is important to others.

The person born under this sign of the Zodiac is usually quite fond of children. They understand children and children usually feel close to them. Aries himself usually has something youthful about his nature. Children have no difficulty in getting along with them and generally enjoy having them join them in some of their activities. Aries know the value of a good joke and children love them for this. A sense of humor that is rich and well-balanced makes them a favorite with children. Aries people seldom forget the joys of their own youth and enjoy living somewhat vicariously through the adventures and games of their own children.

Although the Aries man or woman is not much of a disciplinarian, they do become rather disappointed if their children do not live up to their expectations in later life. Aries generally thinks he knows what is best for his children and can become rather overbearing if his children are not inclined to agree. Aries is a person who enjoys being popular and respected and he can be a proud parent.

Social Relationships

The Aries person usually has no trouble in making new friends. He is generally outgoing and generous. He enjoys having many friends. People are easily attracted to the Aries because of his bright and pleasant personality. He knows how to make people feel at ease and encourages them in their self-expression. People often turn to an Aries when they are in trouble. The Aries man or woman knows how to counsel a friend in trouble; he or she is sometimes willing to share the burden or responsibilities of a good friend.

On the other hand, Aries people often make a habit of jumping from one friend to another. As long as a person remains new, interesting, and somewhat mysterious, he remains a friend. As soon as an Aries becomes aware of this friend's limitations, he is apt to try to find someone new to replace him. This is the pattern an uncultivated Aries follows in work. As long as the project is new, it absorbs his interest. As soon as it becomes old hat, he turns it over to someone else and starts something new.

Aries make friends quickly. If they are really impressed, they will place the new friend on a very high pedestal. Some Aries become very possessive of their friends and if someone else shows an interest in them, they become rather jealous and resentful. If a friend becomes tiresome or dull, the tactless Aries will not hesitate to handle him in an inconsiderate manner.

Although Aries generally have a talent for making friends quickly, they also are apt to lose them rather fast if they are not careful. Some Aries tend to neglect their friends and acquaintances as soon as something new catches their fancies. The weak Aries is sometimes a bit of a gossip and finds it hard not to supply others with the secrets of their friends. This sort of Aries person generally takes people for what they appear to be and not for what they actually are.

Love and Marriage

Aries men and women need the spirit of adventure in romance. Aries can pretend to surrender to love's idyllic dream, seemingly peaceful and lamb-like but never sheepish. Yet the Ram in love is really playing possum, ready to leap passionately toward their heart's desire.

Aries is generally involved in strong relationships usually with powerful partners, individuals who might be either ruthless or deeply wise. The key to a successful relationship is equality, but many Aries will jockey for position with a mate. It is often impossible to tell who is the stronger partner. Sometimes the more outwardly bold and aggressive member of the pair is really the more dependent, deep down.

The Aries man or woman can become quite possessive and at times intensely jealous. Also, Aries can become fixated on a loved one who fails to appreciate their worth, someone who does not love or honor them the way they expect to be loved and honored. A mate or partner may find it hard to understand why Aries will feel slighted or wronged for no apparent reason. Sometimes Aries may resort to unreasonable or childish behavior, pouting and sulking relentlessly, when they feel that a lover is taking them for granted.

Romance and the Aries Woman

The Aries woman is more often than not charming. The opposite sex generally find her attractive, even glamorous. She is a woman who is very interested in love and romance. The female Aries has plenty of affection to give to the right man—when she meets him. Women born under this sign are usually very active and vigorous; their intelligence and strong character are also qualities which make them attractive to men. The Aries woman has no trouble in communicating with a man on an intellectual plane; she can easily hold her own in any conversation. She should, however, try to curb her eagerness to talk; quite often she winds up dominating the conversation. The Aries who has cultivated the talent of being a good listener generally does not have any trouble in attracting the sort of man who might propose to her.

The Aries woman is not the sort to sit back and wait for the right man to come along. If she sees someone who interests her, she will more than likely take the lead. She can usually do this in such a charming fashion, that the object of her affection hardly notices that he is being coaxed into a romance.

The Aries woman has no trouble in being true to the man she loves. She is true to herself and believes in remaining faithful to the man she has chosen. She usually makes a thoughtful and considerate companion. When her man is in need of advice she is often able to give him wise counsel. Aries women are generally able to voice an intelligent opinion on just about any subject. Their range of knowledge—just as their range of interests—is quite broad. They are imaginative and know how to keep a relationship alive and interesting.

The woman born under the sign of the Ram makes an excellent wife. It is seldom that she will bother her mate or partner with matters that she can easily handle herself. She has a way of transforming almost any house or apartment into a very comfortable home. With household budgeting, she often turns out to be a mastermind. All in all, the Aries woman is very considerate and dependable; she has all the qualities it takes to make an excellent wife or partner. She knows how to bring up children correctly. She is fond of children and affectionate. She is often the kind of mother who enjoys a large family.

Romance and the Aries Man

The Aries man is often quite romantic and charming when court-ing the opposite sex. He knows how to win the heart of the woman he loves. The Aries in love is as persuasive and energetic as he is in anything else that interests him. He makes an attentive and consid-erate lover. A direct and positive person, he has no trouble in at-tracting women. They are often taken by his charming and dashing manner. The opposite sex feels very safe and confident when with an Aries man—for he knows how to make a woman feel wanted and appreciated. However, the Aries man is sometimes so sure of himself that he frightens the more sensitive woman away.

Although the man born under the sign of the Ram is usually quite faithful when married, he does not mind playing the field as long as he remains single. He can be quite a flirt; sometimes the Aries man goes from one romance to the other until he finds the right girl. Making conquests on the battlefield of love is apt to give his ego quite a boost. The Aries man never has very much trouble with rivals. When he is intent on love he knows how to do away with all opposition—and in short order. The Aries is a man who is very much in need of love and affection; he is quite open about this and goes about attaining it in a very open way.

He may be quite adventurous in love while he is single, but once he settles down, he becomes a very reliable and responsible mate. The Aries man is really a family-type man. He enjoys the company of his immediate family; he appreciates the comforts of home. A well-furnished and inviting home is important to a man born under this sign. Some of the furnishings may be a little on the luxurious side; the Aries feels often inspired to do better if he is surrounded by a show of material comfort. Success-oriented, he likes his home to radiate success.

The Aries man often likes to putter around the house, making minor repairs and installing new household utensils. He is a man who does not mind being tied down as long as he does not really feel it. He will be the head of the house; he does not like the woman to wear the pants in the family. He wants to be the one who keeps things in order. He remains romantic, even after marriage. He is tremendously fond of children and is quite apt to spoil them a bit. He makes an affectionate father. Children make him happy when they make him feel proud of them.

Woman—Man

ARIES WOMAN
ARIES MAN

The mating of Aries with Aries could lead to some pretty frantic fireworks, but it does not necessarily have to. As strong in her ways as he is in his, the Aries woman will make her Aries man happiest by supplementing his drives and dreams. An Aries woman can understand and respect a man born under the same sign if she puts her mind to it. He could be that knight in shining armor that Aries women are often in search of. Women born under the sign of the Ram are hard to please and are not interested in just getting a man. They know just what kind of a man he should be and usually do not settle for anything less than their ideal. They are particular. As far as love goes, neither of them shilly-shally with passion. They play for keeps. An Aries-Aries union could be something strong, secure, and romantic. If both of them have their sights fixed in the same direction and have mutual appreciation for each other, there is almost nothing they could not accomplish. It is a blockbuster of a combination.

However, if the Aries wife chooses to place her own interests before those of her husband, she can be sure of rocking the boat ... and perhaps eventually torpedoing it. The career-minded Aries woman, out to do better than her Aries husband, generally winds up doing herself in. He won't stand for it and your relationship won't stand the strain it will bring about. The Aries wife who devotes herself to evenings of bridge will find that she's burned the one bridge she didn't intend to. The home-loving Aries man finds hastily scribbled notes on the dining-room table and TV dinners in the freezer equally indigestible. When you get home from that night out with the girls, he'll take his heartburn out on you in a succession of petty arguments. If you want to avoid burps and bumps in your marriage, be on hand with his favorite meals, snacks, plus a generous amount of affection. The way to an Aries' stomach is through his heart.

Homemaking, though, should present no problems to the Aries wife. With her, it's second nature. With a pot of paint and some paper, she can transform the dreariest domicile into a place of beauty and snug comfort. The perfect hostess—even when friends just happen by—she knows how to make guests feel at home and this is what makes her Aries man beam with pride.

The Aries father is young at heart and will spoil the children every chance he gets. Kids take to him like ducks to water. His quick mind and energetic behavior appeal to the youngsters and will keep them active and alert.

ARIES WOMAN
TAURUS MAN

It is the Aries woman who has more than a pinch of patience and reserve who can find her dream-come-true in a man born under the sign of the Bull.

The steady and deliberate Taurus is a little slow on the draw; it may take him quite a while before he gets around to popping that question. For the Aries women who has learned the art of twiddling her thumbs and who doesn't care if her love life seems like a parody of "Waiting for Godot," the waiting and anticipating almost always pays off in the end. Taurus men take their time. Every slow step they take is a sure one—they see to that, especially when they feel that the path they're on could lead them to the altar.

Any Aries woman looking for a whirlwind romance had better cast her net in shallower waters. Moreover, most Taurus prefer to do the angling themselves. They're not keen on women taking the lead—once she does, he's likely to drop her like a dead fish. Once the Aries woman lets herself get caught on his terms, she'll find that her Taurus has fallen for her: hook, line and sinker.

The Taurus man is fond of comfortable home life. It's as important to him as it is to the Aries woman. The Aries who centers her main activities on keeping those home fires burning will have no worries about keeping that flame in her hubby's heart aglow. The Aries woman, with her talent for homemaking and harmony, is sometimes the perfect match for the strong, steady, and protective Bull. He can be the anchor for her dreams and plans, and can help her acquire a more balanced outlook and approach to her life and her goals. Not one for wild schemes, himself, Taurus can constructively help her to curb her impulsiveness. He's the man who is always there when you need him. Taurus are rather fond of staying put, especially when it's near someone they love and cherish. When tying her knot with a Taurus, the Aries woman can put away all fears about creditors pounding on the front door. Taurus are practical about everything including bill paying. When he carries you over that threshold, you can be certain that the entire house is paid for.

As a housewife, the Aries married to a Taurus man need not worry about having to put aside her many interests for the sake of back-breaking house chores. He'll see to it that you have all the latest time-saving appliances and comforts.

The Taurus spouse or lover is generous, patient, and easygoing. He's no slouch and it can lead to disaster if the ambitious Aries wife misinterprets his plodding ways for plain laziness. He knows where he's going. He appreciates her interest in his work, and pays heed to her helpful suggestions because they pay off. Taurus are faithful and never flirt. All his love and attention are riveted to the woman of his choice, as long as she's deserving.

The Aries mother can forget about acquiring premature gray hairs due to unruly, ruckus-raising children under her feet. Papa Taurus is a master at keeping children in line. He's crazy about his kids, but he also knows what's good for them. And although he may never resort to the rod, he'll never allow himself to spoil his child, either. Children respect Taurus authority and will usually do their best to make papa proud of them.

ARIES WOMAN
GEMINI MAN

The Aries woman and the Gemini man are a twosome that can make beautiful music together. Perhaps that is due to the fact that they are alike in certain respects. Both are intelligent, witty, outgoing, and tend to be rather versatile. An Aries woman can be the Ms. Right that Mr. Gemini has been looking for—his prospective better half, as it were. One thing that causes a Twin's mind and affection to wander is a bore, and it's highly unlikely that an Aries would ever be accused of that. He'll admire the Ram for her ideas and intellect—perhaps even more than her good cooking and flawless talent for homemaking. She needn't feel that once she's made that vow that she'll have to store her interests and ambition in the attic somewhere. He'll admire her for her zeal and liveliness. He's the kind of guy who won't pout and scowl if he has to shift for himself in the kitchen once in a while.

The fleet-of-foot Gemini man is always on the go. But this does not fluster the speedy, spry Ram who is usually in a hurry herself. She's always a couple of jumps ahead of him—and if she's the helpful wife Aries usually are, she won't mind telling him when and how to jump. They're both dreamers, planners, and idealists.

The woman born under the sign of the Ram, though, is more thorough and possesses more stick-to-it-iveness. She can easily fill the role of rudder for her Gemini's ship-without-a-sail. He won't mind it too much, either. If he's an intelligent Twin, he'll be well aware of his shortcomings and won't mind it if somebody gives him a shove in the right direction—when it's needed. The average Gemini does not have serious ego hang-ups and will even accept a well-deserved chewing out from his mate quite gracefully.

You'll probably always have a houseful of interesting people to entertain. Geminis find it hard to tolerate sluggish minds and dispositions. You'll never be at a loss for finding new faces in your living room. Geminis are great friend-collectors and sometimes go about it the same way kids go about collecting marbles—the more they sparkle and dazzle, the greater their value to him. But then in a day or two, it's not unusual to find that he has traded yesterday's favorites for still brighter and newer ones. The diplomatic Aries can bring her willy-nilly Gemini to reason and point out his folly in friendships in such a way that he'll think twice before considering an exchange of old lamps for new.

Gemini men are always attractive to the opposite sex and vice versa. The Aries woman with her proud nature will have to bend a little and allow her Gemini man an occasional harmless flirtation—it will help to keep his spirits up. An out-of-sorts Twin is capable of brewing up a whirlwind of trouble. Better to let him hanky-pank—within eyeshot, of course—than to lose your cool; it might cause you to lose your man.

As far as children are concerned, it's quite likely that the Aries wife will have to fill the role of house disciplinarian. Geminis are pushovers for children, perhaps because they understand them so well and have that childlike side to their nature which keeps them youthful and optimistic. They have no interest in keeping a child's vigor in check.

ARIES WOMAN
CANCER MAN

It's quite possible that a man born under this sign of the Crab may be a little too crabby for the average Aries woman; but then, Cupid has been known to perform some pretty unlikely feats with his wayward bow and arrow. Again, it's the Aries with her wits about her who can make the most out of a relationship with the sensitive and occasionally moody Cancer. He may not be altogether her cup of tea, but when it comes to security and faithfulness—qualities Aries women often value highly—she couldn't have made a better choice.

It's the perceptive Aries who will not mistake the Crab's quietness for sullenness, or his thriftiness for penny-pinching. In some respects he can be like the wise old owl out on a limb; he may look like he's dozing but actually he hasn't missed a thing. Cancers often possess a storehouse of knowledge about human behavior; they can come across with some pretty helpful advice for those troubled and in need of an understanding shoulder to cry on. The Aries gal about to rush off for new fields to conquer had better turn to her Cancer mate first. Chances are he can save her from making unwise investments in time and—especially—money. He may not say much, but he's capable of being on his toes even while his feet are flat on the ground.

The Crab may not be the match or catch for many a Ram; in fact, he might seem downright dull to the ambitious, on-the-move Aries. True to his sign, he can be fairly cranky and crabby when handled in the wrong way. He's sensitive, perhaps more sensitive than is good for him. The talkative Aries who has a habit of saying what is on her mind had better think twice before letting loose with a personal criticism of any kind, particularly if she's got her heart set on a Cancer. If she's smart as a whip, she'd better be careful that she never in any way conveys the idea that she considers her Crab a little short on brain power. Browbeating is a surefire way of sending the Crab angrily scurrying back to his shell, and it's quite possible that all of that ground lost might never be recovered.

Home is an area where the Aries woman and the Cancer man are in safe territory. Both have serious respect and deep interest in home life, and do their best to keep things running smoothly and harmoniously there. The Crab is most comfortable at home. Once settled in for the night or the weekend, wild horses couldn't drag him any further than the gate post—that is, unless those wild horses were dispatched by his mother. Cancers are often Momma's boys. If his mate doesn't put her foot down, the Crab will see to it that his mother always comes first whenever possible. No self-respecting Aries would ever allow herself to play second fiddle, even if it is to her old gray-haired mother-in-law. If she's a tactful Ram, she may find that slipping into number-one position can be as easy as pie (that legendary apple pie that his mother used to make).

Crabs make grand daddies. They're protective, patient, and proud of their children. They'll do everything to see that their upbringing is as it should be.

ARIES WOMAN
LEO MAN

For the Aries who doesn't mind being swept off her feet in a royal, head-over-heels fashion, Leo is the sign of love. When the Lion puts his mind to romancing, he doesn't stint. It's all wining, dining, and dancing till the wee hours of the morning—or all poetry and flowers, if you prefer a more conservative kind of wooing. The Lion is all heart and knows how to make his woman feel like a woman. The Aries lass in constant search of a man whom she can admire need go no farther: Leo's ten-feet tall—if not in stature, then in spirit. He's a man not only in full control of his faculties but of just about every situation he may find himself in, including of course, affairs of the heart. He may not look like Tarzan, but he knows how to roar and beat his chest if he has to. The Aries woman who has had her fill of weak-kneed men at last finds in a Leo someone she can lean upon. He can support you not only physically, but also as far as your ideas and plans are concerned. Leos are direct and don't believe in wasting time or effort. They see to it that they seldom make poor investments; something that an Aries is not apt to always do. Many

Leos often rise to the top of their profession, and through their example are a great inspiration to others.

Although he's a ladies' man, he's very particular about his ladies, just as the Aries is particular about her men. His standards are high when it comes to love interests. The idealistic Aries should have no trouble keeping her balance on the pedestal the Lion sets her on, so long as he keeps his balance on hers. Romance between these two signs is fair give-and-take. Neither stands for monkey business when involved in a love relationship. It's all or nothing. Aries and Leo are both frank, off-the-shoulder people. They generally say what is on their hearts and minds.

The Aries woman who does decide upon a Leo mate must be prepared to stand behind her man with all her energies. He expects it, and usually deserves it. He's the head of the house and can handle that position without a hitch. He knows how to go about breadwinning and, if he has his way (and most Leos do have their way), he'll see to it that you'll have all the luxuries you crave and the comforts you need.

It's unlikely that the romance will ever die out of your marriage. Lions need love like flowers need sunshine. They're amorous and generally expect similar amounts of attention and affection from their mates. Fond of going out occasionally, and party-giving, the Lion is a very sociable being and will expect you to share his interest in this direction. Your home will be something to be proud of. The Joneses will have to worry about keeping up with you.

Leos are fond of their children but sometimes are a little too strict in handling them. The tactful Aries spouse, though, can step in and soothe her children's roughed-up feelings if need be.

ARIES WOMAN
VIRGO MAN

Quite often the Virgo man will seem like too much of a fussbudget to wake up deep romantic interests in an Aries. Generally, he's cool, calm, and very collected. Torrid romancing to him is just so much sentimental mush. He can do without it and can make that quite evident in short order. He's keen on chastity and if necessary can lead a sedentary, sexless life without caring too much about the fun others think he's missing. In short, the average Aries woman is quite likely to find him a first-class dud. His lack of imagination and dislike for flights of fancy can grate on an Aries nerves no end. He's correct and likes to be handled correctly. Most things about him will be orderly. "There's a place for everything and everything in its place," is likely an adage he'll fall on quite regularly.

He does have a heart, however, and the Aries woman who finds herself attracted to his cool, feet-flat-on-the-ground ways will find that his is a constant heart, not one that cares for flings or sordid affairs. Virgos take an awfully long time before they start trying to rhyme moon with spoon and June, but when and if they get around to it, they know what they're talking about.

The impulsive Aries had better not make the mistake of kissing her Virgo friend on the street—even if it's only a peck on the cheek. He's not at all demonstrative and hates public displays of affection. Love, according to him, should be kept within the confines of one's home, with the curtains drawn. Once he believes that you're on the level with him, as far as your love is concerned, you'll see how fast he can lose his cool. Virgos are considerate, gentle lovers. He'll spend a long time, though, getting to know you. He'll like you before he loves you.

An Aries-Virgo romance can be a lifetime thing. If the bottom ever falls out, don't bother to reach for the mending tape. Nine times out of ten, he won't care about patching up. He's a once-burnt-twice-shy guy. When he crosses your telephone number out of his address book, he's crossing you out of his life for good.

Neat as a pin, he's thumbs-down on what he considers sloppy housekeeping. An ashtray with just one stubbed-out cigarette in it can be annoying to him, even if it's just two-seconds old. Glassware should always sparkle and shine. No smudges please.

If you marry a Virgo, keep your kids spick-and-span, at least by the time he gets home from work. Chocolate-coated kisses from Daddy's little girl go over like a lead balloon. He'll expect his children to observe their "thank yous" and "pleases."

ARIES WOMAN
LIBRA MAN

Although the Libra in your life may be very compatible, you may find this relationship lacking in some of the things you highly value.

You, who look for constancy in romance, may find him a puzzlement as a lover. One moment he comes on hard and strong with "I love you," the next moment you find that he's left you like yesterday's mashed potatoes. It does no good to wonder "What did I do now?" You most likely haven't done anything. It's just one of Libra's ways.

On the other hand, you'll appreciate his admiration of harmony and beauty. If you're all decked out in your fanciest gown or have a tastefully arranged bouquet on the dining-room table, you'll get a ready compliment—and one that's really deserved. Libras don't pass out compliments indiscriminately and generally they're tactful enough to remain silent if they find something is distasteful.

Where you're a straight-off-the-shoulder, let's-put-our-cards-on-the-table person, Libras generally hate arguing. They'll go to great lengths just to maintain peace and harmony—even lie if necessary. The frank Aries woman is all for getting it off her chest and into the open, even if it does come out all wrong. To the Libra, making a clean breast of everything sometimes seems like sheer folly.

The Aries woman may find it difficult to understand a Libra's frequent indecisiveness—he weighs both sides carefully before committing himself to anything. To you, this may seem like just plain stalling.

Although you, too, greatly respect order and beauty, you would never let it stand in the way of "getting ahead." Not one who dillydallies, the Aries may find it difficult to accept a Libra's hesitation to act on what may seem like a very simple matter.

Money burns a hole in many a Libra's pocket; his Aries spouse will have to manage the budgeting and bookkeeping. You don't have to worry about him throwing his money around all over the place; most likely he'll spend it all on you—and lavishly.

Because he's quite interested in getting along harmoniously chances are he won't mind an Aries wife taking over the reins once in a while—so long as she doesn't make a habit of it.

The Libra father is most always gentle and patient. They allow their children to develop naturally, still they see to it that they never become spoiled.

ARIES WOMAN
SCORPIO MAN

Many find the Scorpio's sting a fate worse than death. The Aries woman quite often is no exception. When he comes on like "gang-busters," the average Aries woman had better clear out of the vicinity.

The Scorpio man may strike the Aries woman as being a brute and a fiend. It's quite likely he'll ignore your respect for colorful arrangements and harmonious order. If you do anything to irritate him—just anything—you'll wish you hadn't. He'll give you a sounding out that would make you pack your bags and go back to mother—if you were that kind of a girl. Your deep interest in your home and the activities that take place there will most likely affect him indifferently. The Scorpio man hates being tied down to a home—no matter how comfortable his Aries wife has made it. He'd rather be out on the battlefield of life, belting away at what he feels is a just and worthy cause. Don't try to keep those homefires burning too brightly too long—you may just run out of firewood.

As passionate as he is in business affairs and politics, he's got plenty of pep and ginger stored away for romance. Most women are easily attracted to him, and the Aries woman is no exception. That is, at least before she knows what she might be getting into. Those who allow a man of this sign to sweep them off their feet shortly find that they're dealing with a cauldron of seething excitement. He's passion with a capital P, make no bones about that.

Scorpio and Aries can be an exciting yet dangerous combination, astrologically related through the dynamic planet Mars. Energies can be turned against each other, or used constructively to create and inspire. You both can complement each other's strengths, or prey on each other's weaknesses. Scorpio is blunt; his insults can be razor-sharp and cutting. The Aries woman has to keep a stiff upper lip at times and prepare for a lot of ups and downs. Chances are you won't have as much time for your own interests and activities as you would like. Scorpio's love of power may cause you to be at his constant beck and call.

Scorpios often father large families and generally love their children even though they may not seem to give them the attention they should.

ARIES WOMAN
SAGITTARIUS MAN

The Aries woman who's set her cap for a man born under this sign of Sagittarius may have to apply an awful amount of strategy before being able to make him say "I do." Although Sagittarius may be marriage-shy, they're not ones to shy away from romance. An Aries woman may find a relationship with a Sagittarius—whether a fling or the real thing—a very enjoyable experience.

As a rule, Sagittarius are bright, happy, and healthy people; they can be a source of inspiration to the busy, bustling Aries woman. Their deep sense of fair play will please you, too. They're full of ideas and drive. You'll be taken by the infectious Sagittarius grin and the lighthearted friendly attitude. If you do choose to be the woman in his life, you'll find that he's apt to treat you more like a buddy than like the woman he deeply loves. But it is not intentional; it's just the way he is. You'll admire his broad-mindedness in most matters—including that of the heart. If, while you're dating, he claims he still wants to play the field, he'll expect you to do the same. The same holds true when you're both playing for keeps. However, once he's promised to love, honor, and obey, he does just that. Marriage for him, once he's taken that big step, is very serious business. The Aries woman with her keen imagination and love of freedom will not be disappointed if she does tie up with a Sagittarius. They're quick-witted, generally, and they have a genuine interest in equality. If he insists on a night out with the boys, he won't scowl if you let him shift for himself while you go out with the girls.

You'll find he's not much of a homebody. Quite often he's oc-

cupied with faraway places either in daydreams or reality. He enjoys—just as you do—being on the go or on the move. He's got
ants in his pants and refuses to sit still for long stretches at a time.
Humdrum routine—especially at home—bores him. At the drop
of a hat, he may ask you to whip off your apron and dine out for
a change instead. He'll take great pride in showing you off to his
friends; he'll always be a considerate mate and never embarrass or
disappoint you intentionally. His friendly, sunshiny nature is capable of attracting many people. Like you, he's very tolerant when it
comes to friends and you'll most likely spend a great deal of time
entertaining people. He'll expect his friends to be your friends, too,
and vice versa. The Aries woman who often prefers male company
to that of her own sex will not be shunted aside when the fellows
are deep in "man talk." Her Sagittarius will see to it that she's made
to feel like one of the gang and treated equally.

When it comes to children, you may find that you've been left to
handle that area of your marriage single-handedly. Sagittarius are
all thumbs when it comes to tots.

ARIES WOMAN
CAPRICORN MAN

Chances are the Aries woman will find a relationship with a Capricorn man a bit of a drag. He can be quite opposite to the things
you stand for and value. Where you are generally frank and open,
you'll find the man born under the sign of the Goat closed or difficult to get to know—or not very interesting once you've gotten to
know him. He may be quite rusty in the romance department, too,
and may take quite a bit of drawing out. You may find his seemingly
plodding manner irritating, and his conservative, traditional ways
downright maddening. He's not one to take chances on anything.
"If it was good enough for my father, it's good enough for me" may
be his motto. He follows a way that is tried and true.

Whenever adventure rears its tantalizing head, the Goat will ring
up a No Sale sign; he's just not interested. He may be just as ambitious as you are—perhaps even more so—but his ways of accom-
plishing his aims are more subterranean, or at least seem so. He
operates from the background a good deal of the time. At a gathering you may never even notice him, but he's there taking everything
in and sizing everyone up, planning his next careful move. Although
Capricorns may be intellectual, it is generally not the kind of intelligence an Aries appreciates. You may find they're not quick-witted
and are a little slow to understand a simple joke. The Aries woman
who finds herself involved with a Capricorn may find that she has
to be pretty good in the "cheering up" department, as the man in
her love life may act as though he's constantly being followed by a

cloud of gloom. If the Aries and the Capricorn do decide to tie the knot, the area of their greatest compatibility will most likely be in the home and decisions centered around the home. You'll find that your spouse is most himself when under the roof of home sweet home. Just being there, comfortable and secure, will make him a happy man. He'll spend as much time there as he can and if he has to work overtime, he'll bring his work home.

You'll most likely find yourself frequently confronted by his relatives—family is very important to the Capricorn, his family, that is—and they had better take a pretty important place in your life, too, if you want to keep your home a happy one.

Although his caution in most matters may all but drive you up the wall, you'll find his concerned way with money justified most of the time. He is no squanderer. Everything is planned right down to the last red penny. He'll see to it that you never want.

As far as children are concerned, you may find that you have to step in from time to time when he scolds. Although he generally knows what is good for his children, he can overdo somewhat when it comes to disciplining them.

ARIES WOMAN
AQUARIUS MAN

The Aries is likely to find the man born under Aquarius dazzling. As a rule, Aquarius are extremely friendly and open; of all the signs, they are perhaps the most tolerant. In the thinking department they are often miles ahead of others, and with very little effort, it seems. The Aries woman will most likely not only find her Aquarius friend intriguing and interesting, but will find the relationship challenging as well. Your high respect for intelligence and fair play may be reason enough for you to settle your heart on a Water Bearer. There's an awful lot to be learned from him, if you're quick enough. Aquarius love everybody—even their worst enemies, sometimes. Through your relationship with the Aquarius you'll find yourself running into all sorts of people, ranging from near-genius to downright insane—and they're all friends of his.

In the holding hands stage of your romance you may find that your Water Bearer friend has cold feet that may take quite a bit of warming up before he gets around to that first goodnight kiss. More than likely he'll just want to be your pal in the beginning. For him, that's an important step in any relationship—even love. The "poetry and flowers" stage will come later, perhaps many years later. The Aquarius is all heart. Yet when it comes to tying himself down to one person and for keeps, he is likely to hesitate. He may even try to get out of it if you breathe too hard down his neck. He's no Valentino and wouldn't want to be. The Aries woman is likely to be more attracted by his broad-mindedness and high moral standards than by his abilities to romance. She won't find it difficult to look up to a man born under the sign of the Water Bearer—but she may find the challenge of trying to keep up with him dizzying. He can pierce through the most complicated problem. You may find him a little too lofty and high-minded, however. But don't judge him too harshly if that's the case; he's way ahead of his time.

In marriage you need never be afraid that his affection will wander. It stays put once he's hitched. He'll certainly admire you for your intelligence and drive; don't think that once you're in the kitchen you have to stay there. He'll want you to go on and pursue whatever you want in your quest for knowledge. He's understanding on that point. You'll most likely have a minor squabble with him now and again, but never anything serious.

You may find his forgetfulness a little bothersome. His head is full of ideas and plans. Kids love him and vice versa. He's tolerant and open-minded with everybody, from the very young to the very old.

ARIES WOMAN
PISCES MAN

The man born under the sign of Pisces may be a little too passive for the average Aries woman. He's often wrapped up in his dreams and difficult to reach at times. He's an idealist like you, but unlike you, he will not jump up on a soapbox and champion a cause he feels is just. Difficult for you to understand at times, he may seem like a weakling to you. He'll entertain all kinds of views and opinions from just about anyone, nodding or smiling vaguely, giving the impression that he's with them one hundred percent. In reality, that may not be the case at all. His attitude may be "why bother" to tell someone he's wrong when he so strongly believes that he's right. This kind of attitude can make an Aries furious. You speak your mind; he'll seldom speak his unless he thinks there'll be no opposition. He's oversensitive at times—rather afraid of getting his feelings hurt. He'll sometimes imagine a personal injury when none is intended. Chances are you'll find this sort of behavior maddening and may feel like giving your Pisces friend a swift kick where it hurts the most. It won't do any good, though. It may just add fire to his persecution complex.

One thing you'll admire about this man is his concern and understanding of people who are sickly or who have serious (often emotional) problems. It's his nature to make his shoulder available to anyone in the mood for a good cry. He can listen to one hard-luck story after another without seeming to tire and if his advice is asked he's capable of coming across with some very well-balanced common sense. He often knows what is upsetting a person before that person knows it himself. It's amost intuitive with a Pisces, it seems. Still, at the end of the day, he'll want some peace and quiet and if his Aries friend has some problem or project on her mind that she would like to unload in his lap, she's likely to find him short-tempered. He's a good listener but he can only take so much.

Pisces are not aimless, although they may often appear to be when viewed through Aries eyes. The positive sort of Pisces man is quite often successful in his profession and is likely to wind up rich and influential—even though material gain is never a direct goal for a man born under this sign.

The weaker Pisces are usually content to stay put on the level they find themselves. They won't complain too much if the roof leaks and the fence is in need of repair. He's capable of shrugging his shoulders and sighing "that's life."

Because of their seemingly free-and-easy manner, people under this sign, needless to say, are immensely popular with children. For tots they play the double role of confidant and playmate.

Man—Woman

ARIES MAN
ARIES WOMAN

The Aries man will be contented with the Aries woman so long as she reflects his qualities and interests without trying to outshine him. Although he may be progressive and modern in many things, when it comes to pants-wearing, he's downright conventional: it's strictly male attire. The best position an Aries woman can take in the relationship is a supporting one. He's the boss and that's that. Once that is settled and thoroughly accepted by his Aries spouse, then it's clear sailing.

The Aries man, with his seemingly endless drive and energy, likes to relax in the comfort of his home at the end of an action-packed day, and the Aries wife who is a good homemaker can be sure of his undying affection. He likes to watch the evening news from a comfortable armchair. The Aries wife who sees to it that everything in the house is where her man expects to find it—including herself—will have no difficulty keeping the relationship shipshape.

When it comes to love, the Aries man is serious and constant, and the object of his affection should be likewise. He is generally not interested in a clinging-vine kind of wife; he justs wants someone who is there when he needs her; someone who listens and understands what he says; someone who can give advice if he should ever have to ask for it—which is not likely to be often. Although he can appreciate a woman who can intelligently discuss things that matter to him, he is more interested in expressing his opinions than in listening to another's.

The Aries man wants a woman who is a good companion and a good sport; someone who will look good on his arm without hanging on it too heavily. He is looking for a woman who has both feet on the ground and yet is mysterious and enticing . . . a kind of domestic Helen of Troy whose face or fine dinner can launch a thousand business deals if need be. The cultivated Aries woman should have no difficulty in filling such a role.

The Aries man and woman have similar tastes when it comes to family style: they both like large ones. The Aries woman is crazy about kids and the more she has, the more she feels like a wife. Children love and admire the affectionate Aries mother. She knows how to play with them and how to understand them. She's very anxious that they do well in life and reflect their good home life and upbringing. However, both Aries parents should try not to smother their children with too much love. Kids should be urged to make their own decisions—especially as they grow older—and not rely unnecessarily on the advice of their parents.

ARIES MAN
TAURUS WOMAN

The woman born under Taurus may lack the sparkle or dazzle you often like your women to have. In many respects, she's very basic— never flighty—and puts great store in keeping her feet flat on the ground. She may fail to appreciate your willingness to jump here, then there, especially if she's under the impression that there's no profit in it. On the other hand, if you do manage to hit it off with a Taurus woman you won't be disappointed at all in the romance area. The Taurus woman is all woman and proud of it, too. She can be very devoted and loving once she decides that her relationship with you is no fly-by-night romance. She's pretty rugged, too, or can be, when the situation calls for a stiff upper lip. It's almost certain that if the going ever gets too rough she won't go running home to mother. She'll stick by you, talk it out, fight it out, or whatever.

When bent on a particular point of view, she can be as hard as nails—without having it adversely affect her femininity. She can adjust to hard times just as graciously as she can to good times. You may lose your patience with her, though, if she doesn't seem to want to understand or appreciate your enthusiasm and ambition. With your quick wit and itchy feet, you may find yourself miles ahead of your Taurus woman. At times, you are likely to find this distressing. But if you've developed a talent for patience, you won't mind waiting for her to catch up. Never try grabbing her hand and pulling her along at your normal speed—it is likely not to work. It could lead to flying pots and pans and a fireworks display that would put the Fourth of July to shame. The Taurus woman doesn't anger readily but when prodded often enough, she's capable of letting loose with a cyclone of ill will. If you treat her correctly, you'll have no cause for complaint.

The Taurus woman loves doing things for her man. She's a whiz in the kitchen and can whip up feasts fit for a king if she thinks they will be royally appreciated. She may not fully understand you but she'll adore you and be faithful to you if she feels you're worthy of it. She won't see green, either, if you compliment another woman in her presence. When you come home late occasionally and claim that there were a lot of last-minute things to attend to at the office, she won't insinuate that you've been cheating. Her mind doesn't run like that. She's not gullible, but she won't doubt your every word if she feels there is no reason to.

The woman born under Taurus will make a wonderful mother for your children. She's a master at keeping children cuddled, well-loved, and warm. You may find, however, that when your youngsters reach the adolescent stage you'll have to intervene. A Taurus mother is not very sympathetic to the whims of ever-changing teenagers.

ARIES MAN
GEMINI WOMAN
You may find a romance with a woman born under the sign of the Twins a many-splendored thing. In her you can find the intellectual companionship you often crave and so seldom find. A Gemini girlfriend can appreciate your aims and desires because she travels pretty much the same route as you do, intellectually . . . that is, at least part of the way. She may share your interests, but she will lack your stick-to-it-iveness. Her feet are much itchier than yours, and as a result, she can be here, there—all over the place, and all at the same time, or so it seems. It may make you dizzy. However, you'll enjoy and appreciate her liveliness and mental agility.

Geminis often have sparkling personalities; you'll be attracted by her warmth and grace. While she's on your arm, you'll probably notice that many male eyes are drawn to her—she may even return a gaze or two, but don't let that worry you. All women born under this sign have nothing against a harmless flirtation; they enjoy this sort of attention and, if they feel they're already spoken for, they'll never let it get out of hand.

Although she may not be as handy in the kitchen as you'd like, you'll never go hungry for a filling and tasty meal. She's in as much a hurry as you and won't feel like she's cheating by breaking out the instant mashed potatoes or the frozen vegetables. She may not be handy at the kitchen range but she can be clever—and with a dash of this and a suggestion of that, she can make an uninteresting TV dinner taste like something out of a cookbook. Then again, maybe you've struck it rich with your Gemini and have one who finds complicated recipes a challenge to her intellect. If so, you'll find every meal a tantalizing and mouth-watering surprise.

When you're exercising your brain over the Sunday crossword puzzle and find yourself bamboozled over 23 Down and 11 Across, just ask your Gemini friend; she'll give you the right answers without batting an eye. Chances are she probably went through the crossword phase herself years ago and gave them up because she found them too easy.

She loves all kinds of people—just like you do. Still, you're apt to find that you're more particular than she. Often, all that a Gemini requires is that her friends be interesting—and stay interesting. One thing she's not able to abide is a dullard.

Leave the party organizing to your Gemini sweetheart or mate and you'll never know what a dull moment is. She'll bring the swinger out in you if you give her half a chance.

With kids, women born under Gemini seem to work wonders. Perhaps this is because they are a bit like children themselves: restless, adventurous, and easily bored. At any rate, the Gemini mother is loving, gentle, and affectionate with her children.

ARIES MAN
CANCER WOMAN

Romancing a woman born under the sign of Cancer can occasionally give you a case of the jitters. It may leave you with one of those "Oh, brother . . . what did I get into now" feelings. In one hour she can unravel a whole gamut of emotions that will leave you in a tizzy. If you do fall in love with a Moon Child, be prepared for anything. She'll keep you guessing, that's for sure. You may find her a little too uncertain and sensitive for your tastes. You'll most likely have to spend a good deal of your time encouraging her, helping her to erase her foolish fears. Tell her she's a living doll a dozen times a day and you'll be well-loved in return. Be careful of the jokes you make when you are with her—and for heaven's sake don't let any of them revolve around her, her personal interests, or her relatives. Chances are if you do, you'll reduce her to tears. She can't stand being made fun of. It will take bushels of roses and tons of chocolates, not to mention the "I'm sorrys", to get you back in her good graces again.

In matters of money managing, she may not easily come around to your way of thinking. Aries are often apt to let money burn a hole in their pockets. Cancers are just the opposite. You may think your

Cancer sweetheart or mate is a direct descendant of Scrooge. If she has it her way, she'll hang onto that first dollar you ever earned. She's not only that way with money, but with everything from bakery string right on to jelly jars. She's a saver and never discards anything no matter how trivial.

Once she returns your "I love you", you'll find that you have a very loving, self-sacrificing and devoted friend on your hands. Her love for you will never alter unless you want it to. She'll put you high up on a pedestal and will do everything—even if it's against your will—to see that you stay up there.

Cancer women make reputedly the best mothers of all the signs of the Zodiac. She'll consider every minor complaint of her child a major catastrophe. She's not the kind of mother who will do anything to get her children off her hands; with her, kids come first. You'll run a close second. You'll perhaps see her as too devoted and you may have a hard time convincing her that the length of her apron strings is a little too long. When Junior or Sis is ready for that first date, you may have to lock your Cancer wife in the broom closet to keep her from going along. As an Aries you are apt to understand your children more as individuals than your wife. No matter how many times your Cancer wife insists that no man is good enough for your daughter, you'll know it's all nonsense. If you don't help her to curb her super-maternal tendencies, your Cancer wife may turn into a formidable mother-in-law.

ARIES MAN
LEO WOMAN

If you can manage a gal who likes to kick up her heels every once in a while, the Leo woman's your mate. You'll have to learn how to put away your jealous fears—or at least forget about them—when you take up with a woman born under this sign, because she's often the sort that makes heads turn and sometimes tongues wag. You don't necessarily have to believe any of what you hear; it's most likely just jealous gossip or wishful thinking. She's usually got more than a good share of grace and glamour. She knows it, generally, and knows how to put it to good use. Needless to say, other women in her vicinity turn green with envy and will try anything short of shoving her into the nearest lake in order to put her out of commission, especially if she appears to be cramping their style.

If she has captured your heart and fancy, woo her full force if your intention is to eventually win her. Shower her with expensive gifts, take her out regularly, and promise her the stars—if you're in a position to go that far—and you'll find that a Leo's resistance will begin to weaken. It's not that she's so difficult—she'll probably make a lot over you once she's decided you're the man for her—

but she does enjoy a lot of attention. What's more, she feels she's entitled to it. Her mild arrogance, though, is becoming. The Leo woman knows how to transform the crime of excessive pride into a very charming misdemeanor. It sweeps most men right off their feet . . . in fact, all men. Those that do not succumb to her leonine charm are few and far between.

If you've got an important business deal to clinch and you have doubts as to whether it will go over well or not, bring your Leo wife along to that business luncheon or cocktail party and it will be a cinch that you'll have that contract in your pocket before the meeting is over. She won't have to say or do anything . . . just be there at your side. The grouchiest oil magnate can be transformed into a gushing, dutiful schoolboy if there's a Leo woman in the room.

If you're a rich Aries, you may have to see to it that your Leo wife doesn't become too heavy-handed with the charge accounts and credit cards. When it comes to spending, Leos tend to overdo. If you're a poor Aries, then you have nothing to fear—for a Leo, with her love of luxury, will most likely never give you the time of day, let alone exchange vows.

As a mother, she can be strict and easygoing at the same time. She can pal around with her children and still see to it that they know their places.

ARIES MAN
VIRGO WOMAN

The Virgo woman may be a little too difficult for you to understand at first. Her waters run deep. Even when you think that you do know her, don't take any bets on it: she's capable of keeping things hidden in the deep recesses of her womanly soul—things she'll only reveal when she is sure that you're the one she's been looking for. It may take her some time to come around to this decision. Virgo women are finicky about almost everything; everything has to be letter-perfect before they're satisfied. Many of them have the idea that the only people who can do things correctly are other Virgos. Nothing offends a Virgo woman more than sloppy dress or behavior or careless display of affection. Be sure your tie's not crooked and your shoes sport a bright shine before you go calling on this lady. Keep your off-color jokes for the locker room; she'll have none of that. Take her arm when crossing the street. Don't rush the romance. Trying to corner her in the back of a cab may be one way of striking out. Never criticize the way she looks—in fact, the best policy would be to agree with her as much as possible. The Aries, however, with his outspoken, direct, and sensible nature, may find a Virgo relationship too trying. All those Do's and Don't's you'll have to observe if you want to get to first base with a Virgo may be just a little too much to ask of you. After a few dates, you may come to the conclusion that she just isn't worth all that trouble. However, the Virgo woman is mysterious enough to keep her men running back for more. Chances are you'll be intrigued by her.

Love means a lot to you and you may be disappointed at first in Virgo's cool ways. However, underneath that glacial facade lies a hot cauldron of seething excitement. If you're patient and artful in your romantic approach, you'll find that all that caution was well worth the trouble. When Virgos love, they don't stint. It's all or nothing as far as they're concerned. Once they're convinced that they love you, they go all the way right off the bat, tossing all cares to the wind. One thing a Virgo can't stand in love is hypocrisy. They don't give a hoot about what the neighbors might say as long as their hearts tell them "go ahead." They're very concerned with human truths. So much so that if their hearts stumble upon another fancy, they're likely to take up with that new heartthrob and leave you standing in the rain. She's that honest—to her own heart, at any rate. But if you are earnest about your interests in her, she'll know, and will respect and reciprocate your love. Do her wrong once, however, and you can be sure she'll come up with a pair of sharp scissors and cut the soiled ribbon of your relationship.

As a housewife, she'll be neat and orderly. With children, she can be tender and strict at the same time. She can be a devoted and loving wife—it all depends on you.

ARIES MAN
LIBRA WOMAN

A woman born under the sign of Libra is worth more than her weight in gold. She's a woman after your own heart. With her, you'll always come first, make no mistake about that. She'll always be behind you, no matter what you do. And when you ask her for advice about almost anything, you'll most likely get a very balanced and realistic opinion. She's good at thinking things out and never lets her emotions run away with her when clear logic is called for. As a homemaker, she's hard to beat. She is very concerned with harmony and balance; your home will be tastefully furnished and decorated. A Libra cannot stand filth or disarray—it gives her goose bumps. Anything that does not radiate harmony, in fact, runs against her orderly grain.

She's chock-full of charm and womanly ways; she can sweep just about any man off his feet with one winning smile. When it comes to using her brains, she can outthink anyone and sometimes with half the effort. She's diplomatic enough, though, never to let this become glaringly apparent. She may even turn the conversation so that you think that you were the one who did all the brain work.

She couldn't care less, really, just as long as you wind up doing what is right. She's got you up there on a pretty high pedestal. You're her man and she's happy if you make all the decisions, big and small—with a little help from her if necessary. In spite of her masculine approach to reason, she remains all woman in her approach to love and affection. You'll literally be showered with hugs and kisses during your romance with a Libra woman. She doesn't believe in holding out. You shouldn't, either, if you want to hang on to her. She's the perfect lover who likes to snuggle up to you in front of the fire on chilly autumn nights. She'll bring you breakfast in bed Sundays, then cuddle beside you and tuck a napkin under your chin so you won't get any crumbs on the blankets.

She's very thoughtful about anything that concerns you. If anyone dares suggest that you're not the grandest guy in the world, your Libra is bound to defend you. She'll defend you with her dying breath. When she makes those marriage vows she means every word. As an Aries who also has a tendency to place people you like on a pedestal, you won't be let down by your Libra mate. She'll be everything you believe she is and more.

As a mother of your children, Libra will be attentive and loving. However, you won't have to take the backseat when Junior comes along. You'll always come first with her—no matter if it's the kids, the dog, or her favorite relative. Your children will be well-mannered and respectful. She'll do everything in her power to see that you're treated like a prince.

ARIES MAN
SCORPIO WOMAN

The Scorpio woman can be a whirlwind of passion—perhaps too much passion to suit you. When her temper flies, better lock up the family heirlooms and take cover. When she chooses to be sweet, you're apt to think that butter wouldn't melt in her mouth . . . but of course, it would. She can be as hot as a tamale or as cool as a cucumber, but whatever mood she is in, it's no pose. She doesn't believe in putting on airs.

Scorpio women are often quite seductive and sultry—their charm can pierce through the hardest of hearts like a laser ray. She doesn't have to look like Mata Hari (quite often Scorpio women resemble the tomboy next door) but once you've looked into those tantalizing eyes, you're a goner. Life with her won't be all smiles and smooth sailing; when prompted she can unleash a gale of venom. Generally, she will have the good grace to keep family battles within the walls of your home; when company visits she's apt to give the impression that married life with you is one great big joyride. It's just one of her ways of expressing her loyalty to you—at least in front of others.

She may fight you tooth and nail in the confines of your living room but at a ball or during an evening out, she'll hang on your arm and have stars in her eyes. She doesn't consider this hypocrisy; she just firmly believes that family quarrels should stay a private matter.

She's pretty good at keeping secrets. She may even keep a few hidden from you if she feels like it. This sort of attitude, of course, goes against the Aries grain; you believe in being open and straight-from-the-shoulder.

Never cross her up, not even in little things; when it comes to revenge, she's an eye-for-an-eye woman. She's not keen on forgiveness if she feels she's been done wrong. You'd be well-advised not to give her cause to be jealous, either. When she sees green, your life will be made far from rosy. Once she's put you in the doghouse, you can be sure that you're going to stay there an awfully long time.

There's a good possibility that you may find your relationship with a Scorpio too draining. You'd prefer someone gentler and softer, someone more direct and less secretive, someone who's flexible and understanding. If you've got your sights set on a shapely Scorpio, you'd better forget that sweet soul mate of your dreams. True: a woman born under Scorpio can be heavenly, but she can also be the very devil when she chooses.

The Scorpio mother is protective yet encouraging. She is devoted to developing her youngsters' talents without spoiling them. Under her skillful guidance, the children will learn how to cope with extremes and will grow up to become well-rounded individuals. She will teach her young ones to be courageous and steadfast.

ARIES MAN
SAGITTARIUS WOMAN

You most likely won't come across a more good-natured girl than the one born under the sign of Sagittarius. Generally, they're full of bounce and good cheer. Their sunny dispositions seem almost permanent and can be relied upon even on the rainiest of days. No matter what she'll ever say or do, you'll know that she always means well. Women born under this sign are almost never malicious. If ever they seem to be, it is only superficial. Sagittarius are quite often a little short on tact and say literally anything that comes into their minds—no matter what the occasion might be. Sometimes the words that tumble out of their mouths seem downright cutting and cruel. They're quite capable of losing their friends—and perhaps even yours—through a careless slip of the lip. On the other hand, you can surely appreciate their honesty and good intentions. To you, qualities of this sort play an important part in life. With a little patience and practice, you can probably help cure your Sagittarius of her loose tongue; in most cases, it will be worth the effort.

Chances are she'll be the outdoors type of girlfriend; long hikes, fishing trips, and water skiing will most likely appeal to her. She's a busy person; she could never be called a slouch. She sets great store in being able to move around. She's like you in that respect: she has itchy feet. You won't mind taking her along on camping or hunting trips. She is great company most of the time and generally a lot of fun. Even if your buddies drop by for an evening of poker and beer, she'll manage to fit right in. In fact, they'll probably resent it if she doesn't join in the game. On the whole, she is a very kind and sympathetic woman. If she feels she's made a mistake she'll be the first to call your attention to it. She's not afraid of taking the blame for a foolish deed.

You might lose your patience with her once or twice, but after she's seen how upset you get over her shortsightedness, and her tendency to talk too much, chances are she'll do everything in her power not to do it again. She is not the kind of wife who will pry into your business affairs. But she'll always be there, ready to offer advice if you ask for it. If you come home from a night out with the boys and tell your Sagittarius wife that the red stains on your collar came from cranberry sauce, she'll believe you. She'll seldom be suspicious; your word will almost always be good enough for her.

Although she can be a good housewife, her interests are generally too far-reaching and broad to allow her to confine her activities to just taking care of the house. She's interested in what is going on everywhere.

As a mother, she'll be a wonderful and loving friend to her children. She's apt to spoil them if she is not careful.

ARIES MAN
CAPRICORN WOMAN

If you're not a successful businessman or at least on your way to success, it's quite possible that a Capricorn woman will have no interest in entering your life. She's generally a very security-minded female and will see to it that she only invests her time and interest in sure things. Men who whittle away their time and energy on one unsuccessful scheme or another seldom attract a Capricorn. Men who are interested in getting somewhere in life and keep their noses close to the grindstone quite often have a Capricorn woman behind them, helping them to get ahead.

Though Capricorn can be a social climber, she cannot be called cruel or hard-hearted. Beneath that cool, seemingly calculating exterior there's a warm and desirable woman. She just happens to feel that it's just as easy to fall in love with a rich or ambitious man as it is with a poor or lazy one. She's practical. Although she is keenly interested in rising to the top, she's not aggressive about it. She'll seldom step on someone's feet or nudge competitors away with her elbows. She's quiet about her wishes. She sits, waits, and watches. When an opening or an opportunity does appear, she'll latch on to it immediately. For an on-the-go Aries, an ambitious Capricorn wife or girlfriend can be quite an asset. She can probably give you some very good advice about your business affairs and when you invite the boss and his wife to dinner, she'll charm them both right off the ground. She's generally thorough in whatever she undertakes. She'll see to it that she is second to none in good housekeeping.

Capricorn women make excellent hostesses as well as guests. Generally, they are very well-mannered and gracious, no matter what their background is. They seem to have a built-in sense of what is right and proper. Crude behavior or a careless comment can offend them no end.

If you should marry a woman born under Capricorn you need never worry about her going on a wild shopping spree. Capricorns are very careful about every cent that comes into their hands. They understand the value of money better than most women and have no room in their lives for careless spending. If you turn over your paycheck to her at the end of the week, you can be sure that a good hunk of it will wind up in the bank.

Capricorn women are generally devoted to family—their own, that is. With them, family ties run very deep. Never say a cross or sarcastic word about her mother. She won't stand for that sort of nonsense and will let you know by not speaking to you for days. In fact, you'd better check her family out before you decide to get down on bended knee, because after you've taken that trip down the aisle, you'll undoubtedly be seeing an awful lot of them.

With children, she's loving and correct. They'll be well brought up and polite.

ARIES MAN
AQUARIUS WOMAN

If you find that you've fallen head over heels for the woman born under the sign of the Water Bearer, better fasten your safety belt. It may take a while before you actually discover what she's like and even then you may have nothing to go on but a string of vague hunches. Aquarius is like the rainbow—full of bright and shining hues; she's like no other girl you've known. There's something elusive about her, something delightfully mysterious—you'll most likely never be able to put your finger on it. It's nothing calculated, either; Aquarius don't believe in phony charm. There will never be a dull moment in your romance with the Water Bearer woman. She seems to radiate adventure, magic, and without even half trying. She'll most likely be the most open-minded woman you've ever met. She—like you—has a strong dislike of injustice and prejudice. Narrow-mindedness runs against her grain.

She is very independent by nature and is quite capable of shifting for herself if necessary. She may receive many proposals for marriage and from all sorts of people. Marriage is definitely a big step for her; she wants to be sure she knows what she's getting into. If she thinks that it will seriously curb her independence and her love of freedom, she's likely to shake her head and give you back your engagement ring—if she's let the romance get that far.

The line between friendship and romance is a pretty fuzzy one for an Aquarius. It's not difficult for her to remain buddy-buddy with someone with whom she's just broken off. She's tolerant, remember? So, if you should ever see her on the arm of an ex-lover, don't jump to any hasty conclusions.

She's not a jealous person, and doesn't expect you to be, either. You'll find her pretty much of a free spirit most of the time. Just when you think you know her inside out, you'll discover that you don't really know her at all.

Very sympathetic and warm, she can be helpful to people in need of assistance and advice.

She's often like a chameleon and can fit in anywhere without looking like she doesn't belong.

She'll seldom be suspicious even if she has every right to be. If the man she loves slips and allows himself a little fling, chances are she'll just turn her head the other way and pretend not to notice that the gleam in his eyes is not meant for her. That's pretty understanding. Still, a man married to a woman born under Aquarius should never press his luck in hanky-panky. After all, she is a woman—and a very sensitive one at that.

She makes a fine mother, of course, and can easily transmit her positive and generous qualities to her children.

ARIES MAN
PISCES WOMAN

Many a man dreams of a Pisces partner—and an Aries is no exception. The Pisces woman is soft and cuddly, and very domestic. She'll let you be the brains of the family; she's content to just lean on your shoulder and let you be master of the household. She can be very ladylike and proper; your business associates and friends will be dazzled by her warmth and femininity. She's a charmer, though, and there's much more to her, generally, than just her pretty exterior. There's a brain ticking away in that soft, womanly body. You may never become aware of it, that is, until you're married to her. It's no cause for alarm, however; she'll most likely never use it against you. Still, if she feels that you're botching up your marriage through inconsiderate behavior, or if she feels you could be earning more money than you do, she'll tell you about it. But, then, any wife would, really.

She'll never try to usurp your position as breadwinner of the family. She'll admire you for your ambition and drive. No one had better dare say one bad word about you in her presence. It's likely to cause her to break into tears. Pisces women are usually very sensitive beings and their reactions to adverse situations is sometimes nothing more than a plain, good, old-fashioned cry. They can weep buckets when inclined.

She'll have an extra-special dinner waiting for you to celebrate your landing a new and important account. Don't bother to go into the details, though, at the dinner table; she is only too happy to leave the details of business to you.

She can do wonders with a home. She's very fond of soft and beautiful things. There will always be a vase of fresh flowers on the hall table. She'll see to it that you always have plenty of socks and handkerchiefs in the top drawer of your dresser. You'll never have to shout downstairs, "Don't I have any clean shirts left?" She'll always see to it that you have. Treat her with tenderness and the relationship will be an enjoyable one.

She'll most likely be fond of chocolates. A bunch of beautiful flowers will make her eyes light up. See to it that you never forget her birthday or your anniversary. These things are very important to her. If you ever let them slip your mind, you can be sure of sending her off to the bedroom for an hour-long crying fit. An Aries with patience and tenderness can keep a Pisces woman happy for a lifetime.

She's not without faults herself, however, and after the glow of love-at-first-sight has faded away, you may find yourself standing in a tubful of hot water. You may find her lacking in imagination and zest. Her sensitivity is likely to get on your nerves after a while. You may even feel that she only uses tears in order to get her own way.

Pisces make strong, sacrificing mothers. She will teach the children the value of service to the community.

ARIES
LUCKY NUMBERS 2011

Lucky numbers and astrology can be linked through the movements of the Moon. Each phase of the thirteen Moon cycles vibrates with a sequence of numbers for your Sign of the Zodiac over the course of the year. Using your lucky numbers is a fun system that connects you with tradition.

New Moon	First Quarter	Full Moon	Last Quarter
Jan. 4	Jan. 12	Jan. 19	Jan. 26
5492	2374	4014	4229
Feb. 2	Feb. 11	Feb. 18	Feb. 24
4578	8396	6075	5338
March 4	March 12	March 19	March 26
1026	6394	4757	5513
April 3	April 11	April 17	April 24
3085	5260	0972	1790
May 3	May 10	May 17	May 24
4528	8364	4201	1689
June 1	June 8	June 15	June 23
8072	2533	3096	8561
July 1	July 8	June 15	June 23
5489	2997	7635	6196
July 30	August 6	August 13	August 21
2708	8865	6245	5907
August 28	Sept. 4	Sept. 12	Sept. 20
6953	3096	6894	4173
Sept. 27	Oct. 3	Oct. 11	Oct. 19
0944	2179	9152	2830
Oct. 26	Nov. 2	Nov. 10	Nov. 18
7754	5134	4852	6971
Nov. 25	Dec. 2	Dec. 10	Dec. 17
7874	4672	2859	9316
Dec. 24	Jan. 1 ('12)	Jan. 9 ('12)	Jan. 16 ('12)
6539	8374	1294	2498

ARIES
YEARLY FORECAST 2011

Forecast for 2011 Concerning Business
and Financial Affairs, Job Prospects,
Travel, Health, Romance and Marriage
for Persons born with the Sun
in the Zodiacal Sign of Aries.
March 21–April 20

For those born under the influence of the Sun in the zodiacal sign of Aries, ruled by Mars, planet of action and energy, 2011 promises to be a year of unexpected challenges and opportunities for significant change. Whether the change hits you suddenly, causing total chaos or revolutionary new insights and understanding, or whether it's a restlessness that pushes you to start making changes, your world is about to be altered. Be open to learning new things, let go of your expectations, and be honest with yourself about your true ambitions and needs. Then you have a very good chance of obtaining goals that seemed to be beyond your reach.

Uranus, the planet of sudden change and enlightenment, returns to visit your sign of Aries on March 11 and will stay in Aries for the next seven years. Uranus is often referred to as the awakener. Situations that you have simply accepted before can now become inhibiting and restricting. Your need for personal freedom becomes greater, forcing you to make changes to the way you handle yourself and the world around you. Out of these changes will come a new outlook and understanding of your reality. With Uranus in Aries you can expect changes to occur in all areas of your life, because essentially what you desire from life will change. You will desire more freedom and excitement in your daily routine, in relationships, in work, and in study. Business and career arrangements are all likely to undergo significant adjustments or even total transformation. Health will be affected more than ever by your stress level and emotional state. Travel may be a perfect way for you to escape the mundane and restrictive ties of your daily life.

Pluto, the planet of transformation, is now moving through Capricorn, your sector of achievement and life outside the family unit. Pluto will reside in Capricorn for sixteen years. Your willpower and your ambition to succeed in your area of expertise will increase. Even if you were shy in the past, this Pluto transit will fuel your desire to prove what you can do. You want your accomplishments to be recognized and your talents to be appreciated. If you do not know your goals, you will probably change your path. You may change jobs often and spend several years feeling quite lost until you find out what you are supposed to be doing. Business contacts with people of great wealth or influence can be established. You're almost sure to be involved with loans, taxes, insurance, inheritances, joint finances, corporate money, or secret weapons. The chance of becoming a public figure is a possibility. On the negative side you should avoid any illegal dealings, nurture your reputation, and learn to deal with authority figures. Otherwise, you can come up against public situations that may damage your chances of fame and fortune forever.

Business and finance for the year look to be fairly positive. Jupiter, the planet of expansion, moves into your sign of Aries on January 22, triggering a major cycle of personal growth. This is an auspicious time to start new projects and expand old ones. So if you are starting your own business or gathering money to expand an already existing business, the signs are all positive. With Pluto giving you access to powerful figures, you should make the most of what people will offer you. Do be sure that you are basing your figures and reputation on a viable base. As an Aries you tend to rush things and not think them through properly. If you don't have the patience or the expertise to do due diligence, engage a professional to help set your business on a solid foundation. Many Aries individuals may decide to go back to school. Further study and the right credentials give you a chance to progress toward your ambitions and life goals. You will learn that no matter how out of reach a goal may seem, you will find a way to reach it. If you are having trouble, someone will come along and give you a hand. So don't be afraid to ask for help.

Jupiter moves into Taurus, your solar house of money and self-worth, on June 4. Jupiter visits Taurus for the rest of the year, bringing its gifts of luck and expansion to all money matters. Jupiter forms a positive aspect with Pluto and career matters in July, making this a perfect time to apply for a dream position or a promotion, or to change your goals. This Jupiter transit often coincides with professional success, political power, or tremendous gains in personal wealth or resources. On a more humble level, this transit can give you the chance to straighten out situations in your life that have been sources of trouble for you. As an Aries you tend to be self-indulgent and arrogant and may overcommit your resources, spend unwisely, act impulsively, or take unnecessary risks. If these negative effects occur, you are in danger of losing whatever you make and then some more, especially if you have borrowed to fund your business venture. Note the periods when Mercury, the planet of communication, commerce, and contracts, turns retrograde. These periods are not recommended times to try to start or finalize any business or finance. In 2011 these Mercury retrograde periods are March 30 through April 22, August 3 through August 26, and November 24 through December 13.

Job prospects for 2011 look very good. You are likely to progress up a rung or two if you are settled in your employment. During August and September you can have the chance to be more creative and start working in areas of design, advertising, fashion, or human resources. Your abilities and talents are likely to stand out more at this time, and you may gain financial or other favors quite unexpectedly from your employer. Relations with coworkers can be very good at this time, and if you do not already work with other people this is when you can start. Cooperation and teamwork will come easily, giving you a reputation of favor among your workmates. Good social relations with workmates can lead you to join a company sports team or sponsorship group. Your ruling planet Mars moves into Virgo, your sector of work, health, and service, for the last two months of the year. Mars in Virgo signals an enjoyment of physical work. You may earn money playing a sport or you could take on a leadership role. With this Mars transit you may experience conflicts with coworkers and superiors, so try to leave your ego at home. And be careful in any physical activity that might lead to injury on the job.

Health matters can remain stable, and good health should be the order of the day for those of you who do not have a chronic condition. You do have to watch your lifestyle, though. Too much fatty food, or just too much food, could be a problem for you early in the year. Extra weight adds all sorts of risks to your long-term health, not to mention your physical ability and self-confidence. Keep a constant exercise regimen happening. If you can manage it, go to the gym regularly so that you stay on top of your physical fitness. You will be under a lot of pressure all year, with nervous tension and stress clouding your judgment. Rushing jobs that should be handled carefully poses the risk of mishaps and accidents. Headaches and fatigue could make life hard at times. It is essential to your good health that you get exercise and a well-rounded diet. Cut down on stimulants such as caffeine and sugar, and minimize your intake of drugs and alcohol. These substances may help you deal with emotional situations momentarily, but they actually add to your stress levels over time. The changes that are occurring in your life this year are too promising to risk wasting such a valuable opportunity on oral gratification.

Spiritual matters can be more important to you this year, and they will have a positive effect on your health. With Saturn and

Neptune making positive contact, you can study subjects that raise your consciousness. Yoga, occult metaphysics, spiritualism, and mysticism broaden your understanding. Put them into effective practice in your life. These pursuits will do everything you look for in drugs and alcohol, and then lots more. They are helpful for alleviating stress, calming your mind, and enabling you to make informed and intuitive decisions that are true to your inner self.

Saturn, the planet of responsibility and limitation, moves through Libra, your house of relationships and marriage, all year. Saturn in Libra urges Aries individuals to seek a committed long-term relationship. For those of you who are already married or partnered, this is a year when your relationship can become the source of difficulty. Your partner may be making increasing demands that seem to erode your sense of independence and limit your freedom to express yourself as an individual. Some relationships will end, because they demand more than they are worth. Those that survive can go through confrontations and periods of adjustment as your needs change and the mutual love matures. This year favors seeking guidance counseling. There are some difficulties that will benefit from such mediation, especially if you are unsure what it is you both want from each other and the relationship, as distinct from what you think you want.

Single Aries may yearn to meet someone and form a meaningful relationship. You may feel that the lack of a relationship is tied in with your feelings of self-worth. The important thing to remember is that when the time is right, the right person will come along. Until then you are free to explore the person that you are. There are likely to be many possible partners who come your way. The period from July to mid-October is a prime time for a love relationship to take hold. Aries will be highly creative at this time, seeking fun and entertainment through the arts and play. So you are more likely then to meet a like-minded soul who wants to join in the fun and explore what it means to connect romantically. This is also a promising time for those of you who would like to become a parent. But if you are not ready to be a parent, take precautions to save yourself unwanted consequences.

As an Aries you have the courage and the inventiveness to weather any storm. In this potentially joyful year build a strong foundation and protect it, as the winds of change will shift.

ARIES
DAILY FORECAST

January–December 2011

JANUARY

1. SATURDAY. Happy New Year! Change is in the air and it promises to be very positive for Aries people. Take the time to contemplate the year ahead and note the things that are important, and let this guide you when snap decisions will have to be made. A career move may entail leaving cherished friendships, but the opportunities ahead are too good to miss. A hard decision will be eased if you fall back on your support network. You may find that you have a way out of a tough situation through the skills and kindness of a friend or relative, so don't be too shy to ask for help. If you are heading off on a journey, expect the unexpected and you should be in for the time of your life!

2. SUNDAY. Inspiring. A spiritual or social event can bring you in touch with life-changing ideas and broaden the horizon of experience. Communication with loved ones can be challenging, but open your eyes to subconscious issues that will lead to avenues of resolution. Exciting possibilities in love are also indicated. If you are single now, you may not be soon. Aries in relationships might experience renewed passion and a depth of intimacy like never before. Whether single or not, you need to be mindful of the boundaries you set and make responsible choices, as the lure of romance and fantasy can blind you to situations that are detrimental to your self-esteem if you relax your guard.

3. MONDAY. Powerful. A strong drive to succeed at whatever you are doing will help you push through all odds today. Some Aries may have problems at work and find your employer is asking too much of you. Don't get your back up, though. It could be a passing mood. Your mother might need your support. If you feel she is using emotional blackmail, simply speak to her about it, as you have the chance to transform the way you relate right now. A valuable secret can fall into your hands and give you a key to improving your finances and investment opportunities. But don't go near anything that is dishonest or unlawful, as this would change the situation into one that results in your own undong.

4. TUESDAY. Ambitious. The new Moon in Capricorn early this morning bodes well for the achievement of your goals, but make sure you know what it is you really want. If you are looking for advancement in your career, check out course or training opportunities that will give you the edge over your competitors. Some of you may even be able to talk your employer into paying for your training. Aries wanting to start businesses of your own should get advice from a financial adviser. The backing you need is sure to be available if your business plan is in order. Your popularity might have you busy working late and attending functions, so make sure you don't neglect loved ones at home.

5. WEDNESDAY. Favorable. A slow start to the day will give you time to get your business in order and prepare for the hectic pace to follow. Meetings and conferences could be the order of the day, and you should find business is conducted fairly and in an orderly manner, making this a perfect time to introduce new notions and ideas for the future. A romantic evening could be in the pipeline, and you may receive an invitation from a new suitor that makes you forgetful of your daily duties. A class in yoga and meditation may catch your eye, and this would be a wonderful release from the pressures of life as well as the constant chatter of the mind that leads you from your true path.

6. THURSDAY. Promising. A bright idea should be explored in full. If you are contemplating a new project, get your thoughts down on paper and start laying the foundations because this may be the beginning of something very valuable to your future. If you are having problems in a relationship, talk it over with a close and trusted friend before you start planning drastic action. Friends may have some insight or suggestions that can help you work things out simply and gently. Beware of taking on extra debt at this time. No matter how good the transaction sounds, get expert advice from a financial planner beforehand. A business friendship might start to deepen into the realm of loving intimacy.

7. FRIDAY. Interesting. Aries may be attracted to strange and different people, places, and things today. An art exhibition or music concert might be an instructive and inspiring outing, opening your mind to new ideas and sounds. The travel bug could bite you and turn your mind to faraway places. You might check out work opportunities in odd places, and find a future that heretofore you would never have known about, Keep on your toes at work, though, because your boss is likely to be watching and if you are doing a good job, may even put your name down for a promotion. Do not believe all that people tell you. Use your common sense before getting into situations that may be hard to get out of.

8. SATURDAY. Reactive. Unconscious phenomena can play a role in your responses, so before you give someone an earful or walk off in a huff, pause and consider your role in the situation. Contemplation and meditation can be very useful to your peace of mind. If you are unsure of how to sit with your thoughts, register for a class and add meditation to your spiritual assets. Career issues might be exacerbated through the illness of a colleague, and this might put extra pressure on you to perform. But if you can maintain your focus, you have the chance to make an impression with the people who matter. A love affair could blossom with a friend and cause some jealousy among others. Be true to yourself.

9. SUNDAY. Optimistic. A fortunate understanding of a situation, combined with your Aries gift of being willing to take a chance regardless of fear, will put you in the driver's seat and help you make friends and influence people. A spiritual meeting might be the best medicine for those of you who are troubled. The lesson of surrender may seem hard to learn, but once understood, brings a simple peace of mind and happiness. An upset in your relationship can affect your libido and gnaw at inner feelings of guilt. Try being honest with yourself and just maybe you can start to understand what is going on underneath the surface. Aries parents may receive some expert help from your mothers-in-law!

10. MONDAY. Impulsive. The Moon moves into your own sign of Aries this morning and will stay there until Thursday night. Moon in Aries turns your focus onto your personal and subjective needs. You may be very sensitive, picking up on the moods of those close to you, giving you a sympathetic ear with warmth and understanding. Spend a little time on yourself, too. Spruce up your image with new clothes, a haircut, or visit a masseuse and free up your body. Somebody in a position of power might be trying to manipulate you, and you need to be very careful that you don't end up being the fall guy. Try to subdue your normal enthusiasm long enough to consider your own goals, and don't let anybody lead you astray.

11. TUESDAY. Restricting. Pressure from your partner could cramp your style and limit your spontaneity. This can be a good thing if you understand why this situation is occurring. But if you feel unfairly dealt with, talk it over with them, without losing your temper! This is not a good time to get mixed up with the law, especially in a litigation. Give the matter plenty of thought before engaging an attorney. Aries writers may be offered a contract with a publishing house, but make sure you read all the fine print before signing. Work behind the scenes will be very productive, as it will allow you to express your creative flair without the dampening input of other people's opinions.

12. WEDNESDAY. Healing. Good felings among friends will enable Aries to sort through a personal issue constructively, resolving past resentments and dishonesty. Your partner may be dealing with stresses at work that are affecting your home life. Why not suggest that they have some healing bodywork for relaxation and then see a counselor to help them deal with the matter? Personal security issues could be causing you added strain, but sometimes it is better to meditate on them rather than try to fix things or control them. Put it all in the hands of a higher power. This is an excellent time to start planning your next vacation. Check out the specials; an unbelievable deal could be available.

13. THURSDAY. Expressive. You may be offered a position as spokesperson for your company or business, and this would be a wonderful opportunity for you to develop your communication skills. Mercury, the planet of communication, has moved into Capricorn, your solar house of career and long-term goals. Mercury here makes the next three weeks a good time to concentrate on expanding your knowledge base and getting training in areas of advancement. This is also a good time to approach your boss for a pay increase or talk about the possibilities of promotion. Some of you might be interested in striking out on your own, and a course in small-business management would get you started, but don't talk about your plans at work.

14. FRIDAY. Productive. Spend some time on money matters, and if you are worried about a credit card debt, call the issuer and negotiate a better interest rate. A promotion into a managerial role is highly likely, and you may have to stand up for a colleague who is being mistreated. If you do so, you will find that your popularity and respect for you blossom overnight. A new romance can be interrupted because your new lover has planned an overseas adventure, but this may take a positive twist and encourage you to head overseas also, or conversely, give you time to build your career while you carry on your love affair long-distance. A positive approach to any problem will bear sweet fruit.

15. SATURDAY. Variable. Give yourself plenty of time to make appointments, travel, and organize your business because there are likely to be setbacks and holdups throughout the first half of the day. This is not a good time to apply for a job or send your resume out. Wait, and the stars will be more favorable tomorrow. Aries popularity is on the increase, and more than one invitation for this evening could cause indecision and stress. Breathe deeply and choose the one you think you will enjoy the most, not the one that appeals to your ambition or pride. This evening promises fun and entertainment, and for singles the chance of a romantic introduction. Overindulgence may be your only vice.

16. SUNDAY. Social. Mars, the planet of energy and ego, moves into Aquarius, your social sector, and will emphasize friendships and invitations. But you still need to be conscious of recognizing the needs of others. Your ambition to achieve will get a boost, and you can work extremely hard at this time, especially if you have room for individual initiative and effort. Conflicts with authority figures, such as parents, employers, teachers, or even government officials, might hold you back if you insist on threatening or ignoring their wishes. Be mindful of all the rules and regulations, and you can lay the groundwork now for a cherished dream. No matter how idealistic, it may become a reality sooner than you think.

17. MONDAY. Irritating. Don't get caught up in other people's problems and you will enjoy the day. Spend your morning cleaning away paperwork, paying the bills, and catching up with your tax records, as the afternoon will be full of interruptions. Your workload may be interfering with your home life at the moment, and instruction in effective time management might be the answer. The desire to volunteer to help out in your local neighborhood can also open up opportunities to work in interesting areas, or to start becoming active on a political level. Whatever is grabbing your interest at the moment, there is a danger that you can have a finger in too many pies; concentrate on one area for success.

18. TUESDAY. Demanding. Power trips and control issues could interfere with Aries plans. Keep to yourself and stay out of intrigue and you will do well. Your mother might be glad for your help. If you haven't heard from her, give her a ring and check up. A loved one may have to undergo an operation, and you may end up hanging out at the hospital for hours. Take plenty of snacks and if you have kids, arrange a babysitter to make your day less stressful. A relationship breakdown might mean selling off property, and all the feelings of loss and grief that surround this can get you down. Take your mind off it by looking for your next purchase. With prices so low, you might be surprised at what you find!

19. WEDNESDAY. Eventful. A positive frame of mind should make this day successful, and the chance of a visit from Lady Luck can top it off. Aries may have a project in the pipeline that is about to get the go-ahead and surpass your wildest dreams of success! Today's Full Moon is in Cancer, and shines its loving light on your domestic scene, so you can expect plenty of action on the home front. Some Aries may be moving out of state to take up a new career position, and are experiencing the excitement and trepidation that such a move entails. Nevertheless, you can expect a very social evening, and unexpected visitors might turn your quiet night into an impromptu party. Order takeout and relax!

20. THURSDAY. Gregarious. The Sun joins Mars in Aquarius, your solar house of friends, hopes and wishes, and turns your focus toward groups and ideals. You may decide to take up a team sport at this time and get your exercise and social stimulation at the same time. Aries gamblers may need to keep a close eye on this addiction over the next month as the urge to take risks and spend big is increased now. Aries parents can decide to fill up some of your children's leisure time with classes such as dancing, music, or drama to give them an education and a taste for this creative and fun side of our culture. At the very least, it will give them less time to spend on sibling rivalry.

21. FRIDAY. Wishful. The chances of waking up with a hangover or feeling the onset of a winter virus could make the morning difficult. Artists might value this time and get some really original creative work started. Your imagination and fascination for things less tangible make for some interesting outcomes. A new romance may dominate the day, and some Aries could be tempted to take the day off from work, preferring the sensuous embrace of this new and arousing relationship. Vacation time may be due, and you are preparing for an exciting escape on a fun-filled adventure. Make sure you have your luggage insured to guard against loss, and you should be assured of a great time.

22. SATURDAY. Obsessive. If you already practice meditation, you are lucky. But for those Aries who don't, it is a great time to start learning. Putting your house in order may be a good way to keep your mind off a nagging problem and clear out a bit of space at the same time. Go through all your cupboards and storerooms and you might find a few things you can renovate with a bit of your own creative flair, fresh paint, or the sewing machine. This is also a good time to implement a diet to keep you healthy and lose weight. See your local naturopath for the diet that suits you, and stock up the pantry with the correct fare. It is much easier to stick to it when all the right ingredients are at hand.

23. SUNDAY. Beneficial. Jupiter, the planet of expansion, moves into your own sign of Aries and heralds the beginning of a major cycle of growth in your life. Jupiter will remain in your sign until June, during which time you can accomplish your goals, learn new things, and gain new experience. But it is important not to exaggerate your own importance or be wasteful with your resources. You will find that your luck increases as well as your social circle. You do have to be aware of excesses, as your waistline may also expand and a love of the high life might deplete your savings. Attention to detail will be your forte today, so take care of those jobs that on another day may seem too tedious to focus on.

24. MONDAY. Competitive. A colleague may try to take your position at work if you are not careful. Keep up with your workload and stay away from any power struggles to preserve your integrity. Some Aries might be in the public eye at the moment, and can use this opportunity to expand your business and influence. Just maintain a practical approach and don't let the limelight go to your head. Your relationship may be experiencing difficulties that stem from poor communication. A few visits to a marriage counselor might help you both to see the other side and find amicable and equitable compromises based on understanding. A legal hassle can be settled out of court now.

25. TUESDAY. Uncertain. Sharp words spoken in a dispute can amplify heightened tension in the workplace and make for some unpleasantness that could have been avoided. If you hot-blooded Aries can't hold your tongue, you would be wise to go out for a walk instead. Be very careful when negotiating a business contract to set out the terms and conditions thoroughly, as there can be mix-ups and misunderstandings that will lead to losses. Aries looking for careers might do well to ask around your network of friends and family, as there could be openings in areas that interest you. A self-help group can give you some much-needed support with relationship difficulties.

26. WEDNESDAY. Animated. A hobby or craft can start to cost more than your budget can allow. Ask around your social club for paid work to do, and you might be able to generate extra cash at this place of employment. A close friend may be going through relationship dramas and try to involve you. Apart from giving support, be very careful, as you might end up becoming the scapegoat. As the day progresses, you will notice the tension dissipate, and a relaxed gathering of friends can be full of laughs and interesting debate. A long-term goal could need extra attention, as well as a methodical inventory of expenditure and effort, so that you can appraise your progress factually and precisely.

27. THURSDAY. Deceptive. Someone could be trying to pull the wool over your eyes, so make sure you know what you are talking about before going into any business negotiations. A large bill might warrant being double-checked, as there could be extra charges that are not correct. A new romance is in the air. If you are already infatuated with a colleague to the point where you lose your train of thought every time they walk by, you may be very surprised to find out that they feel the same way toward you. Make sure that you keep your romance separate from the workplace. You could be in for a difficult time if any of your other colleagues catches wind of the situation.

28. FRIDAY. Eventful. Today should be very positive, with the chance of a visit from Lady Luck. An application to a pregtigious college or university might be accepted and get you out and about organizing your clothes and study implements, while booking your accommodations. Travel can dominate your thoughts now. If you can't afford a trip overseas, look locally and go to a health spa where you can relax, feel pampered, and take your mind on a vacation via meditation. An Internet romance might get serious and get you planning a rendezvous in some far-flung corner of the earth; make sure you check out the political climate of the place before you rush off blindly.

29. SATURDAY. Loving. A fascination with a foreign culture might draw you to an interesting cultural or art exhibition, or you may end up in discussion about global economics and politics. Joining up with a group that is concerned about global issues, such as climate change and food shortages, can change your life focus and see you heading off overseas to carry out research or for a recruitment drive. A love affair with someone from an exotic corner of the globe can introduce you to new taste sensations in food and music, enticing you to travel home with them to make your life in this new and challenging environment. But it would be wise to acquaint yourself with their customs beforehand.

30. SUNDAY. Challenging. Aries people involved in sports will have the enjoyment of playing someone who stretches you to the limit in an evenly matched game. On a more social level, you may be mixing with some very intellectual people who stretch your local knowledge with invigorating debates and lively political discussions. Low self-esteem can be an issue if you find yourself feeling inhibited in the presence of others, and some of you might be in a situation of abuse that up until now you haven't been conscious of. Once this becomes obvious, you will find that you can start to stand up for yourself and instead of yelling, you may simply pick up your things and walk away.

31. MONDAY. Focused. A self-help group can be very useful to you now. As you listen to others, you will come to a better understanding of how you feel and think, giving you the answers you seek. Partners of Aries may be having problems at work, and when they are not at work, they are bringing it home with them. Have a talk with them about it, and see if some time can't be organized each day to put aside other tasks and duties and be together for love and intimacy. Sometimes problems seem to disappear when they are shared with another, and perhaps you can share the load. Job security might be an issue, so start looking at alternatives and explore options for a solution.

FEBRUARY

1. TUESDAY. Impulsive. Emotional interchanges can make your blood boil and dissolve your common sense. If you can, pause before you say or do something you will live to regret. A job offer from your company's competition could be just what you want, with the income to match; keep this to yourself until you are ready to hand in your resignation, or you may end up the butt of a coworker's jealousy. Social engagements are likely to be forthcoming for all sorts of activities, and fill up your calendar for the next month. Choose who you mix with carefully and stay away from any people that are always putting you down. Then you won't have to worry about your Aries temper.

2. WEDNESDAY. Inspiring. Mars, your ruling planet, meets up with the Sun in Aquarius, giving you the energy to move mountains and overcome problems. But you might have to watch your natural urge to bulldoze your way through things, as you can tread on toes and make enemies that way. Independent activities suit you best, and if you have a personal project on the drawing board, you can get the ball rolling now and achieve great things. A meeting could become disruptive. If you can maintain diplomacy, your boss will be happy. This is a good time to take up a physical exercise program and work off any excess anger in the gym or on the playing field, rather than in the rest of your life.

3. THURSDAY. Exciting. You are loaded with energy now and being so high-spirited, you'll have a lot of fun juggling all the tasks that other people find too boring to deal with. This makes you very valuable and very popular! Expect people to toss you some easy tasks that you can use to build up your expertise and your resume. They don't have the time to deal with them, but you do. Your usefulness will be rewarded and remembered, so don't think you are doing other people's work for no reason. An unexpected invitation for romance may transport you into fantasyland. Remember that dreams and reality are often quite different. Keep your feet on the ground and you will keep your self-respect intact.

4. FRIDAY. Passionate. Love is in the air for all Aries people. A new relationship can have your heart thumping and make it impossible to concentrate on anything but your loved one. Forget work and hide away together, being close to nature and sharing thoughts, memories, and dreams for the future. This is a special time and deserves to be enjoyed. Of course, some of you may have many responsibilities, and find that you need to take time to organize your duties before you can take off. Get a close friend to cover for you if need be. Your popularity is high. You could be in line for a promotion, gain a position in the public eye, or be recognized for your special skills and expertise.

5. SATURDAY. Rewarding. Benefit will come through associations, and a powerful friend can work wonders behind the scenes to further your career. Spend a bit of time contemplating your future. Make sure you know exactly where you want to go, and you will find that the pieces should all fall into place. A love affair may get serious, turning your thoughts to wedding plans. Don't worry about what your families will want. Think about what suits you two; after all, you are the main players. The best thing to do is to talk it over and find a compromise. In all types of decision making, there may be a problem with consensus. Let everybody express their points of view, and make a decision later.

6. SUNDAY. Irrational. Thoughts and feelings can be at odds, and you find yourself acting on impulse, buying things you don't need, gambling away your extra cash, or accepting an invitation to a gathering you don't want to attend. If you can cancel all of your plans and head off for a hike in the hills or a day at the beach, you will benefit from the calming vibes of nature. Don't even ask your lover, as you will probably just end up arguing anyway. A class in art or dance or a spiritual retreat would be excellent by allowing the expression of your soul without all the irritations of other people's wants and needs. If you have to catch up on a backlog of work, hang out a do-not-disturb sign.

7. MONDAY. Intense. The expectations of others might get you down a bit and hamper your style, but sometimes it is necessary to put other people first. Your partner may need some help to organize a social event, and even though you have to cut corners at work, it will be so much better if you can lend a hand. If your partner is suffering from depression, why not suggest you both go along to counseling together and help your partner get out of the house. You could stop somewhere nice and have lunch on the way, and just the caring intimacy of your company might make all the difference. An exercise program would be beneficial for your health at the moment. Why not check out what's available at your local gym?

8. TUESDAY. Magnetic. Your charisma can be all-powerful, putting you in line to step up a rung or two at work. One of your bosses may be out due to illness, and you may be asked to fill the position while the boss is away. If you tread carefully, it might become permanent. High-quality personal grooming can be all-important, so it might be worthwhile visiting an up-market store and laying out some of your savings on some classy attire. Aries singles can find your heartstrings pulled in a passionate encounter, and end up going places you hadn't planned and meeting people you normally would never meet. It's all part of finding out how interesting life can be when you are one of the beautiful people.

9. WEDNESDAY. Powerful. Your ideals are very important to you now, and it is an excellent time to start to plan the manifestation of your dreams. Put your thoughts down on paper, and start by compiling two or three positive affirmations for achieving your goals. Keep them simple and say them often and you are on your way. Beware of trying to manipulate others, as you could get drawn into a power play like a puppet on a string and you wouldn't know what happened. A raise in pay can give you a false sense of security. Don't use your credit cards, as you are likely to rack up debt now that will take you months to pay back. A passionate embrace could be the start of something hot. Be careful!

10. THURSDAY. Stimulating. All kinds of meetings and social events could be available, and you will be firing on all cylinders when it comes to debate and discussion. Aries students can gain a better grasp of your subjects now through class discussion and tutorials; you might even start up a study group for debate after hours. You have a talent for dealing with people right now, and if you are asked to represent your company at a seminar or be an area representative, you should find your feet quickly and hit the ground running. A disagreement with your partner can be useful if you are willing to own up to your own role in things openly and honestly, clearing the air for true and honest intimacy again.

11. FRIDAY. Dreamy. A strong dream may echo in your mind all day, giving cause to wonder about your spiritual life. It is a good idea to write these dreams down, and you might consider buying a special notepad for this purpose, making this a special part of your life's journey. There can be quite a bit of subconscious phenomena surfacing now, and you will benefit from meditation and other contemplative practices. Romance is highly likely, and Aries singles might begin an alliance that will last your entire lives as you feel like twin souls with this other person. When it comes to keeping your mind on your job, you would be wise to write your tasks down, so that you don't have to rely on your memory too much.

12. SATURDAY. Impressionable. Your mind is like a sponge today, absorbing all sorts of ideas and experience, and this will be perfect for Aries writers or artists, who have been struggling to get your ideas out into your work. A lucrative contract may come your way, and you should have your attorney go over it and make sure you are happy with all the conditions. Otherwise, make changes that suit you better before you sign. A brother or sister could ask for your help to find employment. You might even need to help them out with a place to stay so that they can find the right kind of employment that will set them up for a career. Aries smokers should give up now for lasting success.

13. SUNDAY. Social. This looks to be a wonderful day for Aries people to relax and entertain. If you are snowed under with a backlog of work, why not ask a few colleagues over to work on the matter together. Many minds make light work, and you will have a lot of fun doing it. Some of you may be getting to know your neighborhood, and a local market is a great way to see what's going on and what's available in the area, meeting the neighbors while you shop. Stop at the corner coffee shop while you are out, and catch up on the local gossip. Chances are you will make a new friend who will stay with you for life. Whatever you do today, don't stay home alone and let your worries get you down.

14. MONDAY. Profound. The deepest and most powerful forces within your subconscious mind are influencing your actions, and it can be difficult to avoid acting compulsively. Guilt, jealousy, being overly possessive, or simply the desire to control another's emotions can take control of you, or you may experience these emotions through somebody else. You can be sure that any conflicts between you and another will reveal a great deal about the inner workings of both of you. Meeting the demands of your boss along with your family members could be stretching you to the limit. Call a family meeting and see if you can allocate the jobs and lighten your load, which will benefit the whole family in the long run.

15. TUESDAY. Heartening. Home and family can be your main focus at the moment, and a day at home redecorating and catching up with the gardening might be just what the doctor ordered. Take it easy and spend some time working out a manageable budget that fits your lifestyle and allows you to add some leisure activities for fun and laughter in the home. Unexpected visitors might disrupt your day, so get started on what is important early and you won't mind so much. A meeting may be called off at the last minute, and that might put your nose out of joint. But instead of wasting your trip, you can go see an old friend. Your impromptu visit helps put a smile on their face, too!

16. WEDNESDAY. Expansive. Everything can seem to go your own way now, and a range of options for expansion and learning can open up to you. A change in your life's perspective can change your career goals, and a range of adult study courses can inspire your thinking in a radical direction. Suddenly, you may feel that you can now do what you have believed you were too old or too poorly educated or some such to do. Anything is possible, so harness your dreams and take off! Romance is also a high possibility, with a soul mate walking into your life. Take it easy, though. If it really is true love, it won't disappear in one night. Young couples wanting to start a family might have already started.

17. THURSDAY. Creative. Energy levels can be down a bit over the next few days, so don't take on too many commitments. Some of you may have to look after a sick child and will need to get all the rest you can. Your creativity is high and your imagination should be in full flight. Don't let it take you into a depressive state with imagined slights and guilts getting you down. Rather, use this time to get in touch with the spirit inside yourself simply by praying and allowing your spirit to manifest. Relationships can be difficult, especially if there is any dishonesty between the parties. Consider seeing a counselor and working on your communication issues so that you can share intimately without fear.

18. FRIDAY. Healing. The Full Moon in Leo puts the focus on your individual talents and your ability to help others through these personal gifts. You may feel that you are pretty average, but people enjoy your company and gain a lot of benefit from your energy and spontaneity. Living life in the fast lane can be fun. But if you are feeling a little run-down, check in with the local naturopath and stock up on your vitamins and minerals, or simply change your diet. With the right nourishment and exercise, you will be feeling fantastic in no time. You will respond really well to some psychic healing, and if you have the name of a reputable healer, it will do you wonders.

19. SATURDAY. Reflective. Take it easy this morning reading the papers and allowing your body and mind to come together peacefully. Enjoy being at home and doing your chores, playing with your pets, and nurturing your garden, as this is who and what you really are. Stay away from crowds and enjoy the company of loved ones. Some of you may have to visit your mother, and if she is in a nursing home, take her some lovely fruit and flowers to nourish her soul. You can have issues in your relationship with a partner about having so little time to spend together. With your different work routines and outside interests, you might be time-poor. Plan a couple of hours for you both to relax together.

20. SUNDAY. Indulgent. Whatever you get into today, you are likely to overdo to the hilt. Your boundaries might be weak, so watch the company you keep. If there seems to be abuse of alcohol and drugs going on, escape to a quiet corner where you can do your own thing away from the madness. Keeping a journal can be good for your psyche, and it will be fun to look back at it to see how you have grown, so now would be a great time to start. Or if you find it hard to write, maybe you can take up playing music or doing some painting to develop your sense of self and encourage playfulness. Life is a journey and you are on the road, so stop thinking about the past and the future and start living in the here and now.

21. MONDAY. Affectionate. Keep tabs on your business appointments and commitments this morning because you might miss something extremely important. The rest of the day should be much lighter. If you have done your work well, you might even be celebrating a financially successful business venture. Plan an intimate dinner with your partner. This is the perfect time to talk over any issues you have been dealing with and talk honestly about your feelings and desires for the future. This will be especially helpful if one of you needs to make a career move and the change is going to affect the other partner. Legal matters can be resolved out of court satisfactorily and amicably now.

22. TUESDAY. Revealing. You may feel like going off by yourself to think or study today, and that should work out well. You may also feel like withdrawing into yourself and meditating. Mercury, the planet of communication, enters Pisces and your solar sector of the spirit, joining the Sun in Pisces. This gives you the increased ability to deal with nonrational aspects of reality. If your workplace is too hectic for you to concentrate, find a quiet place to work, or work behind the scenes to do your best. An exciting business deal may have you on the edge of your seat. The need for secrecy can drive you nuts, as you may be so excited you want to tell the world. Your biggest problem is your tax debt.

23. WEDNESDAY. Reclusive. Your ruling planet Mars joins the Sun, Mercury, Chiron, and Uranus in Pisces today, and crowds into your solar sector of the subconscious. With so much going on in your inner world, you may want to withdraw from a lot of your usual outside activities and contemplate your situation. This is a period of gestation, when ideas and sentiments brew inside and can burst forth with new projects and activities as soon as Mars and Mercury move into your own sign next month. So allow yourself some quiet time to nurture these inner needs and desires and use your solitude to get in touch with your sense of self. If this might seem somewhat nebulous, seek counseling for guidance and self-awareness.

24. THURSDAY. Adventurous. An interest in foreign politics might inspire you to investigate faraway places over the Internet and start dreaming about overseas travel. Stop in at the travel agent's during your lunch break and start organizing a trip for your next vacation; it is not as hard as you might think. Some of you may be planning to return to the country of your forebears, and could start by researching your family tree and getting in contact with relatives who are still living there. You will probably be offered accommodations as well. Aries grandparents may be asked to babysit the grandchildren, and you might organize an outing to make their stay more interesting.

25. FRIDAY. Philosophical. A legal problem can be cleared up with a visit to an attorney, giving you cause to ponder on how many of the problems in life are created in our minds. The powers of our thoughts can be harnessed through using affirmations, meditation, and prayer, so start, try it out, and see if it works. A health issue could be making life harder than it should be. Try going to different health professionals for alternatives to the treatments you have already received. Chances are you might be pleasantly surprised with more natural methods. Be extra careful to lock up your home and car when leaving them unattended, and check that your insurance policy is up to date also.

26. SATURDAY. Excitable. Nervous tension is likely to make people around you fidgety or simply annoying. If you are feeling upset, stay away from emotional situations and take yourself for a walk in nature. This will ground you and allow you to see where you end and other people start. Sometimes you can pick up on the energy of others and start to feel quite confused about what is going on. Mixed messages may also throw you off and leave you with a feeling of being deceived. Don't let yourself be aggravated and end up yelling. Try to do some steady breathing and remove yourself from the cause. Lady Luck is on your side today, and a job application can be successful!

27. SUNDAY. Easygoing. A social event may take you all day to organize, but you can lessen the work if you call on some friends for help and you all have fun doing it together. Take lots of photos so you can have a picture night later and laugh while you relive the fun. An impending speech might have you busy planning what you will say and practicing positive self-talk, but don't get yourself worked up. Relax and you are sure to be a hit. Some Aries parents may have a sick child that needs to go to the hospital. Again, if you are worried about the costs, ask your friends to pass around the hat and you will be able to have the treatment that is necessary. Today's lesson is to reach out.

28. MONDAY. Friendly. The Moon dances with Venus today, creating favorable circumstances in your business and professional life, attracting persons and situations that facilitate your work. People in authority are favorably inclined toward you, and most relationships in your professional life will run smoothly. No matter what you do for a living, you might get involved in artistic matters now, such as design work, layout work, office redecorating, even public relations for the purpose of making your business look attractive. Relations with women are especially fortunate, and you may gain some benefits through such associations. This is a good day to see your mother and share love and affection.

MARCH

1. TUESDAY. Fortunate. Concentrate on your hopes and wishes for the future now, as you can start the groundwork for them to manifest in the next two weeks. Positive affirmations and contacting the relevant people and authorities will all go toward a favorable outcome. Friends and associates are important to you. An emotional attachment to one friend in particular could demand extra loving and comfort from you, but you will find the rewards justify your efforts. Business income can get a boost and allow you to start planning a new venture with confidence and support. A stepchild may need your understanding, and any chance you have to share your experience as an equal will win their favor.

2. WEDNESDAY. Loving. While you are not inclined to talk about your feelings, you will not evade them within yourself. If you have a problem, seek out an older person whose wisdom you respect, who can offer emotional support and suggest practical and immediate answers, as you need commonsense answers that can be applied directly. Venus, the planet of love and harmony, moves into Aquarius and your sphere of friends, hopes, and wishes. Venus should bring lots of good feelings into your social realm, making this next three-week period the best time for group activities or activities with friends. Business conferences and meetings are all favored by this Venus transit, and it is a great time to throw a party!

3. THURSDAY. Fatiguing. The chances of waking up tired are high, whether your sleep was full of dreams or your sleep was broken due to worries playing on your mind. Take it easy and allow yourself time to come back to life before you head out. Some of you may be coming down with a virus, and it would be wise to spend the day in bed drinking herbal teas, allowing your body to fight it off unhindered by other activities. A day in front of the television or reading a good book could be the perfect medicine. This is also a perfect day for reflection. If you can allow yourself the luxury of doing nothing, you might be amazed at the insight and understanding that will help you resolve an important issue.

4. FRIDAY. Focused. Work behind the scenes will be very beneficial, and the achievement of long-term goals can start to feel tangible. Stay away from social venues and cancel any invitations for today, as you won't enjoy yourself if you go out anyway. A romance with a friend might be interesting, but annoying at the same time because it has become a group issue, denying you the sense of privacy and intimacy that you desire at the moment. Be honest and ask for your space. If you feel that your friend is resentful of this, then maybe the friend isn't right for you, and better to know now than farther on down the line when it may become far more difficult to extricate yourself from the relationship. Be loving and kind to yourself.

5. SATURDAY. Disruptive. Resentful thoughts or anxiety over a situation can trouble you all day, and the best way to deal with this is to meditate, or simply pray to a higher power for freedom from resentment and worry and for some direction on the matter. The more you can separate yourself from your ego, the more peaceful will be your day. You may be contacted by an old friend, and the chance to get together and reminisce and catch up on all your gossip will be food for your soul right now. Some Aries could be concerned for your mother. If she is in the hospital, make the effort to visit her, and you might find that you can have quite a special conversation that helps dissolve past resentments.

6. SUNDAY. Refreshing. A sense of renewal can wash away yesterday's anxieties and give you a whole new and bright slant on your life. For Aries who have been ill, you are likely to be feeling better and starting to get your energy back with a new and vigorous enthusiasm for life. Physical activity will be beneficial, and the great outdoors will give you inspiration galore. Ask some friends to go on a picnic to a local beauty spot to enjoy outdoor games and adventure together. Take the video camera along and record your fun for future enjoyment as well. If you are applying for a new job, gather as many personal references as possible for success.

7. MONDAY. Expressive. With the Moon in your own sign of Aries, you are sure to be enthusiastic and emotionally involved in whatever you are doing today. Of course with your quick temper, you might need to watch your reactions and moderate your impulses to suit the situation. Otherwise, you could end up in trouble! Young Aries drivers might want to watch your speed around town, and students should be wary of upsetting the teachers. Partnered Aries can have difficulty coming to terms with your partner's needs or demands at this time. Rather than have an argument, you both should agree to postpone making a decision until later when you can sort it out amicably over dinner at a favorite restaurant.

8. TUESDAY. Sensitive. Caring for others will come naturally today, and you may even put your name down to help out with a local charity. You are sensitive to the moods of others, and this can have its drawbacks in that any negative or depressed persons can bring you down, too. Be aware of the moods of others, and keep away from any destructive influences if possible. It will be hard to keep your mind on the job most of the morning, and any important paperwork or decision making should be left until the afternoon for the best results. Don't jump into any long-term commitments right now, especially involving financial debt, as you may not be thinking clearly and could live to regret it.

9. WEDNESDAY. Favorable. An opportunity to move up a rung at work and earn a higher salary may be offered. Don't be shy, put your hand up for the position, and if you have a friend who can pull a few strings, let them know of your intentions as it will be a very positive move for your career. A strong sexual attraction can interrupt your thoughts, and acting on an impulse could overpower what your common sense tells you. So simply stay away from risky situations and preserve you reputation and your feelings of self-worth. An inspiring evening can surprise and delight you. An unexpected visitor, a powerful movie, or a contact via the Internet can bring new ideas and make dreams come alive.

10. THURSDAY. Reflective. What other people think and feel is their problem; you can only be concerned with your own thoughts and feelings. What do you really want? Are you happy doing what you are doing? These are the sorts of questions you might want to ask yourself, rather than trying to work out how to please others. Take care of your physical comfort first, care for yourself with a good diet, nice clothes, and harmonious surroundings, and then you can start to work on your budget and get your financial life in order to match. By the time you have sorted these things out, you might find that you are feeling content and you can look in the mirror and tell yourself that you love yourself!

11. FRIDAY. Outgoing. An opportunity to attend an out-of-town conference or seminar might give you the chance to catch up with some old friends as well. Expand your circle of friends wherever possible, as it will give you a chance to try new things and stimulate your thought processes. Aries people are going through a strong period of personal growth at the moment, and you will find out all sorts of new things, such as abilities and interests, about yourself. New situations, people, and things will allow you room to experiment with the possibilities and experience new adventures. Do not be afraid of losing. Anything that falls away at this time will be replaced by something better.

12. SATURDAY. Major. Uranus, the planet that rules rebellion and change, has just moved into your own sign of Aries. For those of you who were born in the beginning of your sign, this heralds a time when you will try to achieve a new means of self-expression and become freer than you have ever been. Sometimes, circumstances will conspire to force the change upon you and the more you try to fight it, the more difficult it will be. Exciting ideas, new people, and fresh situations are all likely to become part of your daily life. Single Aries are likely to meet somebody who will have a major effect on your life. You may start a relationship that will last a lifetime, albeit one quite different from your expectations.

13. SUNDAY. Interesting. The impulse to quit your job and head off in search of a dream might be overpowering, but visit your family and talk it over with them before you act on your impulse. If you already have your own family, you will need to make sure you can relocate with as little disruption to your loved ones as possible. Your lease may be up and you have to move. Consider buying your own home. Perhaps you could look at purchasing a home that needs work and is cheap, and look at earning money via home renovations. It is amazing what you can do with secondhand materials. A day in the garden might be excellent therapy for your soul right now.

14. MONDAY. Dutiful. Your sense of responsibility is strong. Now you may find yourself helping a neighbor or friend when what you would really like to do is stay at home and sort out your own problems. Still, helping others has a funny way of helping yourself, and while you are out being kind, the problematic side of your life gets sorted out anyway. Your partner may lose their driver's license and make extra work for you driving them to and from work, but at least you can be thankful that they do have a job. Working parents could have a sick child that is worrying you. If you feel the youngster needs extra care, take the day off and heed the advice the doctor gives.

15. TUESDAY. Comforting. A loved one may go on an overseas trip today and leave you feeling a little depressed. You may find yourself sorting through your family pictures and reminiscing over the past. Sort some of your photos into a collage that you can get framed and hang on the wall. It will give you cause to smile every time you look at it. Some of you might start researching your family tree and get into contact with relatives you have never met. Before you know it, you are planning your own trip to meet new relatives and expand your family network. Aries mothers to-be could start to feel the imminent arrival, and should get your bags ready for this exciting event.

16. WEDNESDAY. Enlightening. A new romance could start to cramp your style. Soon, you are bowing out of your next date and planning to do what you want, feeling free from the inhibitions of trying to please. An opportunity to turn a hobby into a job might come your way when friends ask you to start teaching this skill for which you have a real talent. Stay away from gambling venues today as you could get sucked into spending more than you can afford. Instead, buy a lottery ticket with your lucky numbers and you might be successful. An impressive play or concert could be in your town, and it might be worth buying tickets with a friend and going to the show together.

17. THURSDAY. Fanciful. This is an excellent time to seek out some counseling that will help you sort out the dreams from reality. Aries imagination is very strong. Now your sensitivity would benefit from dance movement and art. If you have the opportunity or inclination, either area of self-expression can take you to a strong sense of self and enable you to work out your problems rather than avoid them. Your energy level can be down and your diet could need an overhaul. Check in with a naturopath and nutritionist. You will be surprised how many of your ailments will disappear with the right diet, giving you back your energy and correcting any sleep disorders.

18. FRIDAY. Demanding. Be very careful not to overload your calendar for today, as your nerves and immune system will suffer from the stress. If you live alone, consider buying a small dog to keep you company and force you to get some daily exercise. If you already own a dog, get outdoors with it and have some fun together, breathing in the fresh air and laughing. You may have to play nurse to a loved one, and should take some care with their diet. Beef or bean broth will be particularly nourishing and simple to prepare. A friend might be having a party this evening, so try not to miss it. Your friendship will suffer if you fail to show.

19. SATURDAY. Energetic. Focus on what is important to you today. You can achieve quite a lot, especially if you have a pet personal project to work on that is inspiring your creativity and imagination. A class in self-defensfe might give you a good excuse to get fit and bolster your personal sense of security as well as giving you a chance to make new friends. Some Aries may be considering joining the armed forces. Get in contact with the recruiting office to find out about the real training and job opportunities that would be available to you, as well as the remuneration, before you let your imagination take you on a trip to fantasyland.

20. SUNDAY. Challenging. Disrupted sleep or a touch of the flu could put you out of sorts this morning, lowering your energy levels and making it hard to keep your mind on matters at hand. You may end up having an unpleasant dispute with your partner over something so trivial you can't believe it really happened. But when you feel tired and run-down, rational thought does tend to fly out the window. It might be worth buying them a little present to say you're sorry. But if you feel your partner was unreasonable, give them a chance to make it up to you. An employment opportunity that you would dearly love could become open. Put in your application regardless of your credentials.

21. MONDAY. Significant. Last night, the Sun moved into your sign of Aries, joining Uranus, Jupiter, and Mercury there in your solar house of self. With the Sun in Aries, the emphasis is on your self-expression, giving you an energy boost to move mountains. You may act impulsively right now, and should beware of temper tantrums, as you will not brook any interference or restrictions to your intentions. Pause long enough to consider what you are doing, and take a few slow and relaxed breaths before you act, to avoid accidents and stepping on the wrong toes. Read all the fine print in any deals, contracts, or agreements, as there are sure to be hidden clauses and conditions that you were not made aware of in the negotiations.

22. TUESDAY. Fair. Look at retail therapy for what it is, ineffective bandage for feelings of personal inadequacy, and realize the error of overspending before you break the bank and put your budget in the red. If you want to feel better, you would be wise to use your spare cash to pay down your credit cards and focus on doing things for yourself that you can enjoy without costing you anything. Wash and polish your car instead of going to the car wash; it will save you money and help to keep you fit. Take the kids to the park for an outdoor game instead of to the fast-food outlet. You can spend a lot longer running around having run than it takes to eat fries and a burger, and laugh a lot more, too.

23. WEDNESDAY. Promising. You can inplement personal changes and find they take hold now. But don't try to change the people around you, or they will dig their heels in and get mad at you. By changing yourself, you will affect others without having to do anything. This is not the best time to have any surgical procedures. Put any operations off until next week for the best results. A passionate encounter can take you to the stars and back. But if you are looking for a romance that lasts, you might be disappointed. Enjoy what you have and let it go; it might just be a taste of better things to come. A spiritual healing group can be inspirational and give you an inner glow that lasts.

24. THURSDAY. Practical. Be scientific when gathering information for a court case or legal action of any sort. You may tend to have your own ideas about the situation, but the law could be less emotional about your issues. If applying for a position at a university or other institute of higher learning, be sure to be diligent with all the facts about your eligibility and aptitude. Remember, luck is simply preparation for opportunity. The travel bug can bite you today, and you may spend hours on the Internet perusing all the different travel deals and exotic destinations. You are likely to find job opportunities at the same time, and may start a new career in a foreign land, such as teaching a language there.

25. FRIDAY. Eventful. Watch out for touchy emotions early and you won't put anybody's nose out of joint with your straight-to-the-point approach. A close friend may arrive back from their travels and come around to catch up. Be prepared to lose hours, as they will have some stories to tell and you won't want to interrupt. An impromptu family affair could turn out better than anything that has been planned and bring the whole clan together to celebrate a milestone. Remember to take your video camera and capture the moment for future memories. A new romance can develop between you and a foreigner. Although the allure of their accent and culture can be very attractive, don't lose sight of your own.

26. SATURDAY. Intense. A power struggle at work might leave you wondering if the job is worth all the hassle. Stay away from factions and backbiting, and you might be noticed by your employer for your trustworthiness. Aries who are setting up your own business might want to get some financial advice before you take out a large loan. Any pointers you receive on how to deal with this will be another safeguard for your solvency. Good communication skills will make you a winner in whatever field you are involved in today. You might use this time to approach your employer about your opportunities for promotion and get an idea of what sort of training might be worthwhile.

27. SUNDAY. Charitable. Venus, the planet of love and harmony, moves into Pisces and your solar sector of compassion and receptivity. You can be quite selfless now and take care of a loved one who is in need of help, or become involved in some charitable activity such as working for the underprivileged or in a hospital or similar institution. You could volunteer for a local environmental group and help to clean up your neighborhood, or organize a social activity for fund-raising purposes. Emotional sensitivity is heightened now. You might find it hard to bargain with others on a rational level while you take everything far too personally. Work on a personal project may be advantageous.

28. MONDAY. Gregarious. Contact with others will be far more enjoyable than spending the day on your own. If you play a sport, make sure you get involved in competition. You could meet someone who will be a very valuable contact for you in the future. Networking is the name of the game now. You can end up in places you never intended to be when you leave home, but you should enjoy every moment and glory in the change to your usual humdrum day. Partnered Aries might have to deal with a jealous partner who wants you to stay with them rather than do your own thing. Allot time for both of you to pursue your separate interests. Then save the rest of the day and evening for the two of you to be together.

29. TUESDAY. Supportive. This is a time when you can rely on your friends to help, or you may need to help a friend. Either way, you and your friends will support each other and feel that you belong together. Relations with women are good, and you may encounter someone who can show you a great deal about yourself in a positive sense. You also have patience and extra strength to deal with problem situations and come out feeling very satisfied with your abilities. An older person may be a great help to you now. If you have a problem, ask someone older and wiser for their advice and you are likely to receive practical and immediate answers. A celebration of marriage may be on the cards.

30. WEDNESDAY. Sensitive. Mercury goes retrograde in your sign of Aries today. So communication may be difficult. Your thoughts might not be very clear, and therefore your experiences might be difficult to reduce into words. But poetry and art, especially escapist art or literature, can appeal, and you may find yourself drawn to less conventional types of people. Your personal boundaries can also be a bit weak right now, so do be careful who you mix with. For your safety's sake, don't succumb to peer group pressure or take drugs and alcohol. Your sensitivity to your surroundings is greatly increased, as is your empathy with those around you. You may listen to a friend's problems, or you may discuss your own problems with a friend.

31. THURSDAY. Harmonious. Be gentle on yourself today. If you are feeling low on energy or are recovering from hard physical work, fill up the tub, if you have one, and put in some sea salts and sweet-smelling herbs such as lavender and rosemary for relaxation and rejuvenation. Meditation would be good for your soul, but sitting still might not be easy. So do some physical activity such as tai chi or dance and enjoy the harmonious awareness. Some Aries are moving in unison with another, enjoying the rhythm of each other's body and, on a soul level, drinking in the sights, sounds, and smells of sweet loving. Budding photographers can experience something similar with landscapes.

APRIL

1. FRIDAY. Powerful. Friendships are extremely important to Aries, and they may change your life in a very positive way now. A loved one could be interfering with an important matter. But if you can consider their objections, you might gain a far greater understanding of your undertaking and learn something about teamwork at the same time. Although you feel that you are being practical and pragmatic, under the surface your emotions are likely to be running the whole show. So any attempt at contemplation will be worth far more than any hasty actions. If you can pause before acting on impulse, you will be the winner. Someone behind the scenes can pull a few strings that make your life a lot easier.

2. SATURDAY. Opportune. Mars, your ruling planet, moves into your own sign of Aries, where it joins the Moon and excitable Uranus. This creates an explosive mix of energies that calls for caution, or else you might overreact and pay for your impulse for a long time to come. The Sun, Jupiter, and Mercury are also in Aries, so this is a great time to make significant changes. If you do so in a positive and thoughtful way, your energy levels will be high and you can move mountains if that is what it takes. Do be careful of accidents caused through haste. It is not a good idea to have any surgery done at this time, as there may be more to your malady than is obvious. Get a second opinion, for safety's sake.

3. SUNDAY. Beneficial. This morning's New Moon is in Aries, making this a perfect day for planning your coming month. Your ambition is high, and you can achieve much if you implement foresight and intuition in your undertakings. Your mood is likely to swing with the wind, and the people around you will affect you with their moods also. Stay away from negative and depressed persons unless you are an experienced therapist. The Moon, together with benevolent Jupiter, gives a generous and beneficial flavor to the whole day. But don't let good feelings talk you into gambling more than you can afford, or offering a service that you know you can't provide.

4. MONDAY. Renewing. Today Neptune, the planet of illusion and sensitivity, moves into Pisces and your solar house of the subconscious. You may find that you develop a sense of despair when watching the news, especially about world politics. If so, turn your mind to spiritual matters and read up on the literature you have always wanted to peruse. Or start a course in meditation. You can't do much for the world, but you can do a lot for yourself. By making yourself a better person, you will add to the world. Think globally and act locally is the name of the game. Get active in your local area and leave world politics for the politicians to work out. Your health may need some special attention. Take the day off.

5. TUESDAY. Enjoyable. Little things can happen that conspire to enhance your feelings of self-worth and make you feel special. Be prepared to bend your schedule for others, and you will be doubly rewarded with good feelings and friendship. A promotion can be in the offing. If you dress well and put yourself in the front of the line, you will be successful. A health matter may be interfering with your ability to meet deadlines. Try relaxation techniques, as you are quite likely suffering from stress. Breathing exercises, coupled with meditation and early nights, might be all you need to feel on top of everything again. Plan a weekend escape and give yourself something to look forward to.

6. WEDNESDAY. Optimistic. On a physical level, you should be feeling very good and desire experience and activity. Regardless of the obstacles, you will go after what you want with vigor and enthusiasm. You may decide to start studying so that you have the credentials to get the job and position you want. You will have to be aware that you can overdo things at the moment, so plan your day well with plenty of breaks for relaxation and enjoyment. It is not a good time to spend a lot unless you have done all your homework and know the investment is sound. Otherwise, you will live to regret your optimism. For those of you born in the middle of Aries, weight gain could be a problem.

7. THURSDAY. Distracting. Fancies and illusions may seem more important than reality, so much so that this not a good time to make decisions or to embark upon a course of action that requires clear thinking. Memories of a past romance can conjure up sentimental thinking, coloring your present mood and thoughts with regrets. Start a journal and write these things down. The process of doing so can help you to exorcise this outdated baggage from your subconscious and clear the way for new romances and creativity. Stay away from drugs and alcohol and avoid negative thinkers, then you will be able to make the most of the intuition and the insight that accompany a dreamy state of mind.

8. FRIDAY. Enigmatic. Mystery and innuendo can interfere with your need for concrete knowledge and thought. But if you allow yourself to enter into the mood of a situation, you will at least enjoy the secrets. Romantic power struggles can be nasty or exciting. But if you would like to sort out some long-term issues once and for all, now is a good time to start. Perhaps you and your partner could go to a guidance counselor and learn how to listen to each other. A desire to extend your knowledge could be satisfied through home study. That way you can build up your skills, extend your work options, and enjoy exercising your mind while you practice your time-management skills.

9. SATURDAY. Puzzling. Delays and holdups will put you out of sorts and cause all sorts of frustrating situations. Be very careful not to make any promises for today as you are quite likely not going to be able to keep them. Information on a new business venture could dampen your enthusiasm. Don't jump the gun; it will all change again in about two weeks. Get out and about in your local neighborhood. If there is a local market or community event, you will definitely enjoy yourself, make some new friends, and learn of interesting avenues for entertainment and education within your own neighborhood. Planning for the future can be bolstered by reflecting on the past and practicing patience.

10. SUNDAY. Relaxing. You could be a little under the weather or hungover this morning, so enjoy a sleep-in and then the morning papers. If your partner seems to want to pick a fight with you this morning, you are better off not saying anything. Avoid starting something that will last longer than it deserves to. Plan to get away to a local beauty spot and allow nature to reinvigorate you, or else grab a few DVDs from the store and luxuriate at home in fantasyland. Anything that takes your mind off your worries and allows you to relax will be beneficial. Aries parents might enjoy taking the kids to a ball game, so they can yell and scream all they want.

11. MONDAY. Surprising. Events such as the arrival of unexpected visitors can throw your plans for the whole week out of whack and put you on the offensive. Challenges to your ego are highly likely now. Whatever you do, try not to react aggressively. In fact, do the opposite and react accommodatingly, and you should be very pleased with the results. A project started a week ago may come up against a few problems. If you are unsure of how to handle them, ask an expert to fix the problems right the first time. A parent may be in need of extra care to stay at home. Before you make any decisions, check out all the options available and help them to make an informed decision on their future.

12. TUESDAY. Active. Sports, speculation, and fun are all likely to figure highly on today's agenda. A business deal could become tedious due to small details. If you suggest a transfer of venue to a nice restaurant and take a long lunch while you iron out these details, your popularity will rise and the deal will be a success. An interest in a foreign culture might whet your appetite for philosophy, religion, and travel. Start planning your next vacation in advance to give you plenty of time to pay for and prepare an adventure of a lifetime! Apartment hunting might be a lot easier if you are able to pay a higher rent. Why not get a roommate to ease the cost of an expensive lease.

13. WEDNESDAY. Creative. An opportunity to teach the skills you have learned through a hobby can turn this pastime into an enjoyable and lucrative profession. Don't be shy if asked; you will find your feet in this role instantly. A woman in a position of authority can make your day a bit more difficult, so cross your t's and dot your i's in all professional capacities. A new romance is on the cards for passionate Aries. Don't be surprised if you keep getting amorous glances from someone you think is drop-dead gorgeous. You'll go home with stars in your eyes and a hot date for the weekend.

New parents might consider throwing a baby shower to contribute to the nursery.

14. THURSDAY. Tedious. Interest in the fine details will elude you this morning. Get most of your organizing and correspondence done early so you can concentrate on the detailed bits later when you will feel more like it. Be aware of infectious diseases and stock up on your vitamins and minerals. A tonic such as olive leaf extract would be very good, and drink plenty of water to give your immune system the jump on new viruses. The need for some relaxation and recreation might be appeased with music or art classes, allowing all you fast-paced Aries to meditate while doing something you enjoy. Take the dog for a walk and get out into the fresh air. If you don't have a dog, borrow a friend's.

15. FRIDAY. Instructive. An important assignment or a personal ambition could be pressing. But you will find that there are many other things you have to do before you can get down to what is important to you. Don't let your temper get the better of you. You will learn something that will help you through the rest of your life simply by practicing patience and thoroughness. Your partner may be critical of something that you love to do. This is a good time to sit down and discuss how you feel and listen to how they feel, and you can both share a greater understanding. You cope well with conflict at the moment, and your workplace is a good forum for the union of compassion and ambition.

16. SATURDAY. Expressive. Aries emotions may be up and down, and things you think you want don't seem to measure up once you obtain them. You may struggle with feelings of not being good enough, but these feelings are not based on fact and shouldn't be given too much of your time and attention. Plan activities that get you out with others and that you enjoy for a pleasurable and peaceful time. Moderation in all your affairs is the answer today. Nourishing food, trusted friends, and relaxation will be balm for your soul. Competive urges and rushing will only result in accidents and physical depletion. Use your energy constructively and establish goals within your reach.

17. SUNDAY. Stimulating. Romantic encounters and interludes are indicated, but whether they are real or imagined is optional. You will be busy with other people, and may have to deal with in-laws and relations that you don't get along with all that well. Nevertheless, you are sure to be responsible and exercise restraint for the sake of peace. This evening's Full Moon in Libra will bring harmonious vibes. It is a perfect time to plan a moonlight dinner for two, a concert or play, and an evening of lovemaking and talking from the heart. Some of you may have to sit up late and catch up on a backlog of work before the morning's rush, but take the time to enjoy your lover's embrace.

18. MONDAY. Strategic. Business deals and high finance could be on the agenda today. If you think a proposition sounds fantastic, it probably is. But at the moment, it is likely to work. Do your own research, as you might find some people are very unreliable and you will need to be independent when it comes to decision making. A small inheritance might come your way and spark memories of the past as well. People you haven't thought of for years may touch you in ways you have forgotten and bring back lost bits of your soul. An important decision could be weighing on your mind. If you don't know the answer, give it out to the universe, and the right decision will become known in time.

19. TUESDAY. Supportive. Your ability to stand up for your ideals and your fellows in need is threefold right now. Work-related issues may be rankling, since you know the system is corrupt and treats employees unfairly. Visit your local union office and see what rights you have, and you might be surprised at the support you get from the rest of your coworkers. Your strength will be in unity. A business deal could turn sour. Your best course of action would be to let it go, no matter how much you were depending on it. Then the possibility of a better deal might come your way. If you are planning to have surgery, see if you can put it off for another week for safety's sake.

20. WEDNESDAY. Pensive. Waking up with a head full of dreams could put you off stride in your business dealings. Although you are likely to be in an impulsive mood, try to postpone any major decisions until later in the day. Dealings with foreigners or the importation of goods can open your eyes to another way of life and give you a taste for travel and different cultures and perspectives. You may decide to resume your education and finally go after the credentials that will give you a well-paid position. With the Sun now in Taurus and your solar house of money, it is a good time to focus on the things you value and to start making plans to achieve them.

21. THURSDAY. Attractive. Venus, the planet of love and beauty, moves into your own sign of Aries today and brings its gifts to you. You are looking and feeling good and your popularity is rising. Use these next few weeks to add pizzazz to your wardrobe and accentuate your creativity with an art or music course. Relationships are also likely to become your main focus. If you are having some difficulty in this area, you would be wise to seek out counseling for more insight into the dynamics of true interdependence. Independent and rebellious people could attract you, and so you will need to be more aware of the company you keep. Don't get led into dangerous situations.

22. FRIDAY. Intense. Situations that call for diplomacy may be many. It will be very easy to become defensive and retaliate at the first sight of any disapproval of your character and actions. Because of this, try to stand back in all your dealings and retain your objectivity. Instead of being drawn into emotional arm wrestling, you can gain the upper hand. Be careful when out on the roads, as road rage is likely to be rampant, not to mention a few hidden police cameras. Partnered Aries might feel that you have lost your independence. But if you consider the give-and-take in your relationship, you might end up feeling that you gain more than you are losing. A small gift will say a thousand words.

23. SATURDAY. Pleasant. The tension of the last couple of days will start to dissipate now. With Mercury, the planet of communication, moving forward in your own sign of Aries, misunderstandings can be cleared up and any holdups to your negotiations will start to vanish. A long-term ambition might be achieved now. You could be asked to make a speech or be in the public eye due to your associations. A family responsibility could fall on your shoulders. Your desire to uphold the traditions of your forebears will be strong. If you have the chance to visit your parents and take them out for a meal, you'll make their day as well as learn a piece of family wisdom to pass on to your heirs.

24. SUNDAY. Restless. Exciting and stimulating companions will attract you. You might receive a visit from an extraordinary person who introduces you to new forms of entertainment and enjoyment. You may decide to move your furniture around and change the whole appearance of your environment; perhaps a coat of paint will put a splash of color over the ordinary. An impromptu party can be a lot of fun. You are likely to make some new friends who will also enhance your opportunities for career advancement. In fact, any unexpected introduction could sweep you off your feet and signal the start of a new and interesting, perhaps life-changing, romance for Aries singles.

25. MONDAY. Energetic. Be aware of any ruthless or selfish purposes you might have toward others and you can sidestep a confrontation. A business partnership might become more of a power struggle than a joint venture. Call a truce and sit down and discuss your gripes together, or else you could both go down with the ship. This is an excellent time for exerting yourself through work that must be done. As it is done, you will gain more experience and knowledge of yourself, which you can put to good use later on. A friend might need your support, even if it is just a shoulder to cry on. Make some time to sit with them and listen, and you will gain as much emotionally as they will.

26. TUESDAY. Rewarding. Compassion and camaraderie will make today a good day. Be kind to yourself as much as others and try not to expect too much. If you are not already practicing a daily exercise regimen, now is a good time to implement one. Check out the local gyms and use a personal trainer to help you improve your performance and look good at the same time. A secret romance could be taking more out of you than you are getting. Having to tiptoe around and cover up your trail might start to wear a little thin after a while. Be honest with yourself. Best of all, be true to yourself! Travel plans could pick up impetus when a foreign contact offers you free accommodations and sightseeing in their land.

27. WEDNESDAY. Unusual. Something out of the ordinary, such as a chance to go whale watching, could shake you out of your lethargy, especially if you haven't been out in a boat before. Time on your own might not be something you crave. But today you would benefit from the solitude and self-analysis. Perhaps you may be grieving, and the opportunity to let out your emotions unhampered by others will be cleansing and cathartic. If you can get into the great outdoors, you will feel the benefits deep down in your soul. A promotion might make you a benefactor. The desire to help those less fortunate could result in you sponsoring a child overseas or visiting the sick in your local hospitals.

28. THURSDAY. Sentimental. No matter what you do today, you might find yourself being reminded of childhood memories and regrets at past actions. This is always a positive exercise, no matter how painful. But remember, you did your best within the circumstances. You have a lot of energy at the moment, and can achieve just about anything you put your mind to. But watch your risk taking, as there is a chance of accidents and injury. Even if it is simply a pulled muscle, it will hamper your style and you won't appreciate the inaction at this time. Expectant parents should be prepared for the birth. Do not go on any long journey without a practical plan of action in place.

29. FRIDAY. Unpredictable. Expect the unexpected today, and you will be prepared for anything. Rational thought might not get results, and you would be wise to listen to your intuition in important matters. Good friends and high energy can make for impulsive plans and impromptu parties. Some Aries may take off from work and spend the day in passionate embrace with a lusty cohort. Or you might play some pranks on your colleagues and fill the day with fun and laughter. Be mindful of any pranks you do play, as you might inadvertently hurt someone's feelings and turn fun into torture. A new relationship can start to get serious, and you could receive an offer of marriage too good to refuse.

30. SATURDAY. Cooperative. Friendly and harmonious, today offers you a chance to relax and unwind doing exactly whatever you want. Don't let anyone talk you into doing anything different. Love is high on the list of possibles, as is conception. So if you are not ready to start a family, make sure you use protection. Good feelings and a lucky win could entice you to gamble more than you can afford to lose, and therefore you should practice some restraint. A seemingly lucky streak may only be momentary. Aries artists are at peak in creativity and should enjoy a class in technique, an exhibition, or teaching your skills to a few friends; high-quality work will result.

MAY

1. SUNDAY. Intuitive. You will be emotionally right there whenever friends or family need your sympathy, warmth, and understanding, although objectivity when dealing with others may be difficult to come by right now. Weight gain might be one of your main concerns at the moment, and your best course of action is to watch what you eat. Perhaps simply changing the content of what you eat will be easier than changing the amount. Join a group meeting for an excellent program of support that is free and that works. A personal responsibility or obligation can infringe on your plans for fun and upset those close to you, but stick with it for your own peace of mind.

2. MONDAY. Healing. Rules and regulations can get your goat. While you might think you have a better way of doing things, pause and consider all the practicalities first. The methods developed over time must have their benefits. You are likely to have to look after someone close who is suffering either physically, mentally, or emotionally. While you will enjoy being of help, remember to take care of your own needs at the same time. Plans to borrow extra money should be gone over thoroughly before you put them into action. If there is another way to avoid extra debt, you should try it first. Your partner's earning capacity might be limited, forcing you to work extra hours.

3. TUESDAY. Beneficial. This morning's New Moon in Taurus highlights your finances, heralding the beginning of a new lunar cycle and the chance to initiate some changes. One of your talents might offer an opportunity for work, training others in your area of expertise and allowing you to run your own business from home while doing what you love doing. Be kind to yourself today. Buy yourself something that you have wanted and allow yourself to feel wealthy. Some Aries may be experiencing a marriage breakdown, and find the separation of your possessions particularly troublesome. Get some legal advice before you start, so that you know your rights and obligations, which will be to your benefit.

4. WEDNESDAY. Desirous. You may be in a dreamy state of mind in which fancies and illusions can become more important than reality this morning. So be mindful when shopping for big-ticket items or simply enjoying some retail therapy. A desire to get ahead might encourage you to study online and add to your credentials as well as stimulate your mental functions, educating yourself in the use of the Internet and Web communications. Be very careful if you have a driver's test this afternoon, as your reflexes and memory may not be up to scratch. Aries writers might get some good news from a publishing company. But be prepared for the deadlines and restrictive guidelines that follow, which can inhibit creativity.

5. THURSDAY. Social. Communication in all your relationships will be very positive now. If you can sit still for long enough to listen to your partner's perspective, you can end up finding common ground on many issues you have been sidestepping lately. A business deal can go ahead and surprise you with a large profit margin coming your way. In fact, you might get a proposition to go into partnership with one of your advisers, which should turn out to be a positive move for both of you. Beware of chest infections. There may be a virus going around, and your best defense is plenty of walking in the fresh air and drinking pure water. Exams and government applications will be successful.

6. FRIDAY. Supportive. Feelings of not being good enough can make this morning difficult, but don't be shy. Ask for help, and you will be surprised and relieved to know that you have plenty of support around you. An invitation to a party that everybody wants to go to will come your way, and you are bound to be offered plenty of rides so that you don't have to drink and drive as well. A new relationship could get to first base, and when you go home to meet the parents, you feel so comfortable, it's as if you have known them in a past life. Perhaps your newfound family will become a permanent fixture from now on. A win in a lottery could give you a trip to a foreign shore and start a new adventure.

7. SATURDAY. Potent. Control may be the name of the game, but the sooner you let go, the happier you will feel. You could be surprised at how perfectly everything falls into place when you take yourself out of the picture. A crisis in faith can make you question why you bother dong anything. A quest for spiritual meaning might give you the inspiration to start new projects and reinvent yourself once more. Challenges in the workplace or problems on the home front may make your family routine untenable. But instead of allowing the overload to bring you down and wear you out, think outside of the box. Start looking after yourself first and when you feel okay, everything else will be, too.

8. SUNDAY. Responsive. A love of nature can turn your attention to the garden. If you do not have a backyard, you might start an herb garden in pots on your window ledge, planting some extra flowers to attract the birds and butterflies as well. You could call up your extended family and friends and plan a picnic at a local beauty spot, enjoying the good company with the fresh air and outdoor games. Those seeking houses may head out into the country to look at acreage in cheaper areas, but you need to also check out the services. Travel can get expensive, and having to travel long distances for social contact can often take the shine off the low cost of the house. Talk to locals for their insight.

9. MONDAY. Exciting. Butterflies in the stomach can be caused through excitement or anxiety, and either way they feel the same. So even if you are anxious about a pending situation, think of the positive outcome and your anxiety will turn into excitement. You could be putting a large amount of your earnings down on an investment that gives you a mix of both anxiety and excitement. But when you take a risk, you have as much to gain as you have to lose, so stay positive. A new love makes you feel like a different person, and changes your life around overnight. Keep your daily routine going, though. Don't take the day off to make love, and you will manage to keep the passion alive longer and stronger.

10. TUESDAY. Artistic. This is a day for fun and laughter, love and friendship. You should be looking good and feeling at your best right now, so make the most of your day and don't refuse any surprise invitations for a party. Aries singles are likely to meet a new love and race off to get some new clothes, buy a new car, or do something that will make you look better than you think you are. Relax and be yourself today, and you will have a great time. Work can be a hoot. If you are tempted to play a few practical jokes at work, be careful that your boss doesn't catch you and think you aren't doing your job. Beware of breaking the bank on an extravagance!

11. WEDNESDAY. Practical. Start your day off with meditation and reflect on the day ahead, making sure to take care of your own needs as well as the needs of those around you. An eye for detail makes this a good day to tidy up around your home and sort through the cupboards and papers that have become disorganized. Group activities and charity work in hospitals or institutions for sick and disadvantaged people will be enjoyable. Or you might work with a religious or spiritual organization for world peace or to alleviate hunger. Aries energy is strong but compassionate, and the underdog will capture your heart. Just be sensible when it comes to donating to a worthy cause, and make sure you have something left to live on.

12. THURSDAY. Smooth. Everything should run like clockwork. Even though you may be rushed and feel stressed, there is no need for it. Practice meditation and breathing exercises to bring you in tune with your environment. Your good nature has not gone unnoticed and your employer may have you down for a promotion, or there could be a raise in salary on the way. If you have any concerns regarding bank loans, have a chat with your bank manager and see if you can reduce your interest or repayments by refinancing in some way. A new spiritual or psychological outlook could be very inspiring, but be careful not to shove it down the throats of all those who live with you, love you, and work with you.

13. FRIDAY. Tense. Although everything may look all right on the surface, there could be some unspoken matter that is causing tension beneath the surface of your normal routine, and you may snap at subordinates or other innocent souls. For you hotheaded Aries, this could lead to retaliation, so be mindful of those around you. Some of you may not be feeling well, or are suffering from chronic neck or back pain, and reality may force you to get some treatment now. Check out the different types of healing available to you. There could be something out of the ordinary that will fix you once and for all. A lawsuit may be more trouble than it is worth. Think twice before going ahead.

14. SATURDAY. Edgy. A good night's sleep may have eluded you, either through your own neglect or because some worry has been nagging at your mind and not giving you a minute's break. For those of you who might be suffering from a hangover, have a raw egg in milk and go for a walk outside in the fresh air. Take an umbrella just in case it rains, and the umbrella will also act as camouflage if you run into someone you are trying to avoid. It is likely to be hard to be agreeable. If you feel okay, everybody around you might seem extra touchy! Better to keep to yourself, curl up on the lounge with some movies, and order takeout. New Age enthusiasts might take a vacation from your mind and go on a retreat.

15. SUNDAY. Peaceful. What a lovely day to hang out with the people you love and enjoy the sights and sounds of nature. Go sailing, walking, or swimming, and make the most of the intimacy this environment affords. A love affair may be moving onto the next level of commitment, and expressions of marriage and sharing may come into the conversation. A public gathering might be informative and introduce you to new people and ideas, especially if you enjoy politics and networking. The love of debate could go a little too far later in the day. If you find tempers start to fray, back off and go home before the fireworks. Arguments can be based on silly misunderstandings.

16. MONDAY. Resourceful. Mercury, the planet of communication, and Venus, the planet of loving, join your ruler Mars and the Sun in Taurus. These placements put a sharp focus on your values and possessions. How you present yourself now is very important to you. If you take the time to dress smartly, your confidence will get such a boost that you can achieve anything. Be careful not to spend more than you can afford because with spoiled Venus in your sector of money, you might be tempted to buy expensive baubles on a whim. Joint investments might pay dividends, and you could receive a hot tip from someone in the know regarding a new investment. People in powerful places will be on your side and give you the backing you need.

17. TUESDAY. Competitive. The Full Moon in Scorpio this morning highlights commitment in relationship and the division of joint possessions. If you are going through a marriage breakup, you might leave this division until another day, as neither of you are likely to be agreeable about this. Especially if there are children involved, you might need to go to family court. Many Aries could be enjoying just the opposite, however. Love and attachment to your partner can be deepening on a soul level and your sexual experience is broadening. A spiritual experience or some form of déjà vu is likely. Be open to new ideas and emotions; your psyche is very sensitive now.

18. WEDNESDAY. Idealistic. A raise in pay might give you pause to think about what it is you really want out of life. Should you save for a vacation overseas or your own home, or should you live each day as it comes and simply enjoy life? These questions and more can flood your mind and spark interesting conversations in the workplace and among friends, and you can find other people's ideas about life very inspiring. An advertisement for a meditation course can catch your eye, and may be just the thing to ease your troubled mind. Lady Luck is following you around, and you can meet influential people who can help you make a difference in your future. You just have to ask the right questions.

19. THURSDAY. Enjoyable. Relationships and encounters with others should work to your advantage today, and you can organize people, places, and things better than usual. So take this opportunity and get help to finish a large-scale project that has been driving you crazy lately. Contact with foreigners can come through work. You may have to organize the import or export of goods, or help an overseas visitor obtain an extension on their visa. Alternatively, you might be heading off overseas. Amid all the hustle and bustle you find out that a big bon voyage party is being planned for the eve of your departure. Don't stress, just leave early. Everyone else can keep partying.

20. FRIDAY. Strained. Relations between you and your partner can stretch your patience this morning. You would be wise to breathe deeply and try to talk it out calmly, otherwise it will only get worse as the day progresses. The pressure could be on you at work. If you can delegate some of your work to others who are better able to cope with it, you will be acknowledged for your managerial skills. Some of you might be in for a surprise in your paycheck, although the higher pay might just mean more work. But you should be able to get on top of your financial situation at this time, so don't waste your extra cash. A parent might be having trouble financially; ask them over for a chat.

21. SATURDAY. Receptive. Overnight the Sun moved into Gemini, your solar sector ruling communication and commuting. This is a good time to catch up on your correspondence, answer e-mails, and get together with friends, siblings, and neighbors. Just at the moment, though, you might need to write down lists and directions because your memory might not be the best. When following directions, it might be worthwhile to check your map or navigation system, as other people are bound to be just as muddled. The urge to volunteer for a charity or environmental group might open up many doors in your local area. You will be surprised at how rewarding you find the work, adding another dimension to your life.

22. SUNDAY. Dutiful. A promise made in the past may be due for fulfillment. But you find you have already planned something else, leaving you in a very uncomfortable situation of having to say no to one or the other. You will know which choice is the right one, although it might not be the one you would like to make. Nevertheless, your future will be favored if you do what is right now. Partnered Aries could have to accompany your lover on a business engagement that is really going to leave you on the sidelines, but your support will be a great benefit to them. If the situation is reversed and you find your partner is backing out of supporting you, let them go and give yourself all of you completely.

23. MONDAY. Dynamic. Those of you born in the beginning of the sign of Aries are likely to be going through an identity crisis at the moment. You might dare to be different and wear that outfit you simply love, even if no one else likes it. Your courage could have consequences far beyond your wildest imagination. You may speak up in defense of a friend or colleague, even though it could put your job on the line, but you will feel good for having stuck by your own morals. The gossip going around your workplace can be particularly derogatory. But if you buy into it, you might simply give these false ideas extra strength to spread. Leave the gossips to themselves and get back to the real world.

24. TUESDAY. Perplexing. You may be tempted to withdraw and keep your feelings secret by throwing yourself into your work. In fact, you could be a workaholic trying to make enough money to buy beautiful possessions and establish some security. For partnered Aries, this may interfere with your relationship. The need to balance these two areas of your life is important. If you find it too hard to talk to your partner, see a counselor and in no time you will have ironed out any problems. Single Aries can meet someone new and have to tackle the issue of communication from another angle. Simply believe in yourself and speak from the heart, and you will learn to trust another.

25. WEDNESDAY. Responsible. Get off on your own as much as possible today and get your ideas down on paper before you forget them. The solar influences are very creative and playful, and you might get the opportunity to slacken off and follow a selfish pleasure. Resist if you can, and you will feel much better and avoid a future embarrassment. You will like helping people, but you need to learn the boundaries of what they can reasonably expect from you. Otherwise, you are in danger of playing the doormat role and ending up resenting those people. A concert, the theater, or an artistic display would all be balm for your soul. Go along and relax and allow your creative side to be caressed and inspired.

26. THURSDAY. Challenging. An inner understanding is yours this morning. Use it and trust it and you won't be lead astray. A difficult situation could be exacerbated by interfering busybodies. If you decide to get involved, you will have to use every ounce of diplomacy you have, and that may not be enough. So, if you don't want to lose your temper, perhaps you could leave it for someone else to mess up. Expect the pace to pick up as the day goes on, and don't allow others to bully you into cutting corners or rushing; otherwise, accidents will occur and cause even longer delays. If you suffer from headaches, make sure you carry some painkillers, drink plenty of water, and practice your breathing.

27. FRIDAY. Emotional. The Moon is in your own sign of Aries, where it will stay until Sunday morning, highlighting your sensitive side and putting your own personal security center stage in any situation. Your moods and those of the people around you may seem more volatile, and you would do well to make sure you look after yourself, but not at anybody else's expense. Your home and family are important. If you have left home, you might go home for dinner tonight and catch up with the latest happenings and connect with your roots again. This is an excellent time to start implementing a project that's been on the drawing board for a while. Get some advice from experts and go for it.

28. SATURDAY. Auspicious. The opportunity to express your own individuality and talents can set the ball rolling down a career path you have only thought about in dreams, so value your own abilities and have a go. A new relationship can introduce you to another culture and open your eyes to different possibilities for ways of being. If you are inspired to buy a ticket and head off on an overseas adventure, you will learn much. Some of you may not be feeling one hundred per cent and are considering seeing a spiritual healer. Although you may be skeptical, you can't really lose. They will either heal you or they won't. If they heal you, you have gained; if they don't, everything is still the same.

29. SUNDAY. Fanciful. Delight your senses with fun and games and good cheer. Have an impromptu party and invite all your friends for food and drink. If you are a bit poor, ask everyone to bring their own food and drink, and combine the lot into a scrumptious spread. Aries parents might enjoy a theme park with the kids; let your inner child out and play together. Just keep your eye out that you don't lose anyone. Beware of impulse shopping. You are likely to be so swayed by unconscious drives and old thought patterns that you cannot make an intelligent decision about buying something based on your real needs. Passion is on the cards for you passionate Rams.

30. MONDAY. Energetic. Be prepared for a busy day full of spontaneous events. Anything can happen and probably will. Your sexual energy is high, and you might enjoy some arousing words from people you meet. Do be careful about which invitations you take up; there is the chance of aggression in some encounters. Check up on your bank balance and peruse your bills to make sure you are up to date before you take on any more debt. Otherwise, the impulse will hit you to invite everyone to a lavish lunch at the most expensive restaurant in town. The vibe this evening looks to be very romantic and peaceful after your hectic day, and you can get down to some serious loving with the person of your dreams.

31. TUESDAY. Temperamental. Communication can take all sorts of twists. Just when you think you're having a joke with someone, they are likely to get upset and think you are picking on them, or vice versa. If somebody calls you to change their mind about a future engagement, don't worry too much because later in the day they are likely to change their mind back again. Let them know you are giving them that option. News might come from a friend overseas or someone from your past, or someone can drop in and keep you up half the night telling stories. Single Aries in love should watch the tendency to idolize this person; the higher the pedestal you put them on, the farther they have to fall.

JUNE

1. WEDNESDAY. Interesting. A New Moon in Gemini this afternoon signals a new lunar cycle. You can start new projects around the home and initiate change into your daily routines. Don't be afraid to talk to other people about any reservations or insecurities you feel. You don't have to follow their advice, but the value of other people's experiences is worth knowing about. Life should be pretty laid-back, and attending to your work and responsibilities will be relaxing and satisfying in itself. Just be careful not to let your mind race ahead and plan too many activities that will put you in traffic and stretch your nerves. Better to sit down with a good book if you need mental stimulation.

2. THURSDAY. Extravagant. The urge to splurge could sneak up on you when you least expect it. Before you know it, you've broken your budget, or your diet, and you start to feel annoyed with yourself. The trick is to stay focused and don't allow your mind too much control. Once your mind gets in the driver's seat, your ego will get out of control, too. Every time you notice this happening, bring your thoughts back into the moment. Communication with women might be touch-and-go. If you get caught up in power games, you will live to regret it. Use your quick wit in a constructive rather than destructive mode. An interest in journalism can open new doors of enjoyment and friendship.

3. FRIDAY. Sensitive. Mercury, the planet of communication, moves into its own sign of Gemini today, and gives Aries communication a boost. The inspiration to catch up on correspondence and call long-distance friends will have the added benefit of bringing you up to date with the latest news and put you in touch with interesting ideas and events. Don't get caught chatting over the Internet at work, or you might have to look for a new job. Even if you would love to quit, you could have some serious security issues on your plate without your job. Someone may be going behind your back, trying to undermine your position and popularity. If you have a secret, keep it. Don't talk about it.

4. SATURDAY. Productive. Jupiter, the planet of expansion, moves into the sign of Taurus, your solar house of money and self-worth. Jupiter will transit Taurus for the next year, bringing more of the things that you value into your life. It is very important at this time to understand how you use resources, as there is the potential for their mismanagement. News from a distant loved one might concern you, stirring up memories and sentimental emotions. Plan a visit either to renew your ties or give them some help and support if they are in need. An opportunity to move into a management position or some other position of control could be the beginning of a promising career. Smile and enjoy the benefits.

5. SUNDAY. Impetuous. Disagreements with loved ones can trigger the impulse to escape, but pause before rushing off. Consider if this is what you really want to do. Otherwise, you are in danger of overreacting and cutting off your nose to spite your face. High ideals and expectations can make it hard for someone else to please you at the moment. It would be valuable to reflect upon your own behavior. Maybe you have been self-seeking in your motives. Insight is a wonderful thing, and days like today can teach you something about yourself. If you are experiencing emotional pain, try loving it, accepting it as a valid emotion, and expressing it freely.

6. MONDAY. Positive. Take advantage of the positive energies that abound today. If you have been procrastinating over an important decision, now is the time to decide, as you can't go wrong. Love is in the air and whether you are partnered or single, you should enjoy the closeness of that someone special. A child could try your patience, but the answer is to give them some attention. Take them out with you and do something interesting. Then perhaps you can talk to them more as a friend than a parent, and they might open up and let you in on their personal territory. Information can come to light that will win a court case for you, but you might have to consider the long-term consequences.

7. TUESDAY. Fatiguing. Aries energy levels and immune system are down a notch today, and you would be wise to take care of yourself. Go through your appointments and prioritize what needs to be done. If you can postpone some of them until another day, all the better. Stay away from drugs and alcohol and eat wholesome food rather than fast food. If you haven't got time to cook, at least go to a wholesome restaurant for something that will renew your reserves. Communication and understanding should be very good in all your relationships. If you need to talk about a sensitive issue, now is the time to do so and all should be resolved. Send a love letter to your partner and surprise them.

8. WEDNESDAY. Emotional. Feelings and emotions can overwhelm your rational intellect and make it hard to communicate in an objective manner; also, other people's ideas can influence your own and confuse the matter even more. In any important discussions, write your main points down beforehand so that you can keep bringing your mind back to the matter at hand. If you are in the process of finalizing a workplace agreement, stick to your guns and you might come away with a package on the higher end of the scale. Your nervous system could do with a tonic. Speak to your local herbalist for a potion made to suit your unique needs.

9. THURSDAY. Agreeable. Venus, the planet of love and harmony, moves into Gemini and your solar house of communication today. This placement can have the effect of making your everyday surroundings and activities more pleasant than usual. Your social life often will pick up, as you get together with friends and neighbors to have fun or simply socialize and talk. You may consider purchasing a pet if you do not already have one. Take stock of the types of animal that are compatible with your living conditions, and its assimilation into your home will be a lot smoother. This is also a very favorable time to renovate your home, as your eye for art and beauty is great.

10. FRIDAY. Subdued. You will be inclined to keep your feelings and innermost thoughts to yourself. If a sense of loneliness or isolation is felt, it is probably because you are cutting yourself off from others. This is an excellent day to research and study; any important business deals can be thoroughly scrutinized and tightened up to secure your profit. Legal matters also can be finalized now. Even if you think your case isn't that strong, you might come up with some evidence that pushes the scales in your direction. Trust your instincts and have faith in yourself, and you can move mountains today. An evening of loving romance can bring peace and harmony.

11. SATURDAY. Sociable. A political or environmental rally in your area might be interesting entertainment, broadening your mind and introducing you to new and stimulating people. Aries could be inclined to get active in public affairs right now. Your area of influence is growing, bringing more and more opportunities for expansion your way. Travel could be on the agenda. Some of you might be traveling with a partner who has a home across the sea, taking you to meet family and friends for the first time. To show your respect, make sure you understand the fundamentals of their language before you head off. For all occasions, considering the other person and showing them respect will be rewarding.

12. SUNDAY. Favorable. Spiritual pursuits can be very healing for you fire children, soothing hurts, griefs, and losses by giving you another way of dealing with your emotions and a faith in something greater than matter. A desire to give support to others could be instrumental in your joining a voluntary organization. Helping the needy will give you a sense of worth. You can make a difference where it counts. A personal investment can show great gains now, and this may be an investment in your health, career, or finances. Whatever, you will be reaping the benefits for a long time to come. Clearing our your attic or basement can turn up some great items.

13. MONDAY. Entertaining. Aries enthusiasm is high. Lectures, meetings, business deals, and anything that involves at least a few people will be full of fun and interest. You can be very surprised to find that a person you are dreading having to deal with turns out to be easygoing and full of great stories. You may have to do some public speaking also, and will find it easy once you are up on the podium and get the first couple of sentences out. Somebody whom you trust could be acting underhandedly and taking from you behind your back. So keep your eyes out and watch your paper trail to keep a check on all your business. Beware of hasty actions and impulsive movements, as accidents are possible.

14. TUESDAY. Enjoyable. Overindulgence and extravagance are in the cards. If you are worried about your weight, you should probably bow out of any lunch or dinner engagements because you will find it hard to stick to your diet. A shopping trip could be expensive and tempt you to buy clothes that you will only wear once in your lifetime. Or you could be talked into buying something expensive on credit that will take you years to pay off. Be sensible and protect your budget by doing affordable things and enjoying what you already have. A course of study could catch your eye and give you a release from the humdrum of your routine existence, plus giving you a chance at a successful future.

15. WEDNESDAY. Bright. Motivation to further your education or expand your knowledge of world affairs can come from study. Before you know it, you're signing up for a fascinating course. An interest in flying might entice some of you to apply for training in a range of jobs from flight attendant to flight controller. Pioneering Aries are more susceptible to advertising that promises adventure, but you might want to take what the advertising is telling you with a grain of salt before you throw your money at it. A new association can feel as if there is more to it than coincidence. Karmic ties can draw you to certain people, and a new romantic partner met now could be very significant.

16. THURSDAY. Intense. The pursuit of an objective can override any other considerations. Think before you act and you might not step on the toes of other people quite so much. Impulsive Aries are at your best today, and results of your actions become obvious. Whether you are happy with them depends entirely on you. But either way, it affords you the opportunity to do some worthwhile self-evaluation. A government official could be watching you, so make sure you have nothing to hide. Keep everything aboveboard, and you will be safe. Someone may offer you an expensive piece of equipment at a rock-bottom price, but it is probably stolen. Don't be a patsy.

17. FRIDAY. Cautious. It is a good time to examine your personal and domestic life and to make plans to evaluate whether it is meeting your needs and also the needs of your immediate family. Work behind the scenes if possible, and you won't get involved with petty disputes and power struggles. Your creative nature will bring out the best in you without outside influence. One of your parents may be in the hospital, and it would be beneficial to you both if you could visit them now. The type of conversation you are likely to have will clear the air of a lot of baggage from the past, and enlighten you as well. Inside information about a chance for promotion will give you an opportunity worth taking.

18. SATURDAY. Complex. Conflicting desires, intrigue, and personality clashes will test your patience when dealing with your network of friends. A romance with a person with a significant age difference from you can affect your interests, and you may be neglecting some of your close friends as well. Put some time aside to make contact and organize a get-together where you can mull over all the latest gossip and clear the air. It is also important for you to maintain your own friends and interests. Otherwise, you can end up feeling isolated. A hobby group can be of great value to you. Athletic Aries will benefit from the competition and exercise of team sport.

19. SUNDAY. Tense. Freedom to come and go is essential to Aries. Having a parent, partner, or employer start wagging their finger at you might be like waving a red flag at a bull, so try not to rampage too much. On the other hand, there is the danger of succumbing to propaganda or indoctrination designed to change your thinking. So be careful not to get talked into doing something you don't really believe in. A petty resentment can grow into a monster the more you concentrate on it today. Before you know it, you are on the phone shouting at someone. The best activity would be a pleasant outing into nature, to a theme park, or to a concert, where you can leave your thoughts behind you.

20. MONDAY. Pleasant. Networking will be a breeze. If you are asked to represent your company at an out-of-town seminar, you know you will make a great impression. A friend may be going through a very hard time. Put aside part of the day to spend with your friend. You are especially receptive to others at the moment, and can give them valuable feedback. Also, you will come to know yourself better through your interactions. Friendships and love relationships that start now can have important consequences for your future and your attitudes toward life in general. Plan an early night. Take home a movie and cook something nourishing.

21. TUESDAY. Low-key. Feelings of doubt and discouragement can plague you during the day, and the desire to withdraw from the world could override all other commitments. If you decide to take the day off, make sure you cover yourself with your boss. Spiritual pursuits can be a valuable source of peace. If you don't practice meditation, now is as good a time as any to start. Join a local group and enjoy the benefits, which cover the physical, mental, and spiritual. Secret sorrows or regrets can keep coming up. If you find these feelings are interfering with your daily routines, it would be wise to see a counselor or join a self-help group, and you can begin the process of healing.

22. WEDNESDAY. Reclusive. The Sun has moved into Cancer, bringing warmth and inspiration to your solar house of home, family, and personal security. It is a good day for quiet study, especially of metaphysical or spiritual subjects. Security around your home may be an issue also. Get a security company to manage the problem for you and put your mind at ease. If that is out of your price range and you don't have faith in your locks, consider moving to a more secure home. Give yourself plenty of time to make your appointments. Travel delays are indicated, and there could also be a mix-up with the directions. Success can come with little effort if you have faith.

23. THURSDAY. Spontaneous. Hotheaded Aries people are likely to live up to your name. With the Moon in your own sign of Aries coming to join erratic Uranus, your emotions are likely to be out there for everyone to see. Try to be mindful, as there are bound to be times when people push your buttons, but losing your temper is not going to fix it. Look for other methods of releasing your frustrations. Join a gym and work out your resentments on a punching bag. Take up jogging and let every footstep release some emotion. Or practice yoga and meditation to develop mindfulness. Exciting situations can fire you up and get you rushing around, so be careful.

24. FRIDAY. Beneficial. Extra cash is likely to be on hand to help you organize a comfortable home. Renovations can happen easily with the help of people around you. With friends, neighbors, and family all pitching in, have plenty of food on hand to keep everybody happy. New projects can get off the ground and inspire you to be more creative than usual, exploring your own abilities and potentials. Lady Luck is also on your side now, and you might have a win. If you gamble, know when to stop; otherwise, you might give your winnings back to the house. Family discussions can get touchy; try to let everybody have their say so that they feel heard.

25. SATURDAY. Expansive. Self-confidence will help you to put your best foot forward, and a job interview can go really well. Personal objectives can look closer than ever, and you are likely to be multiskilled. However, you need to watch your energy reserves, as the tendency to overdo it can tire you out and interfere with your plans for the evening. Overspending on clothes and personal interests can break your budget, but make you feel like a million dollars, and you will be turning heads everywhere you go. A lavish affair in the evening can put you in the company of millionaires and the famous. Be on your best behavior and you will add some invaluable contacts to your network of friends.

26. SUNDAY. Unsettled. Family tension is on the rise, and there may be disagreements over today's activities. Your partner might have different plans for you, and you would be wise to conform for peace. A public performance or ceremony can be emotionally moving, touching your heart and thoughts for many weeks to come. Politically active Aries can be involved in a public rally and take a turn at the soapbox. Your nerves will give you some problems, but once you get wound up, you are sure to enjoy yourself and move your audience. An influential person in the family can pull a few strings, especially if you are trying to get a teenage child into a good job with career potential.

27. MONDAY. Busy. An important job interview should go better than expected. Leave early, as there could be holdups in travel plans today. An important assignment or position can mean that you have to be away from home and the family for longer hours, putting extra pressure on your budget for child care. But a bit of pain now can mean gain in the future. Some Aries parents may have to take the day off to look after a sick child. If your employer is not very sympathetic, make sure you get the child to a doctor to validate the illness. You might have to make a major move to accept a lucrative promotion; this will be hard at first, but just take one day at a time.

28. TUESDAY. Powerful. Power struggles, especially with people in authority, can force you to stand up for your own position and gain a more solid sense of self. Machinery and gadgets can break down today, and you will have to stop what you are doing and repair them; patching up will not suffice. Difficulties can be caused by communication problems. Think before you speak and know what you want to say, and you will avoid many annoying misunderstandings. Your ambitions and the force for creative change in your life are at their best now, so put in your application for promotion, apply for your dream job, or put in a bid on the home of your dreams.

29. WEDNESDAY. Satisfactory. Get in and organize your paperwork, pay your bills, and make sure your correspondence is up to date. With the Cancer Sun impacting your home sector, this is an excellent time to plan renovations or move to a different place. Some of you may be ready to purchase a house. Visit local real estate agents and check the Internet. Going to open houses is a much better way to get an idea of what your money will buy. If you are going for a driving test, keep your wits about you and be ready for the unexpected. You are bound to come up against a situation you haven't encountered previously.

30. THURSDAY. Diverse. Plan to get away with your lover this weekend. Book a suite at a resort in a romantic spot and pamper yourselves with intimacy and luxury. You deserve a break. Aries writers will find the creative juices are flowing, with original ideas and a spontaneous way with words. Make yourself comfortable for you might be at it all day. An investment in a farm can send you off to buy chickens and a cow. Listen to all the advice the old-timers have to offer because they will know the area and the pitfalls to be wary of. Make sure you are getting value for whatever money you lay out now.

JULY

1. FRIDAY. Nurturing. This morning's New Moon in Cancer shines its loving light on your home and family, as well as your living environment. Researching the family tree could be an interesting exercise to involve the whole family in, and as you discover your distant roots, you can learn about history and gain an understanding of your family traditions. The purchase of a piece of real estate is in the stars, but only if you feel that your present security will last, and if you know you will be able to afford the mortgage. A strong need to nurture or be nurtured can color your attitude in relationships, and you might find yourself offering your services for a cause you really don't care about.

2. SATURDAY. Creative. The Moon catches up with Mercury, the planet of communication, as it moves into Leo and your solar house of fun, lovers, and children, making your communication a bit touchy-feely today. Contact with friends can be very interesting, and you may be introduced to a new area of creativity, or start a class in dance, art, or drama. Aries students could join up with a study group and enjoy socializing while you are learning. The chances of finding a hot fellow student, who is interested in you, too, are high. Young lovers are in danger of getting caught doing something rebellious. Think twice when planning your escapades, and make sure you are safe above all else.

3. SUNDAY. Mischievous. Hanging out and feeling bored is pretty senseless, and your restless thoughts won't let you sit around and mope this morning. Aries sportspeople will really enjoy your sport and have every chance of winning, no matter how new you are to the game. Lady Luck is on your side. Things that happen by chance, no matter how unexpected, can turn out to be better than you could ever have planned. So don't worry, leave it in the lap of the gods. Children's activities could be a feature for Aries parents. You might be celebrating a special achievement, or simply watching them win. Aries couples will be enjoying each other, finding the time to love, laugh, and share together.

4. MONDAY. Responsible. The urge to have fun can still invade your day. Even though you have work to attend to, or things you have to do for your partner or family, jokes and peals of laughter will interrupt at the oddest moments. Your energy level may be down a bit. You would be wise to take stock of your diet and perhaps see your health professional for advice on allergies and deficiencies. Once you know what the problem is, you can work to fix it efficiently, instead of buying expensive vitamins and tonics that might not be needed anyway. A spiritual class can give you a positive boost to your outlook and an ability to understand an aspect to life that up until now has always eluded you.

5. TUESDAY. Active. A plethora of aspects between the planets should keep everybody busy. Mercury in a tough aspect to Jupiter can cause some mischief for Aries people. Your computer can crash, with no tech help available. It's a hectic day, with much moving about and dealing with traffic, people, and things. Your compassionate side is strong, so you will be more willing to stop and help someone, or be patient with holdups that may be due to someone else's misfortune. A vacation or planned trip overseas could be postponed due to extra work, but the extra money will be a soothing panacea.

6. WEDNESDAY. Irritating. Make sure you have everything before you go out the door this morning; chances are you have left something behind. Aries parents could be concerned about the health of a child, but unless they are sick enough to stay at home, it is best to let them out into the fresh air to find whatever the day has in store. Just make sure their day care knows your concerns and will notify you of any changes. Busy Aries career people might consider employing someone to walk the dog if you find you are never home long enough; the extra cost will be worth every cent for your dog's well-being. Petty bills can add up and threaten to destroy your budget; watch the little things.

7. THURSDAY. Receptive. Your perception is heightened, making it very hard for anyone to pull the wool over your eyes, especially your partner. A certain feeling of distance could be making its presence felt, and now is as good a time as any to broach the problem and bring it up into the light of day. This can have the effect of dissolving the seriousness of the matter. But as long as you skirt around the issue, you allow fears to feed the problem. A project or business deal started around a week ago can have a few hiccups, which just need attention to be sorted out satisfactorily. Don't leave anything important for anyone else but yourself. A risky investment is likely to succeed.

8. FRIDAY. Supportive. Associates and acquaintances can add value to your ability to network, and someone among them will give you some of the best advice you can get. Don't be too shy to ask for help if you need it; it will give someone a chance to do a good deed. Aries students should take the opportunity to attend a discussion group on something you are studying so that you get a broader viewpoint than the one you have; it will give you an edge when it comes to your exams. You or your partner may have to work out of town. If you are worried about the separation, don't be, as distance can make the heart grow fonder. Plan to rendezvous for romantic and passionate weekends in out-of-the-way places.

9. SATURDAY. Fortunate. Many harmonious aspects suggest that even if you play with fire today, you won't get burned. But do be careful to skirt any danger about. Because of a powerful or lustful attraction, there is a risk of indiscretion in love relationships. Stop and consider if other people are likely to get hurt before you take that first step. Some of you are mixing with the movers and shakers, and a hot deal could be too good to miss. But you also need to consider its legality and what your liability in the whole deal is. If you are suffering grief through the loss of someone dear, pick up the phone and use the support of others; perhaps seek a healing group focused around grief.

10. SUNDAY. Renewing. A weekend project to revamp your garden and clear away a lot of old junk could end up being worth more than you ever imagined, as the treasures you uncover show. Even if some old things aren't worth much in dollars, they may be restored into an object of art to beautify your home or garden, giving you hours of pleasure. Partnered Aries might be reaching a deepening of commitment within the relationship, and decide to celebrate this wonderful love and get married. If you are worried about the cost, simply get the family or friends involved and you will have a celebration worthy of royalty. A spiritual meeting can be very moving, renewing your faith and adding a bit more.

11. MONDAY. Lively. Long-term plans can set your future achievements in place and give you a blueprint to follow that will assure you of success. Patience and concentration are in abundance, something you impulsive Aries can sometimes lack. If you add to that a willingness to listen to advice, you can't go wrong and you can achieve much. Fortunately, there looks to be a lot going on, and plenty that interests you as well. If you are at loose ends and looking for work, go down to your local college and check out the courses. You might find one that will interest you and lead you into the workforce. Romance with someone unusual or foreign could be the start of something big.

12. TUESDAY. Rewarding. A love of dance or art could influence your decision when planning your study program; don't let people sway you into thinking you have to study something serious such as law or medicine. Satisfaction, skill, and self-expression are likely to reward you more than mere dollars anyway. Driving on the highway can be stressful at the moment; be especially careful not to get caught up in road rage, as it could backfire on you more than you realize. A promotion to a position of more control can give you the independence you have been craving, as well as the privacy to work undistracted. Let your creative side out and explore your potential.

13. WEDNESDAY. Productive. Prepare for a day that tests your abilities, accountability, and patience. Unexpected disruptions and self-opinionated know-it-alls contribute to the mayhem. The Aries extremist qualities will thrive when your mind takes up the challenge to bring order where there is only chaos. The fast pace will also add excitement to the mix, and you may find that you do your best work under pressure. Be careful that you don't step on the toes of an influential woman. Reconsider plans for an evening out. After the strain and nervous anxiety expended during your workday, your body will need plenty of rest and soothing nourishment.

14. THURSDAY. Sociable. Your popularity looks to be on the rise. After your efficient handling of a stressful situation yesterday, you could be next in line for a promotion. Be sensible when shopping with your credit card, as you are likely to be attracted to fairly expensive and lavish items. What you buy may be a future investment on the one hand, but that doesn't make up for the fact that for now it is just another debt you can't afford. Confidence should be at your disposal when out in the world. The Full Moon in Capricorn late tonight will add to the party atmosphere. Dress to kill, and you are bound to be the person everybody watches and wants to know.

15. FRIDAY. Uneasy. Tension on the home front can be a product of a long-standing dispute, which causes you to stew over resentments and doubts. If you are unable to discuss this matter with the person involved, work through it with a counselor until you can see your own role in it. Carrying around resentments only hurts you, no one else. Illegal activities are sure to be found out, and if you get involved in anything underhanded, you will probably end up the fall guy. Aries with partners may have the opportunity to feel very proud of them. As your partners gain a surprise promotion or positive publicity for a generous act, make sure you show them how pleased you are.

16. SATURDAY. Diverse. An overloaded social calendar is an indication of someone who burns the candle at both ends. But you may be thriving from this busy timetable of events since the action appeals to you as an energetic Aries. Your time schedule could be threatened by many little annoyances. As you get behind, the stress buildup can kill the fun and relaxation. Your network of friends is growing, and you can meet some very influential and powerful people. If you are single, a new romance can broaden your circle even more, plus take you up a rung or two in your social set. Concentrate on your hopes and wishes; they are about to come true.

17. SUNDAY. Uneven. Emotional ups and downs can be expected. If you are a member of a social group or club, there is likely to be some disagreement among the members. If you get involved, you will find your buttons being pushed. Some of you may have to care for a stepchild and find the emotional relationship trying. But if you stop to wonder what it must be like for the child, you might find it easier to be kind and not take their behavior personally. A lunchtime get-together can turn into an all-day party. Watch your alcohol intake, as this can affect your judgment and you can't be sure where you will end up. Try to get an early night or at least rest on the couch reading.

18. MONDAY. Intuitive. Volunteering your services for a needy cause, even though you have a busy schedule, will be worth the extra effort. You have an intuitive understanding of the psychological makeup of people. You may surprise yourself by saying yes to somebody you have never really liked. Trust your instincts, they will invariably be right. An interest in the occult could dominate your attention, and you may visit a psychic or spiritual intuitive for some insight into what makes up the unconscious part of your psyche. You are bound to gain some valuable insight. Hopeful Aries parents can receive some good news on a little bundle of joy coming into your life.

19. TUESDAY. Sentimental. Concentrate on a pet project. The stars suggest difficulties around commuting and a danger of conflicts with immediate neighbors, relatives, and other persons whom you encounter daily. Any interference will interrupt your train of thought. If you can, take your work home or work behind the scenes away from the gossip and innuendo. House hunting and home renovations are favored, and you can make some fantastic headway in this area. Love and romance are likely to occupy your thoughts, as you yearn for an ideal partner or think up ways to give your love life renewed passion. Perhaps you could look at ways to love yourself more.

20. WEDNESDAY. Stressful. An important appointment or function could be weighing on your mind, sending your anxiety levels sky high. This is a perfect time to practice yoga and meditation and reap the benefits of relaxation. Do not allow your temper to rise and suffer the tension and the stress that go along with that. The Moon moves into your own sign of Aries today, and your moods may be all over the place. Be kind to yourself, stay away from aggressive people, and don't drink too much coffee. People around you can seem unreliable and impulsive. Relax, don't expect too much, and enjoy the spontaneity, which should make you feel right at home.

21. THURSDAY. Uncertain. The sense that a powerful change is afoot can intensify your mood and make decisions harder. Relationship difficulties may arise over the most trivial things. Even business partners are not immune to senseless nit-picking. It could be hard to see where you end and the other person begins, so refrain from judgments and criticisms lest they come back to bite you. News from a close friend or relative who is away can brighten the day and give you fresh ideas for your next journey. Hassles over a personal problem can try your patience, but a conscientious approach will be more effective than losing your temper. Focus on your to-do list, and accomplishments are assured.

22. FRIDAY. Sparkling. The Moon meets informative Mercury and energetic Mars in a friendly and creative mix. Good friends and new associations will bring interesting new activities and ideas into your sphere of activity. You are likely to dress up and enjoy adding zing to your persona with trendy costume jewelry, using yourself as a canvas to create an interesting picture. Needless to say, you are looking good and turning eyes wherever you go. Communication is your forte today. Training to be a salesperson could bring out the best in you, not only giving you scope to be original, but helping you earn big bucks at the same time. Daydreaming could be an exercise in virtual travel.

23. SATURDAY. Playful. The life-giving Sun moves into Leo and your solar sector of fun and lovers. Meanwhile, the Moon meets up with expansive Jupiter, pointing to abundance in your preferred area of life. A chance encounter with someone hot and gorgeous can have the single Aries heart beating fast, which may be followed by a whirlwind affair. Aries people in a permanent union are likely to experience a new surge of romantic passion and adventure. Money matters can need attention. Be careful shopping that you don't go over budget. The good vibes can override your better judgment and leave you facing problems tomorrow that could have been avoided today.

24. SUNDAY. Varied. A groggy state this morning may be due to lack of sleep or overindulgence the night before. Stay in bed and enjoy the rest, or the arms of your lover. This is a great day for socializing, getting out and about meeting people and exploring the local neighborhood. A play or concert later on could be an enjoyable climax to an interesting day. A spiritual meeting might inspire you to join a volunteer group or sign up for a retreat. Or you might prefer getting out into nature on your own or with an intimate partner to commune with the elements. Whatever you do, there is sure to be a sense of the supernatural to it. A change of image is indicated, a new hobby perhaps.

25. MONDAY. Imaginative. A dream-filled sleep can leave you feeling under the weather and make any attempt at clarity extremely difficult. Some of you might not be feeling your best, and should see a doctor just in case there is a physical reason for your emotional state. Unfounded feelings of distrust and disillusion could start to pollute the intimacy of a new relationship and leave you in a quandary about what to do. This is not the day for clarity, so it would be better to wait and see what tomorrow brings. Aries artists should find this an excellent day for generating new and creative ideas and designs. Get them down on paper before they disappear.

26. TUESDAY. Suspenseful. A sense that something is about to happen can stay with you all day, and your intuition is probably right. Relationship difficulties can be overcome with honesty and clarity within your communication, giving you a sense of commitment and long-term loving. There is a focus on learning, and whether you are a student or not, you are likely to learn a skill that will be valuable for the rest of your life. A car trip to visit a friend or relative you haven't seen for ages is bound to be pleasant. It will give you and your lover or close friend the privacy and the time for intimate conversation, sharing feelings and thoughts that will form a bond for life. A secret can be uncovered also.

27. WEDNESDAY. Tricky. An abundance of energy is assured as the Moon joins your ruling planet Mars, the warrior god, but the downside is that your hasty actions may not tolerate anyone or anything that gets in your way. Try to be patient and give a thought to those who lack your initiative and bravado, and you will have a calmer day. The nature of this Mars aspect also suggests caution because of the increased risk of accidents. As hastiness does not allow much room for safety, do be careful driving or operating machinery. Passion is also indicated, and your love affair is sure to be hot and steamy. You may be tempted into indiscretions that have future consequences.

28. THURSDAY. Mellow. After the hectic pace of yesterday, you can take a break and enjoy an easy day. Loving feelings and good friends will make for smooth sailing. Your creative streak should be firing, giving you high productivity regardless of your slower pace. Spend the day at home if you can. You might want to start your own home-based business, which will make life a lot easier for working parents. Financing can be approved for a home or business loan, and any doubts about your abilities should be wiped away by success in your chosen field or career. Those of you who might be looking for a time share are likely to find the perfect setting.

29. FRIDAY. Deceptive. Avoid making any important decisions, as today's combination of Mercury and Neptune points to inner confusion and lack of clarity. Enjoy exploring your imagination and creative side instead. In fact, it is an excellent time to learn a musical instrument or take a painting class. Love is in the air, and a new relationship could take up your whole day as you whisper sweet nothings in each other's ears and hang out the do-not-disturb sign. A desire for travel might instigate a trip to the travel agency, or perusal of the Internet for destinations that conjure up adventure and romance. Don't hold back. Plan way in advance so you have time to save for the cost of your dream trip.

30. SATURDAY. Harmonious. The feeling of love, the power of attraction, and popularity are all indicated as the New Moon joins loving Venus and the inspiring Sun in the creative sign of Leo. One negative of such a wonderful aspect is overindulgence. So be careful not to eat or drink to excess, as the effects may be long-term. Parties and entertainment are in abundance, and new friends will fill out your contacts and interests. Single Aries are sure to find romance and the start of young love, but there is a strong indication for conception, so take precautions if you are not ready to make babies. But for prospective parents, this is a great time to start a family.

31. SUNDAY. Contented. Creative and artistic juices are flowing freely now. A neighborhood class in the healing arts and metaphysics may give you something new to learn about. You will not take kindly to anybody trying to interrupt what you are interested in. Enjoy your own company early in the day. Visitors are bound to arrive later on and create an impromptu party that will inspire some creativity in the kitchen. A new lover may have some strange and annoying habits that make you think twice about continuing the relationship. Don't let visitors stay too late, as you need all the sleep you can get tonight.

AUGUST

1. MONDAY. Strategic. You have the energy to get ahead in almost any way that you desire as long as you are disciplined and avoid obvious excess. This means not taking on more than you can handle, as you are likely to involve yourself in projects that are beyond your resources. Your ability to be precise and clear makes this an excellent time for mapping out your future plans and laying the foundations, rather than rushing in wholesale and trying to get everything done at once. A health issue may be cured more effectively through counseling than physical medication at the moment. Your state of mind is just as powerful as a virus at causing disease. Meditation and affirmations can also be good.

2. TUESDAY. Uneasy. The unpleasant feeling that the daily grind is not suited to your psychological makeup can upset your sense of well-being. Coworkers can annoy you, and you might have to bite your tongue more times than you would like. An original and creative flair can make you temperamental and less likely to want to please others. A course of study that will encourage your artistic flair and give you more control over your working day could be the answer. The monetary rewards are not as important as enjoyment right now. A love affair can be too extravagant for your bank balance. If your partner won't adjust to your needs, then maybe you need to let them go and look after yourself.

3. WEDNESDAY. Tense. Anticipation and expectation can combine to make a volatile mix. Waiting for the outcome of a court case, the signing of an agreement or contract, or the go-ahead on an important deal are among the sorts of things that will likely put stress on your domestic life and cause arguments or short fuses. Remember that you and your partner, or the people you share your home with, all have needs. Make sure you consider everybody and not just yourself in the current climate. You may have a secret that is weighing heavily on your conscience, and it might be the time to weigh the pros and cons of coming clean and being responsible for your actions.

4. THURSDAY. Confusing. With Mercury, the planet ruling the mind, moving backward in Virgo, there is extra delay and reflection involved in all matters of communication. A holdup in agreements and contracts, delays in meetings, adjournments in court cases, and even problems setting a date for a wedding are all things that can cause frustration. With Mercury in close association with nebulous Neptune, you have a perfect storm of mixed messages, lost valuables, and memory loss. Try not to drink or take drugs, and you will have an edge over those who do. Make sure you write anything important down. Look after your health, eat nourishing food, exercise sensibly, and get plenty of rest.

5. FRIDAY. Romantic. New relationships are likely to blossom under the influence of today's stars, and some Aries are destined for love at first sight as your soul mate comes into your life. Relationships can move to another level of commitment as your understanding of each other deepens and grows. Some of you who may have been having relationship difficulties can start counseling and find another way of relating that opens doors to a loving future. If you are going through a difficult divorce, matters can come to light that help to clear through the nastiness and disillusionment. A home business can get off the ground with funding and zoning approval.

6. SATURDAY. Heartening. Although your financial situation may leave a little to be desired, the universe is sending messages of love to Aries souls. With the Sun and Venus in intimate embrace in Leo, your sector of love and romance, the chance to be lucky in love is better than ever before. Artistic projects and hobbies can go ahead in leaps and bounds, along with public recognition for originality and design. If ever there is a time for exhibiting your work, it is now. Revamping your wardrobe or beautifying your home is favored. Look for ways to do so without spending large sums of money. Keep your investments where they are, and don't extend credit limits except for an emergency.

7. SUNDAY. Impressionable. Ideas and opportunities, although exciting, can take you out of your comfort zone. It is not a good period for action or initiating new plans. Give yourself plenty of time to mull over change. In fact, until Mercury goes direct again on August 27, you should learn as much as you can and digest all the possibilities of what you are about to do. Then you will make the right decision. Married Aries can have problems relating to the in-laws. You are probably better off letting your partner discuss anything important with them while you stay out of family disagreements. An urge for emotional excitement can be met in the public arena rather than on the domestic front.

8. MONDAY. Philosophical. Adjusting your ideas to fit in with those around you is your best approach to life today. Vacation plans can get the go-ahead, or you might book that trip of a lifetime on an impulse and have to reorganize your next couple of months so that you can prepare. Your partner may have social commitments that they are not pleased about. But if you go along, you can turn the commitments around into enjoyable and interesting outings. So lend a hand and keep everyone laughing. A spiritual or philosophical meeting can be inspiring later on, introducing you to new ideas as well as moving you into more influential circles that can open doors and help with marketing your talents.

9. TUESDAY. Ambitious. Although you know that you are good at what you do, you may lack confidence when it comes to selling yourself. When applying for a job, you should go through an employment agency. Get their assistance in resume presentation and interview decorum for sure success. Problems on the home front could be holding you back from getting the position that you would love, but don't complain about it. Focus on solving these problems, and then you can go forward in your career. Undercurrents in the workplace can be blocking your chances of promotion. If you cannot see any way around these blockages, think about changing employers, going to a company that offers what you want.

10. WEDNESDAY. Intense. Aries teenagers can feel that your parents are being unreasonable. But if you consider all the facts, you might understand where they are coming from. Similarly, Aries parents can find it hard to reach any middle ground with a teenager, and might have to resort to bargaining to keep your child safe. Unstable influences are around. Through friends, fellow students, or coworkers, rebellious ideas can make the straight and narrow look like a straitjacket. Disruptive ideas can come from people who are jealous of your position and try to undermine your security by making you feel dissatisfied. Be your own person and make up your own mind about your situation.

11. THURSDAY. Opportune. Your popularity is on the rise. Although with inflated egos and power plays all around you, it might make you a target for jealous emotions. Watch what you say in any angry exchanges lest you let something slip that you would rather have kept to yourself. Remember, your emotions are on display at the moment. A friend who is going through a tough time might ask you for a loan. But unless you can afford to do without the amount they are asking for, you should be wary as they may not be in a position to pay you back for a long time. Those of you who are roommates might be wise to look at ways to move into your own place. You will benefit from the independence and the space.

12. FRIDAY. Fair. Activities involving teamwork or a group of people are indicated, though this might not be to your liking. If people rub you the wrong way, just stick to your job and don't take their comments seriously, and you can enjoy the interchange. Sportspeople will be especially competitive. You might be inclined to expand your training program, but do be careful of overdoing things and straining a muscle. If you won't be able to compete, your frustration will be even worse. Aries couples can be inclined to leave the madding crowd behind and enjoy the intimacy of a loving relationship, but it might be best to postpone joint ventures until another day.

13. SATURDAY. Friendly. Social activities should be very enjoyable, and active Aries people are likely to have a full calendar for the weekend. Your love for theatrics will especially be drawn to such things as fancy-dress balls and street theater. Get out and about, peruse the entertainment section in your weekend paper, and explore the full range of what is being offered. New interests can arise from experiencing new things, and new friends are likely as well. Romance is also a high possibility. If you are single, be prepared to be swept off your feet by a dark and passionate stranger. Aries couples might plan a weekend escape and disappear for two days of lovemaking and indulgence.

14. SUNDAY. Quiet. Overindulgence from the night before might bring a painful recovery today. Spend the morning in bed and watch movies, or catch up with friends over the phone. An Internet romance can make your back ache and your eyes hurt from too many hours in front of the screen. Plan a get-together and find out what the other person is really like. Stories of last night's escapades could make you want to hide, and certainly all of you will benefit from quiet time at home. A domestic project can give you hours of enjoyment, allowing your creative side free rein and keeping you active. Children may need to be chauffeured around; carpool with the other parents and save gas.

15. MONDAY. Pressured. Finding the balance between work commitments and family commitments could be driving you nuts. Try delegating tasks and see if that helps your workload. A business deal or contract can be causing you stress, as its importance colors all things. Perhaps you can look at life differently and let go of your current expectations and see how that works. A workshop in meditation and relaxation methods might do you a world of good. The stress levels in your body may be creating headaches and fatigue that you could do without. Read up on nutrition, as diet has a lot to do with well-being. If you are unsure, see a professional. The fitter you feel, the easier life will be.

16. TUESDAY. Reflective. A friend from the past can turn up on your doorstep and bring up memories you had forgotten about. Planetary aspects today point to the need for reflection before moving forward and starting new projects. It is worth looking at past actions for indications of where present actions might take you. A lover from the past could return and want to give the relationship another try. Be very wary if you were not happy before; people can change, but not as often as you would like to think. A dreamy mood makes this day unsuitable for important decision making or beginning a new project. Take in a movie or read a book for a safe and enjoyable ride into fantasyland.

17. WEDNESDAY. Eventful. Impulsive behavior should be avoided if at all possible. Try to keep both feet on the ground and your logic intact. Family arguments can be disruptive, and you may find yourself in the middle of a feud. Don't take sides or make judgments if you can help it, and you will have a chance to play the mediation role. If you are involved in domestic violence, report the offense to the law and seek whatever protection you are offered. Remember that you can't help anybody else if you aren't fit yourself. A change of home could be creating havoc with your security. The loss of your social network and your knowledge of the local environment and services can make life hard.

18. THURSDAY. Favorable. Social events will bring many enjoyable hours of meeting and making new contacts. Perhaps there will be an encounter of the loving kind, one that sets sparks of excitement and anticipation up and down your spine. A female friend or associate may have decided to take you under her wing and push you into influential and motivated circles; any inconvenience to you will be a minor annoyance. A business meeting can give you an opportunity to air your knowledge and good business sense. Remember that there will be holdups for the next week or so, and people will think you know something they don't. A chance to take an overseas trip should be grabbed with both hands. Go and enjoy yourself.

19. FRIDAY. Profitable. It is all about using your head today. Don't act on impulse, but consider the pros and cons and listen to sage advice that comes from older and more experienced people; they will not steer you wrong. An important business deal might depend on using your house to finance it. If you have done all your figures properly and sought sound advice, you should end up with a profitable business and a comfortable home. Family disputes are better off avoided, as you will benefit from your family's support right now. If someone has a gripe about you, listen to what they have to say; it will be instructive, as well as show your good character to the people that matter most.

20. SATURDAY. Beneficial. As the Moon comes together with expansive Jupiter, your feelings of self-worth and comfort should grow also. But if you find yourself dissatisfied with these feelings, it is an excellent time to consider a change in approach to life's ups and downs. Romance can be a little shaky. You may be starting to doubt your feelings for your lover and are considering having a talk with them. Or your partner might be demanding a behavior from you that just doesn't fit your character. If you think trying to talk about it will only incite a riot, buy a gift and write what you want to say on the card. Enjoy challenges. Extreme sports is an area where you can excel now.

21. SUNDAY. Good. Spending time on your own could be helpful; a spiritual retreat or meditation workshop would fit today's celestial influences. Find a creative outlet for your imagination. Any creative pursuit that gives you confidence in your own abilities and gives you a focus would be a positive activity. If you let fantasies and romantic illusions control your mind, you can get caught up in a web of deceit and might experience conflict in your personal relationships due to a lack of discernment. A friendly get-together can lead to a discussion around money and how to handle it. Listen well; you may hear some new and successful ways to improve your finances.

22. MONDAY. Diligent. Keep tabs on all the small details, and you will be surprised at how easily your workload flows. Finish off assignments or contracts ready for submission on the due date. Meetings could get caught up in irrelevant details, and you will need to bring the discussion back to the topic if you want to finish on time. If you are asked to take the minutes, accept gladly; it will give you the chance to stay focused on what's being said. Students who are finding it hard to focus should research different study methods; the stimulation of a different approach can revive your interest in your subjects again. Writing blogs or joining an Internet forum can open up a whole new world.

23. TUESDAY. Useful. Your daily routine, health, and work become important now that the Sun has moved into vigilant Virgo, where it joins up with the beautiful and harmonious Venus, bringing balance and harmony to this area of your life. A relationship can develop with a coworker during this time, and life's simple pleasures can be enjoyed. Health routines such as yoga and tai chi can be beneficial. Changing the habit of drinking coffee for herbal teas can shore up your immune system before the bugs strike. A small dog might give you companionship and make you exercise daily. Your wardrobe might need revamping, encouraging you to revive your sewing skills.

24. WEDNESDAY. Bright. A talent for putting people at their ease might surface and give you an edge over your competitors. An absent coworker could leave an opening for you to step up a rung at work and show your managerial skills; you can be sure the boss will notice you. A job opportunity that can further your career may mean moving out of state and leaving friends and family. This will be hard. But if you don't have the opportunities in your local area, then you need to make the choice based on what is most important to you, not everybody else. Once a decision is made, given time, reality always adjusts to suit. A health issue could become chronic if you don't treat the cause now.

25. THURSDAY. Active. The focus is on your immediate living environment as the Moon joins your ruling planet Mars in Cancer, your solar sector of home and family. You have plenty of energy for cleaning up your house and getting out into the garden if you have one. If you don't, you might start an herb garden on the window ledge to enjoy growing and using such plants. Impulsive behavior can cause arguments and accidents, so be a little careful. Put your energy into physical work or exercise, and you can relax with family and friends afterward. If you suffer from high blood pressure, take it easy today, and if you are feeling tired, have a blood test. You may be low in certain vitamins and iron.

26. FRIDAY. Deceptive. People can read you like a book this morning, so take an honest look at the motivations behind your actions. Indulge yourself a little, as you are likely running around after others. If you don't get any of your needs met, you will end up exploding. Aries parents may be worried about a child's performance at school. Go and see the principal before you jump to any conclusions. There may be a simple remedial course of action for you to follow. A fun evening is likely to be planned, and you can expect excitement plus. For single Aries, new possibilities emerge. Speculation can be rewarding. See your stock broker for a tip on where to put your money.

27. SATURDAY. Revealing. Situations can occur that bring memories from the past flooding back with all the sounds, smells, tastes, and colors of the real event. If you find yourself thinking of the past, allow this process. Perhaps you might start a journal into which you can put these reflections for future self-knowledge. Keep a list of what you have to do for today because you are likely to forget important things. A social affair or function could be experiencing all sorts of holdups and delays, and you may have to drive all over town picking up supplies and finishing the final touches. A love of the theater should be encouraged; go down to your local playhouse and volunteer your services.

28. SUNDAY. Intuitive. Aries are action-oriented people who love adventure and excitement. But a late night out may have put you under the weather, and the last thing you feel like is entertaining. You are likely experiencing a vivid dream life. Interesting impressions of your relationships with other people might inspire you to visit a psychic or start studying the occult arts. Trust your intuition, and you can have a small measure of luck with speculation. Stay away from drugs and alcohol, as you are oversensitive to their effects right now. You should also be careful about the company you keep. Tonight's New Moon culminates in Virgo, encouraging diet and lifestyle changes.

29. MONDAY. Lively. Teamwork can be effective and enjoyable, making for fun on the job. A group of your cohorts might take you to a very interesting foreign restaurant for something scrumptious as well as interesting conversation. Information regarding your company's power structure and how to network your way up the ladder can be very helpful to you. Mercury went direct in Virgo Saturday. Now you can expect all agreements and contracts to be finalized, and holdups in communication should start to clear away. A legal matter might need professional handling. See an attorney and get their advice before you do anything. Put a smile on your face and be happy.

30. TUESDAY. Tricky. A new romance could move you into a sophisticated social set and cost you money. Extra stress can be caused through expectations that are not reasonable. Try to let go of the outcome, make sure you have done your part properly, and leave it up to the universe. A certain amount of life's troubles comes from being a control freak. You can be heading off on a trip to the unknown, whether for work or play, but you might not be able to enjoy the moment because you are too busy worrying about forgetting something. Adult learners are in danger of dropping out of the courses of study, but this is just the result of temporary problems. Stick to it and you won't be sorry.

31. WEDNESDAY. Frustrating. Little things can mess up your plans. If ever there is a time where you are in danger of making mountains out of molehills, it is now. An exciting engagement can make waiting tedious and irritating, so try not to snap everyone's head off. A new diet can start to work. If you instigate a shopping spree to deck out your wardrobe with the latest fashions, all this can do wonders for your self-confidence. A new romance could be heating up, and the decision to move in together could be made a bit too fast. Take your time with this, allow the two of you to adjust to each other's daily routines, and enjoy young love a little longer.

SEPTEMBER

1. THURSDAY. Compromising. Success will depend on how far you are willing to go to meet the demands of another. This might entail letting go of some of your pet hates and desires, but the result can amaze you, as letting go of anything usually does. You should be firing on all cylinders today, and your Aries spontaneity will fit with all situations. A business deal may seem to simply evaporate before your eyes, but don't stress. There will be other things to think about. The chance for a romantic interlude may take you away from plans, and don't be surprised if you don't get back to them either. Loving relationships are moving into a deeper area of commitment on a lifelong journey.

2. FRIDAY. Renewing. Change is as good as a rest. Let go of your fears and you will be rewarded with peace of mind. There is plenty of support from friends, coworkers, and the financial sector to get your business deal off the ground. That certain someone who makes your heart miss a beat every time you speak to them quite possibly feels the same way. Ask them to have dinner with you, and if it is meant to be, you won't have to do anything else. Your chemistry will do the rest. A health matter might require minor surgery, and the sooner you get this done the better you will feel. As long as your surgeon is experienced, don't hesitate. The outcome of a lawsuit is likely to be financially pleasing.

3. SATURDAY. Carefree. Feelings of generosity and the simple enjoyment of life are likely to override any other problems. A shopping trip could turn up some beautiful antiques that are a surefire investment for the future, in the meantime adding charm and enjoyment to your home. Be careful about promising your partner or family too much. You might feel quite lazy and want to while away your time with self-indulgence, which would cause a few waves with those close to you. Better to be honest up front and avoid creating expectations. A cultural event or sporting match could be lots of fun this evening, and a way for you and your family to relax, scream away frustrations, and have fun.

4. SUNDAY. Revealing. Act on your feelings and you can't go wrong. Practice revealing your feelings in a loving manner, and a deeper understanding of relationships can develop. A strong urge to get away from your daily routine and go away somewhere might take you off to visit someone out of town, or to a well-known sightseeing destination. Or you may get away in your mind and take in a play or concert, and be transported into a world of art and magic. A spiritual gathering could give you an insight into parts of your life that have always been a mystery, filling your future with excitement and romance. Visitors with tales of adventure can come calling this evening and keep you up late.

5. MONDAY. Eventful. Communicating your thoughts and feelings will come naturally. Beware of trying to manipulate others, as this always backfires at some stage farther down the line. Aries writers could get an offer from one of the publishers you have submitted your work to, giving you the encouragement you need to get into your work with gusto. An application to the college of your choice is likely to be approved, and this will start the preparation for the move into study and college life. Aries travelers might want to watch your pennies, and especially avoid buying too many souvenirs. They may be duty-free, but what you save you will spend on excess baggage. Send a card of love to someone special.

6. TUESDAY. Suspenseful. A feeling that something is about to happen could dog you all morning, adding to your anxiety level. Practice meditation and don't think about the future. Try to be in the moment, and your mind will remain clear and anxiety can fall away. A change in your life's direction can shake you up a bit. But once you get into it, the opportunities that the change brings will far outweigh the negatives. There is an indication of a wage increase or a promotion on the horizon, which could be due to the influence of someone in a powerful position pulling strings for you. A legal matter may not look good on paper. But with a quality lawyer, you should be more than happy with the outcome.

7. WEDNESDAY. Energetic. Highly charged emotions can increase the chance of arguments, especially when you jump in with your opinion before giving it some thought. On the job site or in shared living quarters, you might be better off working on your own if possible. Good feelings between coworkers indicate good cooperative efforts, especially in a dispute with your employer over working conditions, rates of pay, or unfair dismissals. Your ability to achieve is positive, and your hard work might result in a promotion or a surge of prestige in your area of expertise. Avoid giving speeches. If you find yourself in a crowd, the overriding mood can change as quickly as the wind.

8. THURSDAY. Powerful. Stick to your guns and don't let other people confuse you with their ideas and criticisms. Explore your individuality by having faith in your own inventions and imagination. Be very careful when explaining emotions or plans to someone. Messages can be misconstrued and mixed up, causing all sorts of misunderstandings and hurt feelings. Concentrate on your hopes and wishes, and the creation and use of appropriate affirmations would be a powerful tool now. Membership in a hobby group can take you out of your comfort zone and bring fun and new adventures into your life. No matter how busy you may be, lend a hand to a friend in need, and you will benefit, too.

9. FRIDAY. Cheerful. Plenty of good friends and social activity will add up to a fun day. Make sure you keep to the point in business dealings and meetings, as idle gossip and conversation can delay the decision-making process and put the project in jeopardy. Mental Mercury moves into Virgo and your solar house of work and health. Now an interest in diet and exercise might inspire you to start reading a lot and practicing culinary skills that are foreign to your usual routine. Mental activities for their own sake can take up a lot of your time, and sitting in front of the screen playing games with people in cyberspace will put you behind schedule. Internet dating could also intrigue.

10. SATURDAY. Sensitive. The moods of others are likely to affect your own. Just when you think you know what you want, you change your mind. Beware of shysters and dishonest dealings; there are some who are good at giving an impression that is completely misleading. A mood of fantasy and of illusion makes this a great day for watching movies or reading fiction. Parties and romance can dazzle, but make sure you don't overindulge in drugs or alcohol, or you won't know what is up and what is down. Likewise, overindulgence in sweets can destroy your diet and expand the waistline, bringing on depression and a new round of masochistic diets. Enjoy your day with friends you can trust in a safe environment.

11. SUNDAY. Tense. Stay away from crowds and enjoy the peace and quiet of solitude. Some Aries may be mourning the loss of somebody special and find solace in a spiritual retreat or gathering. Rekindling faith in a power greater than yourself can help you accept life on life's terms in a far gentler way than trying to find a rational framework. The same goes for many problems that could be upsetting you right now; relationship breakdowns, money worries, or health issues are all emotionally painful situations that need to be approached one day at a time. If you are feeling out of sorts from overindulgence or a late night, stress headaches and anxiety attacks can be warded off with a good diet and plenty of rest.

12. MONDAY. Emotional. Blocked emotions will eat at your insides and cause you to blurt out all sorts of disgruntled comments. Sometimes it is better to be honest and face your fears of the consequences once and for all. The Full Moon in Pisces early this morning lights up your sector of self-analysis and meditation. So make the most of the vibes to sort out issues that have been worrying you. Start a journal and put your thoughts down daily. This mapping of your emotional landscape can give you insights that are most valuable to building your sense of self. Conflict between you and your partner may be due to a lack of communication; talk about seeing a counselor and learning various coping skills.

13. TUESDAY. Tricky. Just when you think you know what is going on, the whole game can change. Be adaptable and you can stay on top of any situation today. Electrical gadgets can go on the blink. Be very careful not to talk on the phone, or play golf, if you are experiencing an electrical storm. You need to be prepared to make sacrifices to achieve a long-term aim. A craving for fun and sensation might lead you into tense situations, mixing with people you don't normally socialize with and doing unusual and eccentric things. Being out of your comfort zone can put you at risk of making mistakes and having accidents, so practice as much restraint as you can for your safety's sake.

14. WEDNESDAY. Conservative. After yesterday, you are likely to take things slow and steady and try to regroup lost ground. Partnered Aries might start the day off with an argument with your partner and feel remorse and guilt all day long; don't let this happen. If you feel you were in the wrong, call and apologize and the day can start to look up. Financial and career prospects should be looking up, and if you keep your work up to date, your employer will certainly notice. It might be a good idea to update your wardrobe and start working out at the gym, as your appearance is the first impression people receive on meeting you. A new project needs a kick-start, so initiate new plans now.

15. THURSDAY. Loving. Venus is now in Libra, bringing peace and harmony to your relationship sector and putting romance high up on the agenda. Aries people are experiencing many changes lately with Uranus, the planet of change, moving through your sign. These planetary influences may herald changing relationships or a love adventure to add extra spice to your life. You could be more fastidious about everything now. You could call off a business deal because it doesn't suit, or become critical of your partner over some petty irritation. A desire for fun can instigate silly games and lots of fun and laughter in the workplace. Just be careful that the boss doesn't witness some of your antics.

16. FRIDAY. Rewarding. A happy mood and a positive approach can change your fortune. What you expect to be routine work can turn out to be a major activity. Get your important things done as early as possible, as the finger of fortune will move on later in the day. If you are going through a property settlement and need to engage the services of an attorney, choose one who is happy to settle out of court and save you a bundle. It would be a good idea to have your cholesterol levels checked. Also, keep tabs on your diet today. If ever there was a risk of overeating or eating the wrong things, it is now. Watch for exaggeration. Try to apply common sense.

17. SATURDAY. Varied. Security issues can disrupt a close relationship and force you to rethink your values. Tension between lovers demands that you focus on your communication rather than on manipulation and control. An eye for beauty and the exotic will be an asset for home renovators and artists; the work you do today can be a unique blend of balance and harmony. A blind date could turn out be drop-dead gorgeous, so make sure you look your sparkling best and make their night as they've made yours. A sense that your good character is being undermined by an influential colleague may be correct. But this will pass and your good character will remain intact, unless, of course, there is something you are hiding.

18. SUNDAY. Lively. An unexpected visitor can start the day off with a bang, sending jokes and laughter rippling through the scene. An unusual community event might get you out of the house and into the street with a chance to strut your stuff and turn a few heads. Expect a few amorous glances, and perhaps an invitation too good to refuse. An ailing neighbor may be glad for a visit. Pop in and check if they need anything when you are going down the street, and you might be a lifesaver. Students could be falling behind on your studies; burning the candle at both ends certainly won't make you dull, but it sure messes with your ambitions. Try to make time for important work and look after yourself.

19. MONDAY. Interesting. Your ruling planet Mars moves its action into Leo and your solar sector of fun, lovers, and children. A new relationship may have just begun, sending your mind into fantasyland and creating havoc with your workaday thought processes. Start writing a love letter and put your thoughts down on paper; whether you send it or not, it can clear your mind for the mundane things that need to be done. A new subject in the course of your studies could be proving too advanced for you. Contact some of the other students and discuss your problem with them, and you are likely to get a fresh insight. A child that is harassing you for money could be given chores and learn while they earn.

20. TUESDAY. Testing. Emotional tension caused by conflicting opinions is likely; stay away from any situation that may get out of control, and preserve your inner peace. The lesson now is not to take what people say and do personally. A brother or sister could be hard to contact. If you are worried about them, go that extra yard to make sure they are all right. The need to find new living quarters could be causing some grief. But instead of stressing, sit down with pen and paper, jot down the type of home you would really like, and put it out to the universe. Then practice faith. An old childhood friend might turn up on your doorstep and rekindle treasured memories long forgotten.

21. WEDNESDAY. Multifaceted. Partnered Aries having trouble with interfering in-laws might need to seek wise counsel from outside the family. Speaking to your partner could simply cause more problems, unless you know how to approach the matter. Costly legal procedures and a tenuous case can make a lawsuit look like a risky venture, but if you feel you are in the right, stick with it. Miracles can happen. Hopeful Aries parents can get good news and start setting up a nursery. Parents of Aries might not be able to look after themselves effectively anymore, and it might be time to check out nursing homes or other suitable options. Make sure you involve them in your decision making.

22. THURSDAY. Practical. Mental work will be a breeze. Get in early and tidy up all your accounts, filing and laying the foundation for efficient organization. A time-management plan would be an excellent project, and help you to fit as much into your day as fast-paced Aries people like. Daily expenses can be on the rise, and now is a good time to set a budget to keep your finances in the black. A shopping trip might be a form of entertainment. Without thinking, you can get drawn in by the advertising and spend big-time on an item you can really do without. Splashing money around to attract a new beau will not work, and the same goes for trying to impress your peers; you'll just look flashy.

23. FRIDAY. Artistic. The Sun now enters Libra, your opposite sign. New activities and encounters are on their way, some quite unexpected, that will generate both excitement and personal growth. A change in your duties and obligations can free you up to do some things you have always wanted to do but never had the time or space for. Inhibitions might drop away and give you a free rein on your creativity, and you may start a class in painting, writing, dancing, or music. Wild ideas for making money could be the start of a backyard business, and they just might work. Do be careful not to overextend yourself or go beyond your own resources. A loving encounter can change the course of the day.

24. SATURDAY. Enthusiastic. An exciting day of entertaining events should be on the menu for Aries people. Love and romance can bring some interesting changes to your plans. If you are already partnered, there could be some disagreements over what you have planned. Your diplomatic side will shine through and give you a positive edge in any argument. Try not to hurry or push events along, as this will only cause stress and mishaps. Street theater could be very entertaining, even if you are just sitting in a sidewalk café watching people go by. Likewise, an evening at the cinema, the theater, or a concert can give you excitement and strike an inspiring chord in your heart for several days to come.

25. SUNDAY. Advantageous. The effects of a late night can be negated with enjoyable exercise this morning. A walk through a local beauty spot can inspire some interesting ideas for the rest of the day. Work around home can be profitable and satisfying. If you are out and about the local markets looking for objects of art to beautify your home, you may be lucky enough to score a unique antique piece quite cheaply. Steer clear of pet shops unless you want a pet, because you can get attracted to a small puppy or kitten and buy with your heart and not your head. This is an excellent day to catch up on work; your mental faculties are sharp and clarity comes easily.

26. MONDAY. Burdensome. A coworker can irritate and make your working day unpleasant. If you have to correct their mistakes or pick up their slack, you are sure to find it hard to be civil, especially if it is reflecting on you. Have a word with them before it gets to the stage where you can't be nice, before you end up reporting their behavior to the boss. Work in the import and export trades can be made cumbersome by language barriers, and the need for an interpreter is essential, adding more expense. Travelers might also find yourselves in a bind when you can't find anyone who speaks your language. Those of you preparing for an overseas trip might find relevant study guides quite helpful.

27. TUESDAY. Outgoing. The New Moon in Libra this morning highlights relationships of all kinds. With the Sun, communicative Mercury, artistic Venus, and serious Saturn all already in Libra, you can expect plenty of action in various alliances and partnerships. Power struggles can ensue when you find that you can't fit in with other people's expectations of you, but it is also very important for you to impress. Honesty is your best policy right from the start. That way, you avoid the buildup of tension that invariably leads to explosions. A joint venture can get a kick-start now, and advice from someone in the know will be invaluable. Get legal advice before initiating litigation.

28. WEDNESDAY. Intuitive. An insight into what drives people can be a great benefit in a business deal, so trust your instincts. A career move may be necessary to improve your income opportunities, but make sure you fulfill your obligations before moving on. Partnered Aries might be upset by a partner's career move to the point of suffering an identity crisis. It won't take you long to adjust, as you love a challenge and there looks to be plenty of opportunities for you. The need to speak in public can give you the jitters. If you focus on breathing and just watch your body for a few minutes beforehand, you will find that you can allow the words to flow smoothly.

29. THURSDAY. Opportune. Inspiration and success can give you a strong faith in the divine and allow a peace of mind previously unknown. Your ambitious nature is turned up full volume and, combined with the Aries tendency to jump into things, puts you in danger of becoming a patsy for an underhanded shyster. Those famous words advising look before you leap apply to you today. A feeling of dissatisfaction with your relationship might pervade your heart and mind for most of the day. When your mind starts going through the wrongs you feel, write each one down and then ponder your role in the situation, You might get a different take on the relationship and end up with a marvelous night of romance.

30. FRIDAY. Diverse. A secret business deal can fall through and save you from a subsequent loss. Mixing business with pleasure may get you caught up in a web of deceit. Be smart from the start and say no. An interesting new business associate or acquaintance might not be all they say they are; don't lend them any money until you are sure you know them. An invitation to a prestigious social event can give you the chance to build your support network and gain support from key people. If your partner is jealous of the time you spend on your ambitions, ask him or her to come along; together, you can make contact with twice as many people.

OCTOBER

1. SATURDAY. Playful. High spirits and an adventurous mood give this day a positive note. Aries singles look set to meet someone really gorgeous, someone who sparks infatuation and that wonderful feeling of being able to do anything. Friends will be fun, and a group outing can take you to places of new experience. Philosophy and spiritual matters may be of interest. A workshop on a related subject might be the start of a future hobby or talent. Partnered Aries can look forward to peace and harmony in your relationship sphere. Suggest you both go out together, visit an amusement park, and enjoy the buzz of being playful again. If you have children, it is definitely a great way to have fun.

2. SUNDAY. Idealistic. Your focus is likely to be on the future and the many ways you can get where you want to go. Your spontaneous attitude may need to be organized with an effective time-management plan, just to make sure you get the most from your efforts. Make your new motto quality not quantity, and you can't go wrong. A loved one's news can make this an extra special day, and a celebration could be the best way to enjoy the moment. Singles might be bowled over by a sportsperson. For couples, that old adventurous streak can roll back the years. Children may be extra demanding, and need to be brought back to reality; take them to play outdoors. The physical activity will be relaxing, and give you and your children a chance to talk easily and openly as friends.

3. MONDAY. Intense. Regrets over past actions, or resentments over somebody else's actions, can darken the day. Consider your own actions before condemning another's, and you can change the course of events. Power struggles among the hierarchy within your workplace can have effects that last for a long time; try to stay away from the prophets of doom and gloom. Stay positive, and you might be singled out for a promotion. Finances are looking good, and you might pick up extra work doing something you love to cover any shortfalls. A secret affair with hidden passion and undercurrents can lead to slipups and, ultimately, disaster. Reconsider your situation. Above all, love yourself.

4. TUESDAY. Vexing. Small details and minor delays can combine to drive you nuts. A particularly fastidious coworker or partner might be on your case all day long, criticizing your every move. Don't get drawn into an argument, but concentrate on your goals. Your ambition and your staying power will combine to get you past all obstacles to taste the flavor of success. Tired eyes or chronic headaches can be a sign of eyesight strain. Check in at your local optometrist for an eye test. Your popularity may be waning a little because you are always in a hurry or have work to do. Make time for people and revive the romance and mystery of life.

5. WEDNESDAY. Profitable. Catch up on your workload and get an important matter out of the way before people start wanting a piece of you. Self-employed Aries may earn some sizable fees and watch the bank balance rise, enjoying the boost to your confidence and lifestyle. New business associates and social contacts can become valuable allies and help to broaden your sphere of influence. Hopes and wishes can come true; set things in motion and start the ball rolling. They won't manifest if you simply leave them in your dreams. Changes are in the wind and you will not lose by embracing them. Change simply adds to what you already have.

6. THURSDAY. Fair. Membership in a group or club of some sort could become too costly for you to continue. Look around for something to take its place in your social life. There are plenty of free activities that will get you out and about. Relationship difficulties could be the topic of a serious discussion. If you are prepared to listen, rather than try to make your own point, you will gain helpful insight into what is going on. This can enable you to try a different approach, one that your partner will listen to. A business deal could become disorganized, with too many people attempting to make things happen their way. Call a meeting in order to reach a collective decision.

7. FRIDAY. Uplifting. Your imagination is working overtime, and your creativity and enjoyment of life will shine through. Loving feelings between you and your partner can inspire plans for a weekend getaway at a romantic tourist spot. Single Aries might sense something more from an attractive friend, and make overtures about a date for the evening. If you are trying to get off the merry-go-round of party nights or one-night stands, do something that excludes drugs or alcohol and make a lasting connection. If you are alone and feeling depressed, make the extra effort to get out tonight, as you are sure to meet some lovely people. One in particular will be very interesting.

8. SATURDAY. Relaxing. Offload any unnecessary commitments and let yourself unwind. Take a long brisk walk, let your frustrations leave your body, and breathe in the peace of nature as the fresh air revives your tired mind. A spiritual retreat would do you a world of good now, helping you to reconnect with your spiritual self and feel the sense of belonging that sometimes seems so unattainable. Work behind the scenes can be very productive. If you have a new project on the drawing board, sit down with it and fine-tune all the details, and you will be ready to launch it next week. Plans for the evening should be fairly quiet; a romantic movie can end the day in style.

9. SUNDAY. Tricky. An elderly relative might be in the hospital, and a visit from you will cheer their day and give them the chance to tell you stories of your relatives. Lovely Venus now moves into Scorpio and your solar sector of commitment, throwing passion and sexual attraction into your world of relationships. If you are looking at buying a car or a house or investing in a business, you should find that your loan application is approved. Be very careful if the bank offers to up your limit on a credit card. If you can't pay it off now, it will be even harder when you are paying more interest on a larger amount. Keep your finances a secret, only talking to trusted friends and family.

10. MONDAY. Surprising. The Moon moves into your own sign of Aries and joins erratic Uranus in a loving dance with beautiful Venus. This aspect can turn all eyes your way, putting you center stage; groom yourself and dress up for the best effect. A new project can do really well if you get it going now, and you should have no trouble finding a backer to help you get established. You are likely to be very excited and eager in your approach, but be aware of others so that you don't step on any toes in your rush to get things done. Someone close to you can surprise you with a loving gift, or they may ask you out and transport you to cloud nine. A job promotion might be an unexpected surprise.

11. TUESDAY. Invigorating. Tonight's Full Moon in your own sign of Aries is bound to imbue you with enough energy to burn. Nothing will be too much for you, except, perhaps, relaxing. Vacation plans might escalate into an overseas trip that looks like it will cost you an arm and a leg. Start paying for it now and you will be able to enjoy the journey without the pressure of added debt. A proposal of marriage can also become an expensive exercise. Talk it over beforehand so that you know exactly what you want. Then you might not get caught up by the clever advertising that urges a costly ceremony. Enjoy the taste sensations of a foreign cuisine this evening.

12. WEDNESDAY. Passionate. When you think you have made your mind up, it can play tricks on you and conjure up romantic memories that are only partly based on the truth. Stick to your guns on whatever decision you have had to make; emotional issues are always slightly gray. A personal issue could be putting you at odds with those close to you, but you have to follow your own feelings and express your own truth. A friend in your inner circle may be gossiping and complicating an issue that is really quite simple. Instead of getting caught up in the trivia, go straight to the source and be honest. A hot and sexy stranger might sweep you off your feet tonight.

13. THURSDAY. Fortunate. Feeling good about yourself has a domino effect, and your boss will probably feel good about you, too. Some dynamo Aries are likely to get a raise and feel like you are on your way. Informative Mercury now moves into Scorpio and your sector of other people's resources and public money. While Mercury transits Scorpio for the next few weeks, you can hear some very useful information about investments and avenues for finance. You might need to watch your spending habits at this time also. Your attraction to luxury items and the high life can undermine previous hard work. Set a sensible budget without being too strict on yourself, then make sure you stick to it.

14. FRIDAY. Conservative. A relationship with an older person can give you added security, but it may take you into a lifestyle you are not ready for. Be honest with your partner. With their experience and your exuberance, a compromise may be worked out. The alternative is not fair to either one of you. Aries single parents might be having a hard time trying to earn a living. But this is an excellent time to study while you are at home looking after your baby, and it is the best way to get ahead as your baby's needs grow. You have a tremendous creative potential at the moment, and anything you put your mind to is likely to come to fruition. So don't settle for half measures. Aim for the very best.

15. SATURDAY. Successful. Communication is the key to the completion of all matters, and you should take extra care to make sure nobody gets their wires crossed. A hot date could take your mind off important issues, and you need to practice control for success. Some of you may be interested in recycling old clothes or furniture. Use your gift for artistic design to reinvent them or turn them into pieces of art. If you rent a stall at a local street fair, you could make money and a name for yourself now. A close friend might be leaving on an overseas trip, and it is with a heavy heart that you say good-bye. But don't be surprised if it isn't you leaving next.

16. SUNDAY. Uncertain. Half your day could be chatting with people who are probably not what they say they are. A dating service might have you well and truly hooked, and already you have a prospective partner wanting to fly you to some unknown destination. Aries homebodies might discover some exotic recipes and woo your loved ones with tastes from a distant shore. Shopping at various stores can be lots of fun, especially if there are some specialty shops that will introduce you to new fashions and ideas. If you keep running into a rather cute neighbor, you might be right to get suspicious. They may be sizing you up. Don't let flattery lead you astray.

17. MONDAY. Opportune. Shrewd business acumen blends well with an interest in art. Ideas will circulate about business deals that can't lose and unique ways to make money. Listen well to someone with plenty of experience, as you will pick up some invaluable tips. An attraction to a business associate could take you out of your league financially. If they reciprocate, it can give you a boost up the social ladder, although it will cost a lot to keep up appearances. Contractual negotiations, conferences, strategy sessions, and discussions will all go according to plan. But you need to keep your eye on the fine print to make sure that what you sign for is what you are getting. Avoid all illegal dealings.

18. TUESDAY. Revealing. Personal security issues may threaten early in the day. Whether it is an argument with your parents, a partner, or your boss, remain calm and look at your own triggers for valuable insight into a problem that has been boiling under the surface for a long time. A strong desire to stay at home can interrupt your working week, but sometimes it is very healing to nurture yourself. Put yourself first today and treat yourself as you would a lover. A wise investment could pay off and enable you to purchase your own home. Don't hesitate. Visit all your local real estate agents and start the ball rolling, before bills and unexpected costs eat away at your nest egg.

19. WEDNESDAY. Disappointing. Aries people who are going through a relationship separation and property settlement can be disillusioned with the outcome. What the two of you had together may be far more than twice what each of you end up with. Second thoughts over the separation can be discussed with a marriage counselor, and that will make all the difference in the situation. Legal matters will not be straightforward, so don't be surprised to hear some new and unexpected evidence that delays a court hearing. A toothache should be attended to straightaway. A spiritual gathering can lift your thoughts above today's woes and give you perspective.

20. THURSDAY. Chancy. Excitement bubbles over with the anticipation of a coming event. A mystery date could give your mind so much fodder for the imagination that you are useless for any practical enterprise. Artistic juices are flowing, however, and you might decide to take up a class in painting or acting to give you an outlet for your self-expression. A grown-up child may be experiencing marital difficulties and want to come home for sanctuary. This is okay, but if they have young children, make sure you lay down ground rules for your own sanity's sake. Poor personal boundaries can put you in a dangerous situation; be careful and don't go out with anyone you don't know and are unsure of.

21. FRIDAY. Dynamic. You are likely to have energy to burn, and a competitive sport will give you an arena to get it out safely and effectively. Speculation and gambling can be dangerous activities as far as your financial solvency is concerned; stay away from them and you won't miss them. Romantic inclinations can reach delicious physical fulfillment, but beware of a jealous ex hiding behind the scenes. An interest in law is a good enough reason to apply to study at a law school. Your chances of being accepted look great, and you will be pleased with your economic situation once you graduate. A love of dance and theater can be triggered at a social function this evening.

22. SATURDAY. Healing. Highly sensitive planetary vibes this morning suggest that you use this time lazing around and rejuvenating yourself. Take a break from the merry-go-round of the rat race. Meditate on peace and the pure love that created the universe. Abandon your plans and allow the day to run itself. Visit a local beauty spot to enjoy the fresh air and exercise. Stock up your cupboards on the way home, and make sure you have plenty of fresh fruit and veggies to benefit your diet. There are powerful cosmic influences developing that can affect you in a positive manner, so leave yourself open to an invitation to an affair you would normally refuse.

23. SUNDAY. Accepting. Let go of preconceived ideas and you will have a better day. A female friend will be a valuable resource to you, whether it is emotional support or financial help. Don't let your significant other coerce you into changing your plans if they are important to you. It may seem only minor at the time, but farther down the line you can find that you have given away part of yourself for the sake of the relationship, leaving you with a relationship but less of a self. Artistic projects can give you the inner peace you are seeking. Even if you end up simply painting the kitchen, immerse yourself in the color and let yourself enjoy the adventure and fun of it.

24. MONDAY. Stressful. Yesterday the Sun moved into Scorpio and your solar house of sex and money, making you more aware of interpersonal power plays and giving you access to public resources. Trust your own instincts in love and business and you won't be disappointed. But if you listen to others, you might be led astray. Your sensual persona is shining on full beam as the Moon glides into Libra, your house of partnerships; you can afford to be choosy now and find the love you deserve. Later when the Libra Moon and Uranus in Aries come together, there can be stress and distractions. Take a few deep breaths and carry on.

25. TUESDAY. Demanding. The remnants of a dream can stay with you for hours after you wake and add extra meaning to all your encounters. Financial and career commitments might control your life, making you time-poor and interfering with your chances to have meaningful communication with those close to you. Don't allow this to happen. Instead of the material world adding to your life, it can take over. Reclaim the spiritual, the social, and the loving part. A lucrative contract may be cut back by limitations and restrictions, and instead of getting you out of debt, it will just keep you going. Life can sometimes seem unfair, but it just is. Breathe deep and let go of grudges.

26. WEDNESDAY. Interesting. Now the Moon glides out of Libra and into Scorpio. This morning's New Moon is in Scorpio, strongly influencing the areas of your life where you are keeping secrets, or have kept them, and where your issues with power reside. Living fully and being wildly creative is one way to reclaim your power, but how to do that when there are bills to pay? Balance is the answer. Make sure you include all aspects, and try not to keep secrets, especially from yourself. Some Aries are about to come into a windfall. Whether this is an inheritance, insurance payout, or just plain good luck, you will be able to buy something for yourself you have secretly wanted for ages.

27. THURSDAY. Challenging. The inclination to act rashly is better ignored today. Your emotions may be a bit raw, and this will color your thinking with a subjective mood. Writing your thoughts down will be more constructive than speaking them out loud. Energy collides with desire, and arguments may arise. But the making-up process can get you hot and sweaty between the sheets. A friend who is going through a messy divorce might ask you for some advice and before you know it, you are acting as a pseudo counselor. There is nothing wrong with this, but you should be extra careful about the advice you give. Simply let your friend talk. They will come to their own conclusions.

28. FRIDAY. Bright. Even if it's raining cats and dogs in your vicinity, today's energy can be the equivalent of sunny skies. With the Moon lighting up Sagittarius, your house of travel and adventure, life seems full of potential and possibilities. Your efforts should focus on higher education, religion, politics, travel, cultural pursuits, foreign languages, writing, and publishing. An optimistic attitude will be contagious, so spend time with those who are open to all the beautiful ideas you have to share with the world. In fact, you can lead the gang into some pretty wild situations if you so choose. People will be looking to you for adventure, so show them your fearless side.

29. SATURDAY. Lively. Close associations will be important, and you can learn some very interesting ideas and attitudes from people you meet. A childhood dream might look like it has a chance of coming true, although you may have to apply yourself to obtain the prize. Be prepared to work hard for what you want now. Itchy feet and exotic daydreams could make your daily grind tough. Plan a weekend away, or perhaps even a second honeymoon, and put the spice back into life. Sometimes it's just a matter of how you look at things, and little changes can make a big difference. If you are stuck at home, play some rousing music and cook up a feast to treat loved ones.

30. SUNDAY. Sensitive. Your ruler Mars comes under the influence of impressionable Neptune, sapping your resolve as the infinite possibilities of love, life, and karma wash over you. A love adventure can change the look of everything. Instead of logic and reality, things can become blurred with fantasy and elation. A spiritual or political gathering can give you fodder for your mind and have you philosophizing on life, the universe, and all of that for days. But make sure you don't let your commitments slide. Be very careful of drugs and alcohol right now. You are so sensitive to the ideas and emotions of others, it may be hard for you to know where you end and another begins.

31. MONDAY. Focused. The Moon is moving through Capricorn, your house of career and reputation, making you a bit more mindful about your status. It may be hard for you to tone down your approach, but you may need to put a damper on your natural enthusiasm today. It's not that there is anything wrong with your joie de vivre; it's just that society often rewards the more controlled types. Activities seem to lead away from you as an individual and awaken the role you play in the lives of others. Public speaking can be very rewarding and build your reputation. Tonight you can relax and enjoy yourself, so set a candlelit scene. You can connect with your most significant other in very pleasurable way.

NOVEMBER

1. TUESDAY. Harmonious. Work and play can intertwine to make it a lovely relaxed day. Your ability to express yourself in terms that relate to others is an asset, and your boss will be impressed with your style. Aries salespeople are likely to clinch a deal and come out with enough cash to pay down a credit card. The sparks of romance can fly when you run into a new associate; try not to let your work suffer. A social gathering might seem like an impromptu business meeting, as an important issue can be sorted out while everyone is having fun. Your goals can get a bit closer today when you are introduced to a powerful mover and shaker.

2. WEDNESDAY. Imaginative. Luscious Venus moves into Sagittarius and your house of travel and adventure, sparking up your interest in artistic adventures and romantic getaways. A desire to travel combining with your idealistic nature can see you off to a foreign place where you will volunteer your services and give hope to the destitute while you experience the cultural journey. Your mind is hungry to understand and your heart wants to make a difference. This can manifest when you join an advocacy group or start rallying with others for a better world. Some of you might decide to go back to school and achieve your dreams of learning as well as teaching.

3. THURSDAY. Stimulating. A cultural event can have a huge effect on your psyche right now. A relationship with a foreigner can influence you to study their home language and understand the difference in perception another language can give, which will also enable you to understand your lover and see things through their eyes. You might be asked to represent your group, whether it is the company you work for, your coworkers, or a social group. Doing so, you discover you have a talent for public speaking, influencing people's ideas, and organizing—all talents that can further your career goals. A seminar out of town will give you a chance to escape the daily grind.

4. FRIDAY. Tiring. Emotional issues can bring you down. If you are feeling a bit depressed, get out of the house and go for a walk in nature. If you are close to the ocean, there would be nothing better than the fresh sea air and a swim to invigorate your senses and put you in a positive frame of mind. The flu could be running its course in the neighborhood. Get some olive leaf extract to give your immune system an extra boost. If you are just not feeling well, a trip to your local naturopath might be worthwhile. A major change in your life will bring up feelings of grief and loss. If you feel sad, start a journal and write as a form of healing.

5. SATURDAY. Easygoing. Sit back and let things slip past rather than being assertive. You may find communication difficult. Simply speak less and listen more; this often results in others thinking you are clever and wise. Do not engage in any useless conversations. Pure debate is unnecessary and a waste of your time today. Focus only on what must be discussed. Communication improves and secret passions may develop tonight. A little bit of heavenly seclusion under your own roof will be good for the soul. Take advantage of the peace and quiet to watch your thoughts unfold without getting too involved in any of the major plotting and strategic planning that often takes over.

6. SUNDAY. Suspenseful. The day could be spent waiting for something to happen. You might have a loved one undergoing an operation, and have to sit around in the waiting room all day. Pack some food and drink to save you money at the cafeteria. A loved one or dear friend might be arriving from a trip and their plane has been delayed, leaving you at the airport all day. Whatever you are doing, make sure you have a book to read or some puzzles to while away the time, just in case you get held up somewhere. Aries lovers will want to get away to a private location where you can whisper sweet nothings in each other's ears, but you will have to wait for that, too.

7. MONDAY. Expressive. The Moon moves into your sign of Aries today, placing you in the spotlight and give you added emotional energy. Taking a leadership role will be easy for you now, but use your charm and magnetism wisely. Creative pursuits will be right up your alley, and give you a forum for your imagination and sensitive energy. Check around and see if there are any drama groups in your area. Then take the drama out of your life and put it on the stage for a change. Beware of gambling if you have a touch of addiction in this area. A little bit of luck to start with can end up in a major loss if you don't practice restraint. Go shopping and spend it on yourself.

8. TUESDAY. Limiting. Partnered Aries might have a disagreement with your partner over your personal views on an important issue, and the matter is such that you can't agree to disagree. Sit down and write down each other's points and work out a compromise between you. It will be an exercise that will come in handy again in the future. Your responsibilities can get in the way of your plans and push your buttons a bit. Try not to explode or you will blow something really important. A contract could be canceled or fall through and leave you back at square one. You won't mope, though. You'll more than likely start planning something bigger and better to take its place.

9. WEDNESDAY. Beneficial. Today the Moon is part of a powerful cosmic pattern that points to success in money or creativity or career, or a combination of all three. Be confident and put your best foot forward in all endeavors, and you can't fail! A legal matter can be settled out of court in your favor, saving you heavy costs. If you are worried about your level of debt, now is a good time to talk to your bank manager and see if you can roll all your debt together into one low-interest loan. Aries sportspeople will find that a new exercise program is working wonders on your technique and stamina, pushing you into the top level of competition. An award for achievement could be in the offing.

10. THURSDAY. Winning. Today's Full Moon in Taurus shines its light on your house of money, self-worth, and possessions. An income boost can do wonders for your comfort and lifestyle choices. If you work out a budget now, you can get on top of all your problems in no time. An investment made a fortnight ago can come to fruition and pay out better than you had expected. A powerful contact in the financial sector could give you some sage advice, and it might almost verge on insider trading; be careful what you do with it. An artistic project could be almost finished, and you are already receiving bids to buy your work before you had even considered whether it is worth anything. Smile, you are worth it.

11. FRIDAY. Helpful. Think before you speak should be your motto for today. Your ruling planet Mars has just moved into Virgo, your house of work and health. So you will throw yourself into working hard and getting things done. At this time you might start to think about starting your own business, which will enable you to benefit from your hard work. But before you go to the banks, spend time researching the type of business and the prospective income to make sure it is a promising investment. If your health has been less than satisfactory lately, now you will want to do something about it and give up your addiction to the wrong foods. Smokers can decide to quit and start an exercise regimen.

12. SATURDAY. Diverse. A conflict between your heart and your head can make it very hard to make a decision. Your lover could propose marriage, but you are unsure of issues such as cultural differences, age differences, and stepchildren. There is nothing wrong with taking your time and deferring a decision until you can be sure, so don't rush in and cry later. Better to be safe than sorry. Some Aries are bound to be heading off overseas, and you should spend some time on your list of things to pack. Speak to someone you know who has traveled and get the benefit of their experience. An Internet romance could be blossoming so much that you are lacking sunlight. Get outside for a while.

13. SUNDAY. Cheerful. Good friends and loving moments will make this a day to remember. Wherever you are heading today, take your camera to capture moments you can savor for a lifetime. Very adventurous outings such as skydiving, bungee jumping, or deep-sea diving could be on the agenda. If you are taking the teenage kids along, be prepared for extra nervous jitters. This day has a very spiritual aspect to it for everybody, and you may enjoy a religious or philosophical meeting or a class in metaphysics or intuitive healing. Your perception will be moved outside the box and open up many new possibilities in life. A concert can transport you to another realm.

14. MONDAY. Eventful. If you didn't cover all your bases yesterday, you will be faced with upsets today. The powers that be have been watching, so hopefully you have been discreet. If not, you may face censure. Nowadays, forwarding humorous e-mail to your colleagues at work can cost you your position. No matter how strong the urge to share the mirth, hit the delete button instead. Don't let your heart rule your head in a major decision. You need to think about the pros and cons, and not jump wildly into something you haven't looked into. A friend might call you to ask for a favor that you can't give. Don't feel guilty. Just be honest and up front, and don't risk your valuables or your friendship.

15. TUESDAY. Auspicious. Aries house hunters could be pleasantly surprised to find a piece of real estate that is everything you wanted at an affordable price. Get your finances organized and make an application! There may be some problem with communications. Whether it is your Internet or phone service or something worded wrongly, be diligent in whatever you are doing. Take care out on the roads also. Being too busy talking or with your head in the clouds is not a good way to drive a car, and you may be a little accident-prone over the next few weeks. Love is definitely in the air, and you could be out on a date instead of home in bed. No matter how enraptured you are, look after your health now.

16. WEDNESDAY. Varied. Don't expect anything to happen until after lunch, and you will be well prepared for the day. Spend the morning hours organizing yourself and do a few things about the home. Your mother might need a hand and if you can, give her one. She will be so appreciative. A family secret can come out that makes you laugh and see your family in a different light, adding a touch of eccentricity and adventure to your lineage. The pace will pick up as the day progresses, and you could get run off your feet. If you are organizing a social event, you can experience some problems concerning the venue and the entertainment, so make sure you have a backup plan for efficiency and insurance.

17. THURSDAY. Creative. Whatever problems you experience, you will be able to come up with alternatives that seem to be better than the original situations. Aries parents can notice that your child has a talent that should be developed and encouraged. Before you sign up with a local school, check out all the options. You might find a scholarship that will pay for training far in excess of what you can afford and give them a running start; they just have to fit the eligibility criteria. Aries teachers could decide to register for a course to extend your teaching abilities and give your earning capacity a boost, as well as make your work more rewarding. A candlelit dinner would be a perfect end to the day.

18. FRIDAY. Mystical. Nothing may be as it seems, and you could feel like Alice going down the rabbit hole. While waiting for a bus or taxi, an old friend may pick you up and take you somewhere other than where you were going, and you find that it is the right place for you to be. Everything happens for a reason, and the universe has you under its wing. Just let go and enjoy the ride. A romance can get serious with talk of long-term commitment and combining your resources; take some time to talk over expectations about the roles and rights each of you has within this first. Hard work could be rewarded with a promotion that will allow you to have more control over your work and the hours you keep.

19. SATURDAY. Energetic. The emotional Moon and active Mars are both in Virgo, your sector of work, service, and health. So you will feel better sticking to your daily routine no matter what interesting alternatives come your way. A health regimen can be starting to show benefits as your energy levels grow. Your enjoyment in working and getting things done will be very satisfying. Lunch at a local café might prove to be a beneficial social outing, putting you in touch with someone you haven't seen for a while and perhaps letting you meet someone new who will be helpful to you in the future. Some kids might be trying to find homes for their puppies and you can't resist, but do try to be sensible.

20. SUNDAY. Comforting. A bit of housecleaning can be the best thing you've done for a while, making room for you to redecorate and reorganize. Don't be afraid to throw things out. The extra space will free up your thought processes as much as your domestic space. A shopping trip can be enjoyable, but try to leave all the excess sugars on the shelves and buy some wholesome food for home cooking. And don't forget to get a sensible cookbook. New recipes from exotic places will inspire you, giving your digestive system a pleasant change from your usual diet. Young Aries looking for a good career path might check out military service.

21. MONDAY. Confrontational. Differing views on your life's direction between you and your significant other can make for unpleasantness. Avoiding each other won't fix it, although it will give you time to think. Agree to disagree and brainstorm the problem over the coming week. Looking for areas of compromise and being willing to understand the other person's viewpoint will help. You might do a bit of self-analysis and review memories of the past, especially after visiting your grandparents and hearing their version of events that preceded your arrival. It is a wonderful thing to benefit from their wisdom. You are sure to find peace by day's end.

22. TUESDAY. Tense. Negative emotions can color your day and make everything look much worse than it really is. Take heart. This is just a state of mind and it will pass. Domestic problems and feelings of guilt about some past event can bring you down. But by sticking to your commitments and not letting anyone down, you will feel much better at the close of the day. This is an excellent time to make reforms in your life and turn over a new leaf. If you think you may have been selfish or resentful or unforgiving, now you can start to let go and forgive. Don't try to go it alone. Enlist the support of friends, counselors, and elders. Some faith in yourself can help, too.

23. WEDNESDAY. Passionate. You are attracted to strong people who have the courage of their convictions. A new acquaintance can march right into your heart and mind with these attributes. Before you know it, you have accepted their invitation, and passion could be in control of whatever happens next. A desire to make changes in your personal and domestic sphere can result in cleaning, repairing, and reorganizing things in your home. Obsession is also another aspect to the day. Be careful not to set a goal and become so obsessed about it you lose track of everything else. You have plenty of support now, and it is a great time to sort out your finances with an expert.

24. THURSDAY. Reflective. In your emotional encounters with other people you can experience moods and feelings that are quite different from the usual and that give you food for thought. Communicative Mercury turns retrograde now, which makes it harder to express ideas and feelings. Plans and appointments can be held up, be delayed or fall through. This state of affairs will last until Mercury goes direct after December 13. Travel plans can experience problems and have to be changed, but defer making any alternative decision until Mercury is direct. It is a good time for study and reflection; keep a journal for jotting down your thoughts and ideas.

25. FRIDAY. Refreshing. This morning's New Moon in Sagittarius brings a fresh, panoramic vision and a warm fiery time with plenty of optimism floating around. It's a great time to begin projects that are focused on spiritual or educational endeavors. It provides the chance to listen to your own truth and to hear what others have to say without judgment. Meeting people from totally different backgrounds can reveal another aspect of the world, and even the most trivial encounter can be a positive learning experience. The motivation for study could push you in the area of science, technical disciplines, astrology, or other branches of the occult. The more exciting the topic, the more actively you'll pursue it.

26. SATURDAY. Effervescent. This new discipline that you have been thinking of starting, or one that you have already begun, should bring you a great deal of pleasure. This intense energy will help you discover great truths about yourself over time, but today it's best to stay calm and composed. Loving Venus now moves into Capricorn, your solar sector of career. Venus here brings favorable circumstances to your business and professional life, attracting persons and circumstances that facilitate your work. This aspect can involve you in artistic matters such as design, layout work, office redecorating, even public relations for the purpose of making your business or the company look more attractive.

27. SUNDAY. Intense. Emotional experiences are likely to affect you deeply, mostly because they will hit on a nerve that goes to the deepest part of your psyche. If you happen to be with your parents, you could be in for some typical family blackmail or manipulation, so you might want to slip quietly away before there is a scene. Secret plans can be revealed and change everything, leaving you with a sense of betrayal. Or it could be you who upsets another. But once the cards are on the table, you can all come to terms with the facts. So don't lose your cool. You may have domestic chores waiting for you, but they are probably the last thing you feel like doing. Go out and have fun.

28. MONDAY. Enjoyable. Your finances could be in good shape, making it easy to plan lots of fun and outings. You may be having quite a few guests for a celebration over the coming days. You will want to be lavish and have beautiful food and music, but try not to go over the top and become ostentatious. Politics could be your game at the moment. If you are running for office or working for someone who is, you will be out on the road drumming up votes and enjoying the high energy and social activity of the campaign trail. Some Aries may be planning to go into partnership and run a joint venture, giving you and your partner lots to work on together.

29. TUESDAY. Benevolent. Work for a volunteer organization could be very rewarding for you at the moment, besides making some new friends. If you are out of town on business or traveling overseas, your emotional security may depend on you contacting family and friends at home. Visit an Internet café and get online. Feeling lucky can make you generous. A good friend who is having difficulties might get a real hand up from you right now. Even if it is just emotional support, you have plenty to give. Don't spend more money than you can afford. If you have to reach for your credit card, think again, and unless you are purchasing a necessity, say no and save on interest.

30. WEDNESDAY. Social. Your workplace can get really busy today with all sorts of representatives, human resource people, or health and safety inspectors interviewing and checking up on management. A new workplace agreement might be coming your way, so talk to somebody who can give you some tips on maximizing your benefits. A lunchtime get-together can be scheduled to send off a coworker. No matter how much fun you are having, don't drink too much or you will regret it. Interesting people are being drawn to you, but use your common sense and don't let someone's unusual image and charisma blind you to their real nature. Singles might stay single for a while longer.

DECEMBER

1. THURSDAY. Healing. Past actions may catch up with you today. It's best that others do not observe your activities, either because they concern secret matters or because you'll accomplish more working alone. Business or personal power plays emerge, so it's a good time to center yourself. Focus your energy to avoid being used by psychic vampires, and steer clear of psychological manipulators. You may decide to start a class in yoga, tai chi, or meditation to explore and develop your inner strengths as well as take care of the spiritual side of your being. You may even consider a retreat. With the added incentive for spiritual discipline, you can discover a lot about yourself.

2. FRIDAY. Deflating. It may seem as though you can't please anyone, but don't take the foul moods of others personally. The demands of others may place a good deal of pressure on you. If you have to deal with in-laws today, it will be impossible to measure up, so don't even try. Sometimes you just have to relax and let things be. A study commitment can stop you from doing your housework and interrupt your routine. If ever you have felt regrets over taking on this extra workload, it is now. But look to the future and remind yourself of the dreams that can be fulfilled if you are prepared to struggle for it now. Start a journal and give it all your secret sorrows to keep.

3. SATURDAY. Stressful. Deadlines and delays can dog your day and inflate your frustration levels. If you are not feeling well, you would be wise to forsake a day's pay and stay at home and relax. A relationship breakdown could be taking its toll on you, and it might be a good idea to see a counselor if you are starting to worry. There are soothing natural remedies that can help. But if you are taking medication, you need to check these remedies out. If you are still in a relationship, but secretly want out and don't know how to go about it, discuss the process to get clear on basic issues and to bolster your decisiveness.

4. SUNDAY. Pressured. The moody Moon whizzes into your own sign of Aries and threatens to influence your emotional stability. People around you can drive you crazy with their obsessive behavior and demands on your time. Don't lose your cool, though. Simply get outside or away and enjoy being independent. Work around the home can give you a creative outlet to expend pent-up energy. When you are hitting a nail with a hammer, you can consciously let somebody have it in your mind. Sports or an exercise regimen are great pastimes for you today. Aries dieters may have to watch what you eat and drink to placate emotional insecurities.

5. MONDAY. Motivating. Aries artisans and show people can reap the benefits of hard work now. When your work goes on display, the excitement of the crowd adds to the atmosphere of success. Politicians and public speakers may get the opportunity to build a reputation for yourselves and receive extra engagements this month. A strong desire to travel and have adventures can turn your interest toward studying topics such as philosophy and spirituality. These give you the opportunity to travel in your mind, making unusual and exciting discoveries along the way. For those of you who are stuck at home, an adventure novel or movie can take you away from yourself.

6. TUESDAY. Expansive. Material resources look to be growing with the purchase of a big-ticket item. Whether it is a new flat-screen TV or a luxury car, the boost to your ego is obvious. An invitation to an important social event can give your reputation a lift and send you out to the shops to find a trendy outfit. Or someone drop-dead gorgeous who you have been eyeing for a while might ask you out and put you on cloud nine. Whatever happens, your heart can feel like it will burst with joy. Spread your joy to others. You may not be going out anywhere tonight, but that doesn't mean you and yours can't celebrate being alive.

7. WEDNESDAY. Enthusiastic. An important assignment can give you the scope to express yourself freely and creatively. You can show a special talent for your particular area of expertise, and be rewarded with a promotion. Some of you might decide to become a teacher so that you can make money passing on the skills of something you love doing. A business lunch could turn into a fiasco, when you discover there is a language barrier and you are all trying to use sign language without knowing what you are doing. Design work is right up your alley at the moment. You might decide to re-decorate your home and add value for future sale.

8. THURSDAY. Uneven. Your mind can think up all sorts of crazy thoughts. If you are waiting for a loved one to come home, you may be climbing the walls with worry. The worry should be all for nothing, though. Much to your relief your loved one, perhaps a youngster, will arrive home alive and well, although it could be rather late. A good friend may be getting lost in a haze of drinking and drugging. There is not much you can do to help, unless they ask for it. Offer relevant literature for them to read, or suggest a therapy group or rehab where they will be removed from temptation. That's the best you can do. An interest in spiritual matters can be your best medicine right now.

9. FRIDAY. Demanding. An exam can test your knowledge and your memory recall. Take a vitamin tablet and put rosemary oil on your handkerchief to help jump-start your memory. Your mind can be on a thousand and one things, everything but what you are doing, so do take care that it is safe. An overseas contact might get lost, and after you spend hours trying to trace them, you have to admit you've lost track of them. Decide to buy an address book and keep track of numbers and e-mails by hand. Hard copy is a lot harder to lose. No matter how much you try, you may not get a lot done today. If you are trying to give up smoking and having a difficult time, try hypnosis.

10. SATURDAY. Active. The Full Moon in Gemini lights up your solar sector of communication, promising lot of good contacts. Aries people will be at your speediest, out and about in your car crisscrossing town in your hunt for good shopping or a piece of the action. Holdups and delays in traffic might mean you miss the things you are after and the people you want to see, so have a backup plan if everything fails. Some of you might get out of town and visit good friends in an old country house. Enjoy lively conversation and rapid flow of ideas. Or you may find a lovely out-of-the-way place, having a night to remember with your lover.

11. SUNDAY. Tricky. The Moon glides into Cancer, your fourth house of home and family. If you are not at home as part of a happy family, you are probably out visiting a family member or getting involved with your parents even though you would rather be at home. There are signs of power struggles or emotional manipulation. You will have to watch your temper or, regardless of what underhandedness is going on, you will get the blame. Partnered Aries might be rekindling a romance, finding renewed love and romance to restart the fire. Go out on a date, explore your neighborhood, find a romantic restaurant, and act like teenagers on a first date. Young lovers could decide to move in together.

12. MONDAY. Invigorating. A new beginning is indicated, perhaps a new business venture or an interest in a sport. Put plans in motion, and the stars are on your side. Make sure your household insurance is in effect; check your home for possible fire hazards. Watch your step to prevent falls, cuts, and mishaps around the house, and avoid angry domestic scenes. Give yourself a chance to regenerate today by taking a brisk walk and enjoying the sights and sounds of nature. A little bit of heavenly seclusion under your own roof will be good for the soul now. Family and work commitments can collide, and this might be the time to take the in-laws up on their offer to babysit and protect your income.

13. TUESDAY. Sensitive. Whether or not you are alone, you may feel it today. Communication within your relationship could be such that you don't feel you are being heard and your needs are not being met. This feeling is probably only fleeting, but for a few hours you may just feel like you are drowning in your sorrows. This approach to an emotional problem usually only makes things worse, not better. Aries singles might feel that you will never meet anybody, but you know deep down this is not true, so look on the bright side and put a smile on your face. The mere act of moving those specific muscles lifts your mood and before you know it, you'll be smiling of your own accord.

14. WEDNESDAY. Positive. Your horizons look brighter and broader, and the possibilities are all very interesting. Travel and adventure may be on your mind, or a message from an old friend may suggest the chance of romance and lots of fun. Aries students can be inspired by a new teacher, and start to get an interest in your subjects and renewed vigor for achieving your ends. A backlog of work could put a damper on some of your plans, but your energy is high and you won't waste any time finishing off the task at hand. An exercise program is likely to be working, and you might have a personal trainer who has fashioned the perfect workout for your needs. Looking trim, taut, and terrific, you'll find the night is yours.

15. THURSDAY. Varied. Shopping for presents can be lots of fun. You are sure to find some great little sentimental treasures that

won't break the bank and yet will touch the recipient's heart. Someone fascinating could keep crossing your path. Eventually one of
you makes a move, but allow a slow beginning; rushing will only kill
the romance. A gathering of friends can be fun, although someone
might drink too much and make a scene. Make sure it isn't you. You
may accompany your significant other to a work function and have
the time of your life, despite not wanting to go. If you are not feeling one hundred percent, have a nourishing meal, get to bed early,
and beat the bug.

16. FRIDAY. Bright. Informative Mercury is now moving forward, freeing up all contracts, agreements, and business deals and
allowing you to get back to normal. The purchase of a property
might go ahead and give you plenty of work to do, especially
rounding up the finances. An inheritance may include a business,
or investments that give you extra income, which will come in very
handy this season. This is also a perfect time to finalize your holiday plans and check your reservations. Send your gifts and cards
now, and get the whole family involved in putting up your decora-
tions for the festive season; the atmosphere it creates never ceases
to inspire all ages.

17. SATURDAY. Good. The focus at the moment is on how you
can improve yourself and help others. It will be easier to pay closer
attention to your nutrition, plus you should have more energy for
exercise. Relationships with coworkers may become more active as
the emphasis turns to your work environment and your responsibilities to others. You might want to brighten up your normal routine
and add some spice to your surroundings. Ask a few people over for
dinner and play party games for fun and laughter. You might even
try your hand at matchmaking. Keep an eye on your pets, as one
could easily escape and have you and the neighborhood out search-
ing for hours. Keep your doors locked, too.

18. SUNDAY. Fair. Today's energy can be romantic and exciting
for some, but for others it may be a headache. The paradox is that
you can get more enjoyment out of doing things for other people
than you will get when trying to please yourself. Give yourself over
to whatever the day brings. Practice love and harmony, even if you
don't feel it. A partner may be costing you an arm and a leg. Every
time they go shopping, you start worrying. If you find that you can't
talk to them about it, simply open your own bank account and keep
yourself sane. Competition in your career sector can have a positive effect on your efficiency. The more people try to outdo you, the
better you become.

19. MONDAY. Uncertain. Despite your best intentions, not much will move forward today. Indecisiveness can dog you whatever you are doing. Put your faith in the hands of a power greater than you, and trust that the universe will do a better job than you have. Some lucky Aries singles may have two gorgeous possibles vying for your attention. But no matter how good it makes you feel, don't try to string both persons along or you might lose both. Your busy schedule at work can mean lots of overtime and a fat paycheck. But with the silly season just around the corner, you probably have more bills than usual. What goes around comes around; at least you can have a great time.

20. TUESDAY. Fortunate. Today's Scorpio Moon gives you an edge in business and finance, and a lucky break can come your way. An insurance payout can more than compensate for your lost items and see you laughing all the way to the bank. This is a good time to push forward on matters that are important to you. You will have the extra magnetism you need to bring others to your side. If you stay focused, you can make progress in personal areas. Close relationships can benefit if you open up and share your feelings. The pace of life is picking up, so try not to get too caught up in the stress side of the holiday season. Let your gifts be just gifts, not a measure of your self-worth.

21. WEDNESDAY. Hectic. Today's tempo is upbeat and beyond the norm, bringing situations that need snap decisions without enough information to know what is what. Expect to have to organize a large group of people, or to have to find consensus on a subject among people who are widely different. You will love the social aspect to the day, though. Some interesting ideas and information can give you food for thought for weeks to come. Venus, the planet of love and harmony, now transits Aquarius, your solar sector of friends, hopes, and wishes. Venus here is a real bonus for you, indicating a peacemaking role in social gatherings and community meetings.

22. THURSDAY. Expressive. Whatever comes along will tweak your enthusiasm and your ability to talk your way out of anything. The emphasis moves toward articulating your goals as well as upholding family traditions now that the Sun has moved into Capricorn, your solar house of outer security. You might want to contact elderly members of the family to remind them of holiday plans. Make sure older loved ones have all their needs met. Although you might have a wild party to attend this evening, you will rest better if you know that you have fulfilled your duty. Placing presents under the tree could be a problem, especially if the young recipients are likely to peek and poke.

23. FRIDAY. Emotional. Your immune system could be down a little. If you go out in the cold, make sure you bundle up to protect against a chill. Lower energy can lower your tolerance levels, so it would be best if you could avoid overdoing things. Take it easy if you can. If you have to live in the fast lane, take the time for a cup of coffee or tea and the newspaper. Give your mind a break from the continual chatter of organizing and worrying. A wild after-work party may not be worth attending. Anything might happen, and the consequences will have to be faced every day at work. Caroling in the neighborhood is a great spectacle for the kids.

24. SATURDAY. Reassuring. Last-minute shopping is senseless, although you probably will duck in for the excitement of it all and pick up a couple of bargains. Today's New Moon in Capricorn starts a new lunar cycle focusing on underused talents and resources. Let go of objects, activities, values, and people that you no longer need. That way you make room for what you want to come next. Tune in to your elders this Christmas Eve when you all gather around to celebrate your spiritual life and the eternal life of your family's traditions. You will gain guidance and hear wisdom that is priceless. The New Moon heralds the start of a whole new phase in your life, so make your plans carefully.

25. SUNDAY. Merry Christmas! Happy and benevolent vibes give this day a lively and enjoyable feel. Socializing will be full of laughter. There might be intervals amid the noise and bustle when you stop to rejoice in life and love and the mystery of it all. A romantic interlude would add some magic and mystery of its own. Aries people look set to be playing host and perfectly executing the mundane process of preparation and service. You may have a few tense moments with a guest who wants to take over and get in your way. Don't let it fluster you. Simply take control.

26. MONDAY. Relaxed. Whatever your plans, after the responsibility of yesterday, you can feel free and ready to party. Relatives or friends could be staying over and invade your morning rituals unintentionally. Don't let that trouble you. Most of all don't feel that you have to clean up; by lunchtime you won't care and everything will be fine again. Your partner might say the wrong thing and some harsh words may be spoken. Forgiveness won't be long in coming, and making up will be wonderful. Post-holiday sales could seem attractive until you see the crowds at the stores. Go for a walk in peaceful surroundings instead, keep your money in the bank, and prepare for more socializing tonight.

27. TUESDAY. Informative. Interesting information and gossip will entertain and enliven social intercourse. Enjoy a lively debate with friends, neighbors, and acquaintances about matters that affect you all. If you have a problem or situation that you find difficult to handle, now is a good time to talk with a sympathetic friend and get the benefit of their unbiased viewpoint. Of course, for the talk to be beneficial, you have to be prepared to listen. Luck in love is indicated in today's stars. Singles might be pleased at a meeting of old friends to find a few good-looking strangers there. Aries in a committed union can come up with a few surprises to spice up your love life.

28. WEDNESDAY. Mystical. This is an excellent time for studies that can raise your consciousness. You can put yoga, occult metaphysics, spiritualism, and mysticism into practice in your everyday life now. You can get involved in movements and activities for the betterment of humanity or the environment, and work selflessly toward these ends. Make sure when donating any of your hard-earned cash to a deserving cause that you leave yourself enough to live on. You are likely to be a sucker for a sob story. Listen to your intuition first and foremost, not anyone's tale of woe. Be discerning in love. Don't sacrifice your freedom and security for a conditional relationship.

29. THURSDAY. Intense. Intense experiences can force a personal transformation, especially if you are required to stand up for what is right and true against unfair manipulation or the abuse of power. Arguments and disagreements could wear thin, so don't stay around to fight; the sounds of silence in isolation will be music to your ears. Start a painting or music course. Enjoy entertainment that doesn't need anybody's agreement or input at all. You might opt to stay home and do your own thing rather than go out partying with the usual social set. Aries singles are likely to have a new romance to entrance and delight, conjuring up the dream of living happily ever after.

30. FRIDAY. Competitive. Expect the unexpected as the Sun clashes with Pluto. Tempers may flare at work, so keep a low profile. Your health is very much connected to your emotions today; the more calm and centered you can be, the better you will feel. If you allow yourself to be pulled in all different directions, by evening you will have the migraine headache of the year. Personal soul-searching and analyzing your past have been painful, but they have also opened the way for deeper connections. You may be afraid to take the next step, but it really is the right time. Even if all you do is say hello to a coworker you would like to get to know better, you have made progress.

31. SATURDAY. Variable. The Moon slips into your sign of Aries, and gives your personal identity a bit of a shake-up as it moves past erratic Uranus. Emotional issues will get out of hand if you try to deal with them in an intellectual landscape. Emotions are not rational, so it is very hard to rationalize them. Avoid offensive people and you can get through the day unscathed. There is a growing excitement in the air as you anticipate evening plans. Shopping for an eye-catching outfit can turn up some zany fashions and transform your image. Do be careful of accidents; amid the excitement and emotional vigor don't let your guard slip.

ARIES
NOVEMBER–DECEMBER 2010

November 2010

1. MONDAY. Satisfying. Discussions concerning politics and religion often lead to heated arguments, so it may be wise to avoid such subjects unless you want to get caught up in a dispute. There are better uses of your time, especially in helping a partner manage financial affairs for your mutual benefit. Negotiations for a loan or new investment should clear legal hurdles, and official documentation can be put in good order. Make sure all details are exact and precise. Serving a delicious meal is one way to win somebody's heart. Cooking up a culinary storm can be the appetizer for an eve ning of loving passion. Someone close who is returning from a trip will appreciate a warm welcome.

2. TUESDAY. Restricting. Well-laid plans can hit hidden snags. There's no need to blame anyone, or yourself for that matter, because these will be problems that no one could prepare for or see coming. The best approach to obstacles and difficulties is to be flexible, proceeding one step at a time as events unfold. If expecting a rebate or payment, there could be delays due to further institutional red tape. It's possible you weren't fully informed of the maze of requirements that the pro cess entailed. An appropriate adviser can help you deal with such complex matters. A chance encounter with a person you thought was out of town may lead to a deep and revealing conversation as you compare notes.

3. WEDNESDAY. Testing. Schedule meetings that involve the most important matters. If going on interviews for jobs or a promotion, dress the part and be ready for rigorous questioning. If you have the appropriate experience and an impressive record, this should be a mere formality. However, there will be little tolerance for an inadequate per for mance or in sufficient training or experience. Prepare well and you'll be able to handle what ever is thrown at you. If you need any type of professional advice, this is the right day to find quality assistance and useful counsel. Partners and lovers expect affection and attention. They need to feel you're truly committed to the relationship.

4. THURSDAY. Heartening. A partnership that has been growing apart can now be brought closer once again. Slowly but surely, warmth and passion are returning to an intimate connection, as you discover the depth of your feelings for each other. Singles may be drawn into a more lasting affair than was initially intended. Married couples can rekindle emotions that were there in the first place, renewing the original attraction. The heart has its mysterious ways, weaving magic beyond your control. Some Aries may get caught in the unenviable dilemma of having to choose between two people. Make a definite decision. Any deception on your part will be unmasked, possibly leaving you empty-handed.

5. FRIDAY. Happy. To night's Scorpio New Moon presages an opportunity for profound heart-to-heart sharing. Your love for a special person is unmistakable, and you may be making plans for a public declaration of commitment. There could be a bonus in your partner's pay or a windfall inheritance that allows you to travel together on a dream vacation or a honeymoon getaway. Don't be surprised if you receive a gift from a long-standing admirer who wants to show appreciation. Be gracious about accepting this generosity. There's no need to be shy or embarrassed in any way if you truly deserve what you are given. Old debts could come back to haunt you.

6. SATURDAY. Revealing. When someone wants to share their troubles with you, try to be as sympathetic and caring as possible. It's not every day that you hear the details of another person's private life, and you should keep what you are told close to your chest. You are trusted, and confidentiality will be expected. It might not just be an episode of exceptional emotional bonding that may occur. There could be a revelation concerning a technical invention or innovative pro cess that has been under wraps until now. Industrial espionage and trade secrets are in the mix, and you should proceed with utmost care in using what you know or discover. Any backroom wheeling and dealing must be within the limits of the law.

7. SUNDAY. Rejuvenating. It's time to break out of a sustained period of interpersonal contact. You may be feeling claustrophobic and pressured by so much emotional intensity at close quarters.

While these experiences and situations are far from over, there is now an opportunity to get away from it all. Consider planning to travel overseas so that you can disappear for a while. What ever you're leaving behind will either be waiting on your return or may even follow you. If you really want to be left alone, go incognito and don't leave any forwarding address or contact. At the very least, take a break by journeying out of town, or go to a large public event where you will feel anonymous in the crowd.

8. MONDAY. Favorable. If an exam or the culmination of a course is approaching, you'll need to study in an undisturbed environment. This is a time for a thorough review of everything that's been taught in order to make that knowledge your own. Focus also on researching and writing a report or pre sen ta tion that is soon to be delivered publicly. You're sure to locate the right information that's needed to get your views accepted. Wanderlust might be in the blood, and you'll enjoy browsing the Net for great travel deals to exotic destinations that are off the beaten track and not yet in mainstream vacation packages. To night you may become lost in a gripping novel.

9. TUESDAY. Successful. Major moves are happening on the work front, and you'll need to give it your best to make the most of new opportunities. Ambitions that may have been building for the last couple of years are reaching a key point. This is the time to impress management with your potential, so that you can take the next step up the career ladder. If you're running a business of your own, effective advertising is essential to growth and success. What ever you do or sell needs to become a house hold name. This is a period to put into practice what you've been working hard to achieve. This significant career period should not be wasted. Others believe in you and support your aims, which really helps.

10. WEDNESDAY. Pressured. You need a break from a person who has been asking or expecting too much. Being responsible for others, or trying to carry their load, may have become a challenge over the last year or so, since Saturn entered your opposite sign of Libra. However, you can only do so much for anyone else; the rest is up to them. Walk away for the moment and focus on your own priorities and pressing responsibilities. If a friend needs ongoing support, suggest that they seek professional help. Achievement and success have a cutthroat element presently, and you need to be all-out competitive to win. The eve ning offers welcome relaxation with a trusted companion, unwinding from the day's stress.

11. THURSDAY. Resourceful. Help might come from unexpected sources, giving you a boost and putting you ahead of the game. Don't look in the obvious places for what you need or want, especially at work. Somebody may be nice and say what you want to hear, but they'll probably prove in effec tive or unwilling to do anything for you. You may need to call on a favor from a person who is far away, even overseas. Although they're at a distance, they can still be of great ser vice. As much as you want to please a certain person, it is apt to be difficult to know what to do for them. It may be worth taking a chance on a really different approach, using imagination to come up with a whole new way of relating to them.

12. FRIDAY. Cooperative. Teamwork should be solid and productive, making this a starred time to coordinate efforts to get a major project rolling. Beginning to turn a plan or vision into reality will require a clear assignment of roles and a set of strategic goals and associated milestones. Working hand in hand with experienced, capable individual allows much to be set in motion for future achievement. Being part of an effective group should be very satisfying; you'll feel more comfortable with others rather than trying to go it alone. The company of a dear friend is invaluable, offering honest and direct communication without the fear of disapproval or negative consequences.

13. SATURDAY. Social. Your hopes for the day may not coincide with those of your partner, who may disapprove of your intentions to go off your friends. It shouldn't be difficult to divide time between a personal social outing and intimate sharing. The best plan is to get out early, enjoying a vibrant network of friends and acquaintances. No doubt there will be a few relaxing diversions, but don't get carried away. Then take your mate or date out for dinner or to a party, making sure to give quality attention. You won't find it hard to shower them with compliments, as they're sure to be at their attractive best. Singles may move on from one unsuitable companion to another more promising candidate.

14. SUNDAY. Secluded. Despite the temptations of the wider world, with all its entertainment and activities, it seems wiser today to resist. You may have good intentions for an adventure, but it could turn out to be too wild or stressful. Back away from trouble and obviously dangerous people or situations. Nothing will be gained by heroics or confrontation. The hustle of public events is apt to be annoying, and you'll appreciate seeking sanctuary in a secluded place. Today will test your ability to rest and relax, instead of pointlessly burning more energy. Make yourself unavailable by turning off the phone, shutting the blinds, and locking the door.

15. MONDAY. Sensitive. You may feel inclined to take the day off. Recuperation may be wise if you've been extra busy lately, burning the candle at both ends. Part of catching up could involve putting accounts in order and checking that your bud get is on track. If you must go to work, the prevailing mood will be sensitive and solitary. Quiet interaction with a few close people who are tuned in will be enough involvement for the day. If you know something that could help a person who is currently lost or confused, be generous in offering valuable assistance. Deep personal issues and spiritual interests can be all-consuming.

16. TUESDAY. Lucky. Aries people have experienced a lucky streak that's unpredictable but wonderful when it strikes. Today is another one of those days offering exceptional good fortune and happy blessings. Whether you believe in guardian angels or good fairies, you seem to have them on your side at the moment. However, don't rely on luck and take foolish risks, then hope for last-minute salvation. Use your psychic awareness to develop the intuition to take best advantage of this extraordinary energy. Go with the flow, and the best outcomes are assured. By the afternoon or eve ning you'll be brought back to reality and will need to handle a challenge or two.

17. WEDNESDAY. Mixed. Expect criticism or disapproval from a judgmental person who can't help finding fault. The best response is to hear them out and then get on with what needs doing. Battling such types, who won't ever admit to being wrong, is a waste of precious time. They may simply be envious of your ability and achievements. Meanwhile, you've probably got ambitious plans that should be put to good use. There's plenty of enthusiasm for handling tasks at work, and colleagues will be motivated by your energetic example. Planning the great escape can be an exciting prospect. You might be finalizing tickets and itineraries or even be leaving today.

18. THURSDAY. Balancing. Caring about someone doesn't mean always agreeing with them. Part of the attraction in a relationship is having different styles, opinions, and desires. You'll see this clearly today as you try to find a complementary balance and harmony with your mate or partner. Don't be afraid to stand up for your personal views, needs, and what you most definitely want. Just be fair in allowing the other person to have their say. You might find you're on the same page but coming from opposite directions. There are important lessons to be learned about cooperation; otherwise you might as well be alone. If someone is genuinely unsuitable or disagreeable, let them know.

19. FRIDAY. Fortunate. The focus is on making money, and lots of it. Don't be distracted from putting effort into increasing your income and building net wealth. Business should be profitable, so higher-ups will be well pleased with your additions to the bottom line. You may deserve a bigger slice of the pie as a result; ask and you just might get it. Customers have plenty of cash to spend, so make a persuasive pitch to close the sale. When they buy what they want and you receive payment, everybody's happy. No doubt there will be temptations for you to spend as well. Rather than treating yourself, it would be better to offer a gift of love to the person who's closest to your heart.

20. SATURDAY. Uncertain. You might feel out of touch with what's going on around you. Some days are like that, and even the normal dose of weekend retail therapy may not help you now. It would be far wiser to save your money for a better time, rather than throwing it away on what probably won't satisfy. Good deals or bargains, and value for money, could be hard to find. A planned journey might become more expensive than you bud geted. Reassess the whole trip to see where savings can be made without cutting down on potential enjoyment. Loved ones may seem to be a bottomless pit of expense, especially if you're trying to give them everything they want or ask for.

21. SUNDAY. Variable. Today's Full Moon marks the bridge between the Sun in Scorpio and the Sun in Sagittarius, which starts tomorrow, creating a mixed period of endings and beginnings. Complete current projects before jumping into new ones. Take the fruits of recent efforts and feel good about yourself for what's been accomplished, especially financially. Be honest with yourself if you've spent too much and blown the bud get. There's always the need to enjoy your earnings, so long as you don't go too far and drain your savings. A local trip, either driving, walking, or biking, will blow away mental cobwebs. Interesting sites and encounters will stimulate fresh ideas.

22. MONDAY. Eventful. Straight talking combined with nononsense thinking will make things happen. It will be especially satisfying to pull no punches while delivering what needs to be said. A combustible atmosphere fueled by planets in fiery Sagittarius suits Aries people very well. This is a period when action can do the talking, and no one will be mistaken about your opinions. You might feel like you've got a rocket strapped to you, enabling you to blast around and make rapid transit a reality. If there's somewhere you need to be, now's the time to leave. You'll arrive before you know it. Reports, letters, calls and e-mails that need attention can be dealt with efficiently.

23. TUESDAY. Tricky. Being controversial may have been thrilling lately but can also have tricky consequences and difficult reactions. You may have let the cat out of the bag, starting a chain reaction of events that is spiraling out of control. It's too late to back down now, so you'll need to stand by what ever was said or done. Hopefully you've been wherever you were scheduled to go today, because travel can be temporarily frustrating. Stay put if that fits your plans. Misunderstanding something you've read or been told will create confusion. Don't pass wrong information along the chain of command. Personal romantic moments this eve ning will relieve the day's anxiety and stress. Look for love only at home.

24. WEDNESDAY. Reassuring. Familiar places and faces may be somewhat on the boring side, but at least they're safe and secure. There's a lot to be said for sticking with what you know and staying close to home. There are rocky passages ahead that can't be avoided, but stay in a safe haven today. If you're preparing to leave your current home and relocate, get a head start and don't put off the inevitable any longer. Changing where you live could put stress and strain on a special relationship. Nevertheless, it will be better for all concerned if you try hard to work together. Parents and relatives will stand by you, and can be relied on for essential support during tough times.

25. THURSDAY. Intuitive. Listen to your inner promptings and good instincts regarding everything you intend to do at present. As crazy as it seems, obvious directions and actions may not be best. Aries people find it hard to slow down and consider all perspectives. Trust feelings and intuition to steer you along the best path, although you'll need to tune in carefully to get past noise and static. While others expect one action, you might surprise them by doing something they would never have guessed. Make your living space an eccentric reflection of who you truly are, not a carbon copy of what's in every glossy magazine. Crazy design ideas could work really well when you experiment with a range of options.

26. FRIDAY. Enjoyable. You deserve time out for play. What ever is building up at work will be there next week, when you can deal with it refreshed and geared up for action. Meanwhile, activities and recreation which are a plea sure will do you a world of good. Enjoy the outdoors before winter gets a grip. Explore a wilderness area and have an adventure. Or at least get to a park or playground and relax with sports and games. For Aries who are inclined to arts and hobbies, this is a great time for self-expression. Whether it's music and dance, painting and drawing, or poetry and writing, the flow will be easy and straight from the heart. Even if you're not in the most creative mode, you're sure to enjoy what other people have to offer.

27. SATURDAY. Enthusiastic. If you thought you had energy yesterday, you're in for a blast today. Cast caution to the winds and push the envelope of radical experience. Extreme sports of all variety will get your blood pumping and give you the rush you're seeking. Parents can have fun playing with kids and showing them a really good time. An amusement park or nature adventure will provide just the right antidote for too much tele vi sion and time in front of console games and a computer. Taking a spur-of-the-moment trip may appeal to travelers. It's possible to be out of state or around the world before you think twice about it.

28. SUNDAY. Cautious. In contrast to the last few days, caution pays off during the course of today's events. Rein in that gung-ho attitude and be diligent in all activities, especially where precision or an element of danger is involved. A careless or reckless attitude may lead to regret while the Moon moves through painstaking Virgo. If your attitude is appropriate, the right actions will follow. Going at life like a bull in a china shop just won't work currently. There may be a difficult choice to make between staying home to complete house hold chores or going out to a happening. Either way you win and lose, but perhaps domestic demands can wait if there's a truly special event on tap.

29. MONDAY. Uneasy. Keep your cool, because losing it just won't be worth the trouble. This is yet another day to be extra cautious rather than assuming everything will be okay. A clear head and a watchful eye will give you the early warning signals you need to avoid problems. Road rage can strike, so drive defensively. It's possible to stumble onto an angry scenario that has nothing to do with you personally. Rather than trying to save the day, step aside and overlook other people's problems. Trying to be a good Samaritan may seem ideal in theory but could leave much to be desired when it comes to reality. The best you can do is put your head down, work hard, and mind your own business.

30. TUESDAY. Demanding. Your mate or partner may not leave you alone until they get what they want. That doesn't mean you should immediately give in to what ever is demanded. However, realize that sooner rather than later you'll have little choice because they won't let up. It may be an all-or-nothing proposition instead of something cooperative and mutually agreeable. Let those you love and respect have their way, at least this time. If it becomes a regular habit, though, think twice about giving in or being involved with them. A competitor at work could think they have the drop on you, but bide your time before striking back. This is a period to reassess your real feelings about certain individuals.

December 2010

1. WEDNESDAY. Stimulating. This morning's serious approach will quickly give way to a more lively and exhilarating day. Excitement involving something new and different will give you a lot to think about and plan for. You and your mate or partner might want to consider an overseas vacation. Explore possible destinations on the Internet, and be sure to study the different exchange rates for your money. You are surrounded by some very good people, and their connections will be very helpful for your career. Don't hesitate to ask for help; it will be given willingly and can benefit you greatly right now. Although the year is starting to come to an end, you might feel like your life is just beginning. The sky is the limit.

2. THURSDAY. Rousing. Your emotional nature is very strong at the moment, and interactions abound. People you might never have considered romantically may start to look attractive. This will get your thought pro cesses taking some very interesting detours. By using a blend of intellect and intuition you can unlock secrets, but keep your insights to yourself for now. You need to be totally sure of your findings before revealing them to anyone else. Negotiations should go in your favor. This is a good time to talk to the boss regarding a wage increase or a promotion up the ranks. Refuse advances from an amorous colleague or employer; it will not be profitable for you to get involved.

3. FRIDAY. Helpful. Attempt to broaden your horizons in every way possible, through study, new and unfamiliar experiences, travel, or by meeting people from totally different backgrounds who can reveal another aspect of the world. If you strive to make even the most trivial encounter a positive learning experience, the world and all its possibilities will open up for you. Be careful not to be too possessive of your partner. Even if other people are making eyes at your one and only, trust is a must in a relationship in order for it to be enjoyable and lasting. Feelings and memories from the past may be holding you back. Take time to honor them, and then you will be able to lay them to rest.

4. SATURDAY. Refreshing. A particularly annoying situation should pass, leaving the atmosphere clear and sweet. Relationships will resonate harmoniously with your inner wishes, opening the door for intimacy like never before. If you are traveling overseas, expect to battle through customs; the rest of the trip should flow easily. Visitors from abroad might arrive to stay for a few weeks. Plan some enjoyable sightseeing around your hometown as well as to tourist attractions. Older Aries are likely to be babysitting or doing some holiday shopping. An eve ning of storytelling will be relished by your entire house hold, whether young or old.

5. SUNDAY. Instructive. With your investigative capabilities in high form, you can use them now to avoid the risk of regret or embarrassment later. Appraising a situation at first glance can be difficult, but scratch the surface and a clearer picture will emerge. Today's New Moon brings new beginnings your way and opens up opportunities you never knew existed. In-laws can be more helpful than you expect, offering pearls of wisdom that you should heed. Your mate or partner may need more attention than you have been giving. Stop and take real notice of them, listen to what they are asking, and you won't have any trouble providing the kind of support they want, not just what you think they want.

6. MONDAY. Cautious. Think big may be your motto, but you are in danger of overdoing. You could injure yourself through overexercise, push your accounts into the red by overspending, and sideline your friends and family by exaggerating your own abilities and fortune. The positive impact you have on other people should not be underestimated, but if you take a more humble approach you will be well rewarded. Spiritual matters might give you more satisfaction than material efforts. If you practice keeping still and listening, you might receive insight that seems truly divine. A lunchtime meeting could turn into a gastronome's delight, but guard against drinking too much.

7. TUESDAY. Constructive. An orderly environment will be most conducive to working. Before you settle down to the nitty-gritty, spend a while straightening up your environment, focusing on efficiency and cutting out areas of waste. You may think globally and want to join an environmental group, or start volunteering some of your free time to a local good cause. A coworker who has been lagging behind needs some encouragement and a few tips on making their workload easier. If planning to go into business on your own, there is no time like the present. You will enjoy taking control and making the difficult and critical decisions to determine your own destiny.

8. WEDNESDAY. Motivating. It might be hard to focus on seemingly insignificant tasks of daily living. You are likely to be questioning your path in life and looking for an easier way to reach your goals. If you decide to go back to school, the research and investigative work that goes along with studying will be right up your alley. Success is assured due to your dedication and motivation to achieve your goals and be the best. Someone might be critical of you, always seeming to find the right words to belittle you. Instead of avoiding this person, look on the funny side. You obviously fill their thoughts, probably because they are either jealous or obsessed by you.

9. THURSDAY. Successful. Collaboration and cooperation will be beneficial to achieving artistic success. Associates are important, but just be careful that you don't lower your standards to accommodate someone else's expectations. A friend may be trying to talk you into a business investment, but this may not be a wise step to take. Get some advice and you might be able to help your friend avoid the financial pitfalls they are facing. If a recent loss or upset is occupying your thoughts continually, look for a support group. Grief is a normal part of life, but it can help to meet others who are experiencing similar feelings.

10. FRIDAY. Steady. As a long-term project nears completion, you will find that your reserves of patience and strength have grown since the start. You may be more introspective than usual today. Even though you may have plans for a social get-together, you could be making up all sorts of excuses to back out of it. Relax. By this eve ning you are bound to feel more like socializing and will be glad to go out. You are likely to run into somebody from the past and enjoy reminiscing. Or you could end up paired with a close friend, enjoying an honest and deep heart-to-heart talk that will clear up issues you have been carry ing around for a long time. Taking part in a team sport can be beneficial.

11. SATURDAY. Quiet. Your own company might be all you can cope with today. You may be worn out after the busy week of working hard and putting in that extra effort. Cancel any prior engagements so that you can stay home and put your feet up. You will benefit from the rest more than you realize. Be totally entertained by a blockbuster DVD, not having to think or do anything. Or you might be engrossed in a novel or research and need no excuse to sit down and relax. If you know someone in a nursing home, call or drop by for a chat to let them know that you care and to break up the monotony of institutional life. Maybe take a movie with you and watch it together.

12. SUNDAY. Challenging. Hidden tensions can lead to operating in ways not easy to understand. Today these tensions might come to the surface, making you feel ill at ease and not able to get along well with other people. You need to pay more attention to all that is happening if you want to avoid a crisis of some sort. A close friend might confide in you and then give you the opportunity to discuss your own problems, which should be mutually advantageous. Hang around at home and enjoy puttering around in the yard, trying a new recipe that has your taste buds tingling, or giving your home a facelift with a fresh coat of paint.

13. MONDAY. Lively. A restless night might find you up before dawn, getting extra jobs around the house out of the way before you head off to work. Unemployed Aries who have to visit a government agency should be sure to have all papers in order in time for the appointment. Car trouble is foreseen, so check oil, water, and gas levels at the start of the trip. Have insurance papers in the glove box, just in case. If you must be somewhere at a set time, listen to the local traffic report so you know what roads to avoid. You are likely to be in good spirits throughout the day, and no problem will be too much to overcome.

14. TUESDAY. Expressive. You are bound to make quite an impression wherever you go, so before you leave home put a bit of extra thought into what you will wear. There could be a major decision to be made, but just at the moment you may not be able to make up your mind which way to go. This indecision will only last for a short while. Don't let the dilemma worry you; leave it alone and come back to the problem later in the day or at night. A disagreement with your mate or partner about joint finances is likely this eve ning. Talk honestly, and try not to yell if you get upset because that will not help you to reach an agreement. If you disagree regarding disciplining a child, don't let the youngster overhear your discussion.

15. WEDNESDAY. Harmonious. You are likely to take on more than you have the resources for, but your energy level is also high so you will be able to cope. If you haven't already finalized your holiday plans, do so now. Otherwise you might have to compromise on your choices. When it comes to dealing with other people, you will find that cooperating comes a lot easier than usual. This is a good time to talk to loved ones about ongoing differences of opinions, clearing the air in a loving and compassionate way. Celebrate your love by taking your partner to dinner at a favorite restaurant. You might also stop in a club to hear some music or to enjoy some poetry reading on the way home.

16. THURSDAY. Enjoyable. Apart from minor irritations you shouldn't have any problems at the moment. You may be about to receive a pay raise or a promotion at work. It might be hard to plan a family get-together this year because of travel plans. Try to set the reunion date for a time when everyone will be able to attend. Then you can celebrate simply being together, whenever that happens to be. You might decide on the date while talking on the Internet or via a conference call, enabling you all to be together. You could receive a real boost to your self-esteem when a friend gives you a gift to show how much they appreciate your friendship and generosity.

17. FRIDAY. Indulgent. Your impulsive nature is likely to be in fine form, although this might not be good for your bud get. Unless you can curb this Aries personality trait, you will have to start looking for ways to save money where you can't access it at the drop of a hat, which will give you time to consider your actions and options. Work should be keeping you busy and satisfying your competitive urges, and you should be well satisfied with your progress toward your goals. Taking a course to add to your skills or for special training in your preferred area would be a plus for your career. If a family member is in an irritable mood, be supportive.

18. SATURDAY. Healing. A class in a creative pursuit such as painting or music could be very appealing. It would also give you a balance in your life between working and relaxation. Aries need to be physically active, probably in competition. If you are not winning, don't be a poor sport and go home. Enjoy developing your technique until you start to win more consistently, which in itself will do you good. An eve ning out partying and dancing will allow you to let off steam. Even though you may not go to bed until all hours, you will feel reinvigorated by the exercise. A hot date might not work out to be the one, but you will have fun and should at least gain a new friend.

19. SUNDAY. Vital. If an important deal is going down at work, you would be wise to use today to revise facts and figures and to understand the issues inside and out. There could be another bid from an unknown source that threatens yours. Your nerves could be acting up at the moment; going out for a walk in the fresh air can be calming. If you live in town, a trip to the beach or into the countryside will let you breathe in a good supply of oxygen. Savor every word of a letter or e-mail from an old friend of the family you haven't seen in years. There could be some disappointing news, but you will discover this gray cloud has a silver lining hidden within it.

20. MONDAY. Strenuous. If work starts to get a little tedious, taking a break and going for a walk will renew your energy and rejuvenate your inspiration. Stresses and strains may be worrying you and nagging at your thoughts, making it hard to keep your mind on the job at hand, but these will pass and leave success in their wake. Until that occurs, you might be wise to talk to a good friend who can help you work things out in your head; in your heart you know everything is going to be all right. Expect to be in the car a lot today. Listen to favorite music to calm you while negotiating the traffic. Aries who are in the market for a new car will be in luck.

21. TUESDAY. Tense. Worries about your home life may make it hard to focus on your work, or worries about employment could be causing upsets on the domestic scene. You may feel torn between the emotions of a partner and a child, a situation that is fairly normal. The best approach is not to run away from the problem but to seek help from resources available to you. Face your inner feelings honestly. It might be all too easy to blame someone else, but ultimately you are responsible for your situation because you are voting with your feet. Aries writers might gain some recognition, or an important and lucrative contract might finally be signed and sealed.

22. WEDNESDAY. Pleasant. Extravagance is likely to be on display. You might be guilty of overspending on a shopping spree, but what fun you will have doing it. You deserve to treat yourself and those you love after working so hard lately. If house hunting, you may find one property that has all you need to keep warm and snug this winter. Don't worry about the cost. Concentrate on setting up your lifestyle, and the money will come. A partner's investment could show signs of paying off handsomely, and the change you see will do your heart good. Romance is definitely on the cards. Aries singles might meet the person dreams are made of.

23. THURSDAY. Creative. Fun is in the air. No matter who gets cranky or irritable, you will be able to override it and turn the day into fun. You might be taking a child to a play or out to carol by candlelight to night. There is a sense of the supernatural and of magic permeating everything you do. If you are finding it hard to contact someone important to you, don't fret; keep trying and you will get through. Your employer could be irritated, but only because of the pressure they are under, so don't take it personally. Get together with coworkers and order lunch to be delivered so you can all keep working and get what's most important finished on time.

24. FRIDAY. Cooperative. Teamwork will make any task easier. You will be very aware of the bonds between you and your family, friends, and associates. This is the party time of the year, and you will enjoy going out this eve ning to celebrate. Or you might be staying in with your family, relishing all the aspects that make your family unique and finishing preparations for tomorrow. There is a high likelihood of a long-distance phone call from a loved one. Reflection is indicated. Put aside some time to remember someone special who is no longer with you physically but still alive and vibrant in your heart. The beginning of a love relationship is indicated.

25. SATURDAY. Merry Christmas! Whatever you do today, don't let yourself fall into the role of a martyr. Instead, see yourself as giving service to those you love. This may not be an easy role for an Aries, but you will be breaking new ground among your loved ones and be rewarded with their enjoyment. Good company and social fun are strongly indicated. Some old friends or a prodigal child return to the fold after being absent for far too long. Expect some deep emotions to surface that lead to some soul-searching among family members. This will be positive and, if anything, will bring you all closer as family traditions are respected and revered.

26. SUNDAY. Variable. Efforts at communication could be difficult as you become tongue-tied and your words get twisted. You might start to understand your own avoidance techniques. Loving relationships and caring thoughts will prevail, however, and your feelings of security will strengthen. A fortunate new acquaintanceship may enter your life, or you may become involved in a community effort to help less fortunate folk. You might be readying to go to an area of emergency to help the suffering and needy, or be gathering supplies or funds. Someone who owes you money could be tardy with their payment, and it might be best to postpone mentioning it until tomorrow.

27. MONDAY. Problematic. Time spent getting or ga nized and tying up loose ends will be effective. If you are waiting for something important, don't even think about it until this afternoon. You may have to bottle up your feelings when someone with more authority than you takes over and changes decisions you already made. Unless you bite your tongue and do what is required, you could be made to look bad. If you haven't been feeling well, make an appointment with the doctor before the problem develops into something serious. Focus on yourself, and get as much rest as possible. The more you put yourself out for other people, the less appreciation you will get in return.

28. TUESDAY. Uncertain. Being separated from a loved one could be tormenting you at the moment. Difficulties can arise in a partnership, and you will have to be the strong one. Don't bother yourself with imagined worries; get on with the job at hand and the storm clouds will pass. An uneasy feeling that you have forgotten something important may nag at you all day, but this is due more to your self-doubt than to anything based on fact. Seek out a good friend to boost your self-esteem and improve your faith in yourself. A situation might arise that will affect your career choices, but it is too early to start making decisions; everything will be sorted out in its own good time.

29. WEDNESDAY. Optimistic. The doubts of the last few days start to subside, leaving you feeling better about your situation and your opportunities. Someone may make you an offer that is quite unexpected and gives you plenty of food for thought. Do not make any major decisions today, however. Let your opportunities percolate through your mind and see where it all leads. An acquaintance may show signs of deepening into a lover, bringing an extra bonus. Partnership resources can take a turn for the better, putting you in a much stronger bargaining position when it comes to investments. An unexpected inheritance might also surprise and delight you.

30. THURSDAY. Dramatic. Your emotional experiences could be quite intense, and you might find yourself drawn into a lot of drama. Try to avoid backbiting or revealing secrets if you can; this will only come back to haunt you in the future. A surgical procedure will go as planned, with all your nerves and worry seeming like a waste of time. A lawsuit that has been hanging over your head might disappear in the light of some new information. You might decide to make a change for the better within a relationship, and you will find that you have plenty of support for this. A favor from someone will have to be returned. Before accepting, be sure you can do so confidently.

31. FRIDAY. Affectionate. The bonds between you and your close friends and relatives are strong. A get-together could end up being the party of the year. However, some plans for this eve ning may have to be postponed due to a large workload, but this will add rather than detract from your celebration because you will have achieved what you wanted. Stay away from drug takers and heavy drinkers this eve ning in order to avoid confusion and problems. Then you can see in the New Year in a style that portends a loving and hassle-free year to come. If you are spending the day traveling, there should only be a few annoying delays, and you will arrive at your destination safe and totally ready to party.

NOTES

FREE
PARTY LINE

Make new friends, have fun, share idea's never be bored this party never stops! And best of all it's FREE!

Never Any Charges! Call Now!

712-338-7722

WHAT DOES YOUR
FUTURE HOLD?

DISCOVER IT IN *ASTROANALYSIS*—

**COMPLETELY REVISED THROUGH THE YEAR 2015,
THESE GUIDES INCLUDE COLOR-CODED CHARTS FOR
TOTAL ASTROLOGICAL EVALUATION,
PLANET TABLES AND CUSP CHARTS,
AND STREAMLINED INFORMATION.**